1988

Management
for
Supervisors

2nd edition

PAUL PRESTON, University of Texas

THOMAS W. ZIMMERER, Clemson University

Management
for
Supervisors

PRENTICE-HALL, INC., *Englewood Cliffs, New Jersey 07632*

Library of Congress Cataloging in Publication Data

Preston, Paul, (date)
   Management for supervisors.

   Bibliography: p. 317
   Includes index.
   1. Supervision of employees.   2. Supervision of
employees—Case studies.   I. Zimmerer, Thomas.
II. Title.
HF5549.P656   1983   658.3′02   82-18133
ISBN   0-13-549725-6
ISBN   0-13-549717-5 (pbk.)

Editorial/production supervision and interior design by Margaret Rizzi
Cover design by Karolina Harris
Manufacturing buyer: Ed O'Dougherty

Printed in the United States of America

10   9   8   7   6   5   4   3   2   1

ISBN   0-13-549725-6
ISBN   0-13-549717-5 {PBK.}

Prentice-Hall International, Inc., *London*
Prentice-Hall of Australia Pty. Limited, *Sydney*
Editora Prentice-Hall do Brasil, Ltda., *Rio de Janeiro*
Prentice-Hall Canada Inc., *Toronto*
Prentice-Hall of India Private Limited, *New Delhi*
Prentice-Hall of Japan, Inc., *Tokyo*
Prentice-Hall of Southeast Asia Pte. Ltd., *Singapore*
Whitehall Books Limited, *Wellington, New Zealand*

This book is dedicated, with love, to

Kimberly Preston

and

Dawn Zimmerer

Contents

section

FUNCTIONS
OF SUPERVISION

section

PROCESSES
OF SUPERVISION

section 3

PERSONNEL
MANAGEMENT

section

CHALLENGES
OF SUPERVISION

Preface

Today's supervisor is, more than ever before in management history, the person in the center of the storm. All around her or him, people are building up expectations, setting up barriers and holding up ideals. Productivity has become a major goal in our society, and the supervisor or manager is the person who is supposed to deliver improved productivity.

This is really nothing new. Fifty years ago, Fritz Roethlisber, a major contributor to the literature and theory of management, suggested that the supervisor (especially the first-line supervisor) must be a master and is a victim of "double talk." Roethlisberer felt that supervisors must speak two languages—one of the management above, another of the employees below. Higher management and employees have different needs, different goals, indeed different ways of looking at the same organizational world. It is the responsibility of the supervisor to bridge these two different worlds, bringing them together to achieve common purposes for which the organization was designed.

It is a heavy responsibility, one that we feel complimented by being chosen to assist.

Books cannot substitute for real managerial experience. Books can provide us with a quick and effective way of gaining managerial experience, by exposing us to the theories, ideas, successes and failures of other managers who have gone before. In this book, we have taken information, experience and insights from a wide variety of sources. Managers and supervisors with years of experience have shared their experiences with us in seminars, classrooms and in their responses to surveys and questionnaires. This information comes from an equally wide variety of kinds of organizations—manufacturing, hospitals, retail and wholesale merchandising, cattle feeding and ranching, agribusiness, colleges and universities, nursing homes, government and military organizations, banks, savings and loan associations and credit unions, Realtors® and research companies, trade and professional associations. Both authors practice as university teachers and business consultants, teaching management—and learning more about management from managers. The result is, we are convinced, a practical primer on the challenge of management today.

Examples in the chapters come from real life. Cases at the ends of the chapters are also from real managerial situations. As you read and discuss these cases, you'll likely find that you, or one of your managerial colleagues, has been in a similar situation. You'll be able to readily see how the problem in one case can be applied to other circumstances. This is the real value of studying management, and the real purpose we had in bringing this book into being: to assist you, the supervisor, in making better decisions, and in managing better.

Confucious once said that

"I hear and forget,
I see and I remember,
I *do* and I *understand*."

Reading this book is not enough. If you are a student, look for examples of good and poor management around you, and learn from the actions of those managers how to apply the concepts we have been discussing. If you are now in a management position, or if you plan to soon find yourself in a management position, try out some of our ideas, suggestions and approaches. You'll obviously find that some of them do not work for you or your situation. You'll find that most of these ideas *DO* work. Putting them into action will not only help you understand them, it will help you enlarge and refine your "bag of management tools," making you a prime candidate for greater managerial responsibility.

The people we must thank for their help and support on this project are too numerous—if we dedicated one word in this book to each of them, we would run out of words before we ran out of friends and supporters. Suffice to say, we appreciate all the help we've generously been given. We take full credit for having the good sense to ask for their advice, and to then use that advice, just as we take full responsibility for any errors, of either ommission or commission.

We appreciate the support of our families, and the support and confidence of the editorial, production and sales people at Prentice-Hall, Inc.

Finally, a challenge. To each and every reader, this book can be just a book, to be read, enjoyed and forgotten. Or, it can be the beginning of a new and more productive manager, a more productive organization and a more motivated and satisfied workforce.

Good Managing.

Paul L. Preston

Thomas W. Zimmerer

San Antonio, Texas

Management
for
Supervisors

Supervision in a Complex World

When you complete this chapter, you will be able to

1. Identify and discuss the five trends for the future that will affect supervision.
2. Describe the various forces impinging on the supervisor as the "person in the middle."
3. Discuss the supervisory styles and philosophies which have contributed to modern supervision.
4. Explain the major contributions made to management practice by the scientific management school.
5. Discuss the major contributions made by the human relations school.
6. Describe the contingency approach to management.
7. Show how the supervisor can become truly professional.
8. Explain the "ten commandments of management," on which the "challenge to supervision" is based.

EACH OF THE following resources has been important to organizations ever since they were first formed: Money, material, knowledge, and labor. However, in today's ever-changing and increasingly complex world, these basic factors are critical to an organization's success. The nature of the supervisor's job is no longer static. Law, technology, behavioral science, and society itself are in a state of constant change. To keep up with these changes, supervisors must continually review their managerial skills and develop new skills and techniques. Supervisors must move beyond assuming that the people they manage are extensions of the machines they operate. Employees today are complex. Managing them effectively takes more than just a single "one best way." People today are complex. Supervisors must be able to deal with people intelligently as individuals. This is a welcome development, one that requires supervision based on knowledge as well as experience.

Professional Supervision

Along with their increased education and rising expectations, supervisors are increasingly professional in their attitudes and orientation. Only a few years ago, the only "recognized" professions were medicine, law, teaching, and accounting. Today the term "professional" often refers to the attitude of any individual who takes personal pride in his or her career activities and who maintains career-related ties to others who share that feeling. Professionalism is a challenge to many organizations. They find that their best supervisors are identifying more often with their peers in other organizations and are less willing to maintain an insular, isolated view of their jobs. However, most forward-thinking organizations recognize that with professionalism comes the responsibility for individual growth and development. Professional supervisors are better educated, more aware of issues in the world around them, and more sensitive to the needs of their organizations and the workers they supervise than they used to be. For this reason, many organizations have undertaken supervisory development programs to assist in the personal development of their managerial staff. These organizations realize that their continued profitability or effectiveness rests in the hands of their supervisors.

Many organizations are also taking a renewed interest in the process of selection and training of supervisors. This means that present supervisors will be competing with colleagues who are well-trained and who have an attractive mix of skills and personality traits. The competition for recognition and advancement among the supervisory ranks is another challenge of the future, and it is one welcomed by forward-thinking supervisors.

WHAT IS SUPERVISION?

Supervision is defined as the management of a process, a worker or workers, or a project. But supervisors today do far more than simply provide oversight and direction. They are the key link between the policy-making people at the top of the organization and the employees performing work. As such, supervisors must be able to translate the broad general directives and policies of the top policy makers into specific instructions and directions for the employees.

Supervisors are also the most visible and directly accessible representatives of the organization and its management. When employees have difficulties, they take them first to the supervisor. He or she must then determine whether the matter is serious enough to warrant higher management involvement, or whether a solution to the problem can be found immediately. The manner in which the supervisor interprets company policy and organizational goals directly influences the productivity and performance of those doing the work.

Supervisors are often promoted from within the organization. They join the ranks of supervision directly from the organization's nonmanagement work force. Because of their previous position in the organization, those selected from the work force have a better appreciation for and understanding of the problems and viewpoints of the people they supervise. Supervisors thus become the upward communication links, channeling the wishes and feelings of the employees to the higher levels of management; however, they are also an integral part of the management structure of any organization. As mentioned above, the supervisor is responsible for relaying downward the policies and directives of the top management to the employees. This can lead to a serious problem of being caught in the middle, between two forces with different languages, objectives, and attitudes. Fritz Roethlisberger once described the first-line supervisor as the master and victim of double talk.[1] The supervisor must be able to understand the needs and objectives of higher management *and* of the employees and must somehow overcome the natural differences between them. This has always been the unique challenge of supervision. Management theories have evolved and changed over the years. The only constant has been the position of the supervisor at the junction of the two groups.

SUPERVISORY STYLES AND PHILOSOPHIES

The style and philosophy of supervision has changed dramatically during the past years. The early views of the practice of supervision were an outgrowth of the theories and assumptions of scientific management.

Later on, as management thinking shifted first to the human relations approach and finally, in today's view, to the idea of management as a "contingency" process, the practice of supervision has reflected these views. We will briefly review each of these important periods in management and supervisory thought. Naturally, these three views do not reflect all of the many supporting theories and practices of supervisors. Many important ideas in management have developed from mixes of these basic views and categories of thought. Taken together, these views have been responsible for developing the high level of management and supervisory skill that we see in organizations today.

Scientific Management

The concept of scientific management was the first recognizable attempt to develop a unified set of ideas to improve management. Before the development of scientific management, the practice of management and supervision was largely without guidelines. Managers and supervisors did the best they could by using their own limited personal experience. This often led to unproductive actions, expecially in the growing factories and industries that appeared during and after the industrial revolution. Managers could no longer supervise the work of just two or three apprentices or workers. Businesses and other organizations were large, and they were growing larger. Supervisors were now responsible for seeing that hundreds or thousands of units of a product were produced each day. One manager would have to supervise the actions of dozens or perhaps hundreds of workers. The old methods of management, based on experience and direct manager-worker contact, would no longer do the job.

In response to this challenge, management experts and managers themselves began to experiment with ways to simplify work and thereby improve the productivity of workers. Led by F. W. Taylor (an industrial engineer), their efforts came to be recognized as the foundation of scientific management.

Using scientific management methods and assumptions, managers were able to take any job and simplify it until it was possible for a worker with no real training or skill to perform adequately. Even a simple operation, such as assembling a piece of machinery, might be broken up into twenty or thirty operations, with one worker performing each operation. That worker did just the one job, over and over again, all day long. There were a number of advantages to this type of "assembly–line" operation. Because each small part of an operation required little or no skill to perform, there was little need for formal worker training. Unskilled laborers could be hired and become almost immediately productive. If a worker did not perform properly, he or she could easily and quickly be replaced with someone else. Because the worker did the same job repeatedly, it was possible to study the motions required to do the job and remove any unnecessary motions. This led to making each job as simple and productive as possible. Taylor's "work simplification" brought many important cost savings to industry and made mass production and assembly lines possible.

Problems with Scientific Management. There were many problems with this system, and some are obvious if you think about the effects of any assembly-line operation. Work, for most people, became dull and repetitive, and little incentive was given for personal pride of accomplishment. Because workers could be interchanged, it was possible for managers to dismiss uncooperative workers and replace them at will with others who were eager for work. In short, this system permitted a dehumanizing influence to invade business.

However, the system of scientific management also led to some developments that have strengthened organizations and pointed the way to the productive capacity that we enjoy today. Characteristics of organizations such as chain of command, authority and responsibility delegation, and the technologies permitting mass production were either invented or adapted to the needs of a growing and demanding society.

Human Relations

To test some of the concepts of scientific management, researchers set up productivity experiments at the Hawthorne works of the Western Electric Company. While they were doing research, they discovered that people have needs that go far beyond simple economic satisfaction. They found that people are also motivated by needs for relationships with others. The Hawthorne studies led to the development of a school of management thinking that was based on trying to improve productivity through better human relations between management and labor. The human relations era was noted for the development of innovations in work design and in the design of the work place that would enable workers to achieve more satisfaction of their needs for enjoying social contact and personal reward. However, in the era of human relations, the primary motivating force recognized by management was still the workers' desire for economic rewards.

The human relations view was responsible for an awareness of the complexity of working people. This view did not actually result in a change in the work that people did, but it did contribute to healthier management attitudes about motivation and the desire of most people to do a good job when given a chance and a reason. Critics suggest that adopting the *human relations* concept was just another management try at forcing workers to become more productive. In their view, it did not mean that managers cared any more than before for their workers. This view may be partially true. Organizations and their workers must produce to survive and prosper. The utilization of the human relations concept represented a turning point in the evolution of management. It forced managers to pay attention to the needs and aspirations of their workers.

The Legacy of the Human Relations Era.   Since the human relations era, supervisors have come to realize that people are not motivated solely by money. Instead, we are motivated by many things. Certainly money and the security and safety that it can buy are important. Without adequate food, shelter, and security, few of us can function properly. These things are the first concerns of any individual. To obtain them, we must work. However, we are also motivated by a need to be part of a social group. We are motivated by a need for personal recognition or "ego" satisfaction. Each of us likes to be recognized by others for the talents and skills that we possess. When we do a good job, the praise and recognition that sometimes follow are often more important motivators than the money that we are paid.

The human relations concept has brought about an awareness that no two individuals are alike. Each of us is motivated by different things, at different times, and for different reasons. To improve productivity, managers who adopt this concept are encouraged to take a critical look at the nature of the work to which people are assigned. Whenever possible, the job should be redesigned to give employees more of a sense of personal accomplishment. It is difficult to take pride in or get personal satisfaction from continually doing the same dull job. Human relations ideas have slowly begun to force managers to take a new and closer look at the work environment and the work itself.

Supervision Today

The introduction of human relations thinking into management led researchers and management thinkers in many directions. Some continued to explore the technical side of management and developed new and better ways of reducing the involvement of people in the production of products. This path led to the development of automation and highly sophisticated management systems. Other experts refined human relations by concentrating on the complexity of the individual. Because individuals constantly change by contact with their environments, it is almost impossible for a manager to assume they can all be treated or motivated in the same way.

Management today can be described as a combination of the best elements of management experience. However, it is unfair to characterize management as a "salad" of elements that is jumbled into a mixture. What has emerged in management can best be described as a "contingency approach" to management.

Contingency Management

Contingency management is a view that asserts that no one style of leadership, form of organization, or arrangement of resources and personnel is *best* for *all* situations. Instead of adopting a "one best way" approach, modern managers are discovering that the leadership pattern, organization form, and resource flow in an organization must be specifically suited to the business and its environments. Some organizations operate in an environment where innovations and change occur constantly (for example, the fashion industry and the medical products industry). Other organizations are relatively stable, and do not experience much need for drastic or rapid change in their management styles (for example, businesses selling office supplies, farm machinery, or sailboats).

Contingency-oriented managers assume that each business situation requires a unique mix of labor, technology, organization structure, and management style and involvement. Contingency management is not a specific style of management. It is a philosophy of management, one that fits the needs of today's professional supervisors.

Doctors, lawyers, and accountants seldom work with the same cases daily. As "professionals," they use their skills and experience to deal with each patient or client as an individual. They are alert to similarities among cases, but they must also be sensitive to the differences among the people and situations they encounter. Supervisors deal with a variety of different people and situations. To become professionals, supervisors must move away from the view that employees can be managed and motivated solely by reward and punishment. The role of the professional supervisor is to develop new ideas and to look with an open mind at the ideas that are being expressed by the philosophers, theorists, observers, and successful practitioners of management.

TAKING A CLOSE LOOK AT OURSELVES

If you were to describe your job, you would probably think of a number of different answers: "I'm constantly shifting gears and going in new directions." "It's a people business, and we deal with people." "It's different every day, you never know what's coming next." "I'm expected to think on my feet and keep moving." These comments are typical of sentiments shared by managers who are asked to describe how they spend their workdays. Managers seem to move about in a constant blur of motion, only to consider long-range plans when it is absolutely necessary.

The First Managers

As a distinct group of persons in organizations, managers can trace their "roots" back to Moses and the biblical days of ancient Israel. In Exodus 18, we learn

> The next day Moses took his seat to settle disputes among the people, and they were standing round him from morning till evening. When Jethro saw all that he was doing for the people, he said, "What are you doing for all these people? Why do you sit alone with all of them standing round you from morning till evening?" "The people come to me," Moses answered, "to seek God's guidance. Whenever there is a dispute among them, they come to me, and I decide between man and man. I declare the statutes and laws of God." But his father-in-law said to Moses, "This is not the best way to do it. You will only wear yourself out and wear out all the people who are here. The task is too heavy for you; you cannot do it by yourself. Now listen to me: take my advice, and God be with you. It is for you to be the people's representative before God, and bring their disputes to Him. You must instruct them in the statutes and laws, and teach them how they must behave and what they must do. But you must yourself search for capable, God-fearing men among all the people, honest and incorruptable men, and appoint them over the people as officers over units of a thousand, of a hundred, of fifty, or of ten. They shall sit as a permanent court for the people, they must refer difficult cases to you but decide simple cases themselves!"[2]

Jethro (the father-in-law of Moses and the first recorded management consultant) suggests to Moses in this passage that he must decentralize. Moses is advised to hire some managers and to delegate authority to them. He apparently did, because managers have been around ever since.

COORDINATION

Henri Fayol (a turn-of-the-century French industrialist) believed that coordination of a firm's activities was the main objective of a manager. In this view, all activities of an organization are supposed to help the organization reach its predetermined goals. Because all organizations have goals, managers in business, government, and education, and the

Photo courtesy of Eastman Kodak Company.

professions all perform coordinative activities, and coordination requires good communication. Also, managers must keep track of what is happening within their environment and must be sensitive to where and when problems can occur.

A common problem facing all managers is finding time during the daily chores to coordinate properly.

Generally, managers know what their major objectives and responsibilities are, and they seem to carry these goals around in their heads. However, they can lose sight of longer range goals as they go off in what seems to be a dozen different directions in the crush of daily affairs. This view of the manager seems to be in conflict with the traditional or textbook view of management in which managers plan, organize, direct, and control apparently one activity after another.

Because the succeeding chapters of this book deal with communication problems that face "real" managers, it might be useful to examine in detail some of the characteristics of the manager's job today.

In general, the typical manager today seems to work immersed in an unrelenting stream of visitors and telephone calls. Jumping from topic to topic, she or he thrives on interruptions and, more often than not, disposes of items in ten minutes or less. Although the manager may have ten projects going, most of them are delegated. The manager juggles projects, checking each one periodically before sending it back through the system.

The contemporary manager spends as much time dealing with people outside the department as she or he does with subordinates or superiors. These "outside" contacts involve customers, suppliers, trade associations, and government people.

Today's manager is constantly alert for snatches of "soft" information such as gossip, hearsay, and speculation that may help him or her get a step ahead. In addition, passing along such tidbits to the right subordinate is an integral part of the manager's job, because information in organizations is an important "currency of exchange."

The typical manager shuns written reports, skims periodicals, and merely processes mail. Managers have a pronounced liking for doing business face to face or by telephone. This allows the manager to gauge emotions.

The outcome of any serious effort at self-analysis should be comforting to you as a manager, even though it should also raise some important doubts and questions in your mind. The results and conclusions should confirm that much of what you are already doing is typical of many others doing similar jobs. The old "classical" theories about the "proper" behavior of managers leaves many of them feeling that somehow they're doing their jobs all wrong. Although it may be comforting to realize that as a manager you are not alone with your problems and concerns, don't fall into the trap of assuming that there is no need for further self-analysis or change. Instead, examine the many roles you play and compare them with the roles played by other managers. As you do this, you will develop an increased awareness of your personal skills in the most important of managerial activities—communication.

The successful manager today operates in three different areas of activity: interpersonal relations, decision making, and information transmission. Let's look briefly at each area, beginning with the manager's informational activities, and see how communication relates to it.[3]

Informational Activities

In the general area of information, managers perform several activities and, in doing so, play many roles. Among these are

The Disseminator of Information. Managers are viewed by employees as a prime souce of information. This extends both to information that employees need to do their jobs (such as facts, figures, schedules, and specifications) and information that they want about their jobs (How does it affect me? Where do I fit?).

The Linking-Pin to Higher Management. The effective managers are ones whom employees believe are credible and reliable links between employees and those from higher levels in the organization. This means that managers must be skilled in communicating with both superiors and subordinates and must be both senders and receivers of messages. Managers need to be able to accurately and persuasively present their employees' views to the organization's higher management and must also be "tied in" to the employee "grapevine" in order to have all the information necessary for satisfying employees' needs and wants.

The Translator. Managers (especially those supervising nonmanagers) have been described as "masters and victims of double talk." They communicate with two different groups of people. They get and give information to those above them in the organization who manage managers. They must speak the language and understand the viewpoints of their employees who manage no one. The viewpoints of managers and employees are usually quite different, and it falls to the manager to become an effective information bridge between them. Managers and department heads have to translate top management's wishes into terms relevant to employees, and they must summarize and transmit their employees' feeling to upper management in terms that these top managers can understand and appreciate. Of all the roles that the supervisor plays, the "information handler" is perhaps the most difficult.

Interpersonal Relations

Most managers play interpersonal relations roles that include a leader role, a monitor role, and a representative role.

The Leader Role. A manager is the formal leader of a work group or department. She can also be the informal leader (that is, the person to whom others look for personal advice or guidance) if she is adept at interpersonal communication skills and is able to convey that ability to the employees. All leaders can manage people, but not all managers are leaders. In some work groups, a member of the team (an employee) is the real group leader, and the manager is merely the titular "head" of the department. The most effective departments are those in which the manager also plays the "leader" role.

The Monitor Role. A manager is constantly receiving information from all parts of the organization. This means that he keeps in touch with the people as well as the processes involved in an organization while maintaining a watch over changes or new developments. The manager must monitor the people in his department and watch for signals about their needs, their goals, and the factors that motivate them to do a productive job.

The Representative Role.   A manager is the official (and sometimes unofficial) representative of the department or division. He or she is thus a symbol or spokesperson of that group. His or her actions will be viewed by others as indicative of the attitudes or actions of the personnel in his or her department. As a spokesperson, the manager is also responsible for creating a favorable image for the department in the eyes of those who control the department. As in some of the other roles of a manager, the representative role requires that a manager be able to effectively communicate the feelings and the activities of his or her department to those who make decisions about work schedules, budgets, manpower allocations, and other important issues for the employees. As such, the manager's image in the eyes of his or her employees is directly influenced by how well the representative role is handled.

Decision-Making Activities

Managers make many decisions about matters related to their jobs and to the employees working for them. Some of the major decision-making roles include the risk-taker role, the resource allocator role, and the mediator role.

The Risk-Taker Role.   Although managers can't technically be considered entrepreneurs, they often play a role similar to that of an entrepreneur. While making critical decisions, managers have to be willing to accept risk. With decisions involving transferring, hiring, or firing of personnel or choosing one alternative over another, no one can absolutely predict what will happen. Thus, the effective manager is an individual who is willing to accept at least a small element of risk as a natural part of her or his job.

The Resource Allocator Role.   Managers must make decisions involving the appropriate allocation of resources. These resources include money, materials, job assignments, and support personnel. Some managers don't feel that they have any control over resources in their departments. They feel that these decisions are made for them by others higher up in the organization; for many managers at lower levels, such feelings are correct. Yet all managers possess one scarce resource that can and must be allocated—their personal time.

As a manager, you are constantly deciding which employee, project, or problem will get your attention for the next few minutes or

Photo courtesy of Diamond International Corporation.

hours. Often, there are decisions to be made involving conflict over time allocation: "Do I attend the important department head's meeting, or do I stay here and get the credit policies report out?" Sometimes the decision involves choosing between different employee demands on your time: "Do I spend time with the experienced people going over their recommendations and listening to their problems, or do I spend the time with the new employees who need the benefit of my insight and experience?" A manager's time is also allocated between those things that managers are *required* to do, such as reports, memos, meetings, and phone calls, and the things managers *like* to do, such as problem solving, planning for the future, working with and motivating employees, and even pursuing personal self-development. These choices are all part of the resource allocator role of the manager.

The Mediator Role. The word "mediator" is associated with labor-management negotiations to some managers. Yet all managers are called on periodically to settle disputes between individuals or groups. As such, they make "mediator" kinds of decisions about whose position or idea is to be rejected. In some fortunate cases, the decision can be a compromise in which both sides "win." In more difficult conflicts, tough decisions must be made and properly communicated to both winners and losers. It's in this position that a manager's communication skills really come through.

Some of the roles that managers play are assigned by the organization. These roles involve the managers' duties as managers and as supervisors of employees. Other roles are assumed by the managers, and include the roles of counselors, friends, advisors, and even "parents." All of our roles, whether assumed or assigned, influence our communications with others, and when conflicts arise between managers' assumed roles and their assigned roles, the stage is set for some real difficulties.

HOW DO *THEY* SEE *YOU?*

Suppose you asked some people who deal with or work in your organization to draw a verbal picture of you.[4] How would they "draw" you? Would the portraits sound something like this?

THE MANAGER as seen by

THE BOSS	Asleep at the wheel; gopher (as in gopher that report, and so on); a perfect example of the "Peter Principle" (managers rise to their level of incompetence).
YOUR EMPLOYEES	A curmudgeon with whips and claws; perpetually snarling; an ivory tower.
THE FINANCIAL POLICIES COMMITTEE	A Las Vegas dealer; a high roller; river boats and risks.
YOUR BARBER OR HAIR DRESSER	Expects too much; "Resurrection is far more difficult than birth."
THE CUSTOMER OR CLIENT	Gopher (see boss above); management wizard (small minority); ole what' sizname (vast majority); overpaid; who cares? (almost everyone).

Don't be upset by these caricatures. After all, they are not actually what others think of a typical manager. Don't we wish!!

The truth is that perception is a funny business. What people see in other people, situations, experiences, and in themselves is true to them. The validity of one's perceptions is little affected by any absolute standard of accuracy or inaccuracy.

If people can be wrong about perceptions of everyday events, it can be assumed that our perceptions of ourselves can be just as distorted. Thus, the advice to "get into someone else's head" to improve communication should be just as relevant for getting inside our own heads. In short—know thyself.

EASY TO SAY—HARD TO DO

Self-analysis is difficult to do and useful only if it is done honestly. Telling yourself what you want to hear bears about as much relationship to the truth as does the voice of the mirror owned by Snow White's stepmother. Honest, careful, and periodic self-analysis will give you a big head start in improving your communications with others and in enabling you to manage in your organization.

THE CHALLENGE OF SUPERVISION

Successful supervisors have found that the secret to success lies in their willingness to operate by a set of principles; yet they must be willing to learn and to change. In a book dealing with corporate crises, Joel Ross and Michael Kami outline some basic principles that supervisors often overlook.[5] They call their principles the "ten commandments of management." They are

1. Develop and communicate a strategy . . . a unified sense of direction to which all members of the organization can relate.
2. Establish overall controls and cost controls to achieve plans, programs, and policies.
3. Exercise care in selection, and require that individuals actively participate in management.
4. Avoid one-man rule.
5. Provide management depth.
6. Keep informed of change and reach to change.
7. Don't overlook the customer and the customer's new power.
8. Use but don't misuse computers and technological aids.
9. Do not engage in accounting manipulations.
10. Provide for an organizational structure that meets the needs of the people.

The focus of the future of organizations is on people. Their needs and abilities make the difference between a successful organization and an unsuccessful one. Organizations now more than ever need supervisors who are willing and able to go beyond conventional wisdom, standard answers, and tried-and-true methods. This is the challenge of supervision—one that we will address throughout the book.

ACTION GUIDELINES FOR SUPERVISION

1. Supervisors must appreciate the complex nature of the employees. Think of yourself and your employees as unique.
2. Employees should never be managed solely as a group. Deal with

them as individuals. The key to effective supervision is communicating with each employee on a one-to-one basis.

3. All persons are involved in change. Because change usually occurs slowly, our ideas, values, and goals evolve over time. Examine how change affects your employees and respond to it appropriately.

4. Supervisors should accept the challenge of managing both the younger and older employees, although different approaches may be needed for each.

5. Supervisors find that some younger employees do not respect the traditional authority of the supervisor. Challenge yourself to build that respect in others.

6. Supervisors will find that some younger employees are interested in the "whys" of the job. Invest the time necessary to explain why things are done and you will benefit from more dedicated employees.

7. Supervisors find that some older employees resent younger supervisors. If necessary, exercise your authority tactfully to demonstrate your commitment to being a supervisor.

8. Supervisors must recognize that the general level of education of all employees is rising. Avoid using an old standard "brush-off" response to employees. Don't treat employees like children. Better-educated employees expect the straight facts and will usually respond with a sincere attempt to help solve problems.

9. Supervisors will be aided in the future by technology and computers. Learn as much as you can about the technological changes influencing your job. Become a source of knowledge for your employees. Groups taking the lead in welcoming technology are usually more successful than those who let change pull them along.

10. Supervisors find that the employment and promotions of minority persons can cause resentment by some nonminority employees. Develop a firm approach in explaining to all employees the nature of existing laws and the requirement of those laws (and the philosophy of justice and fairness behind the laws).

11. Supervisors should take every opportunity for growth and expansion of their personal training. This development of the supervisor is the first step toward professionalism in management.

12. Supervision has been influenced by many styles and philosophies of management. These philosophies of management reflect the knowledge and values of their time. Although supervision has always existed, it has become more important now than ever before to better define the role and duties of the supervisor. Today the challenge of successful supervision lies within the supervisor as an individual and in his or her ability to manage creatively and wisely. Use this book (and others) as a source of ideas and not as a cookbook.

DISCUSSION QUESTIONS FOR SUPERVISION

1. We discussed money, materials, knowledge, and workforce as the central elements and resources of the supervisor. In your job, which of these elements is most important? Which is least important?

2. What are the new skills supervisors must develop today to handle new trends and problems?

3. What are the contributions of scientific management to the practice of supervision?

4. What are the contributions and lasting effects of human-relations thinking?

5. Can supervision be considered a profession? What would be the hallmarks of a "professional" supervisor?

ACTION EXERCISES FOR SUPERVISION

1. Develop a table listing those trends that you believe are the most important ones affecting your performance as a supervisor.

2. We have presented a definition of supervision. Is this definition adequate when viewed from your experience and knowledge about what supervisors do? Develop your own definition, and compare yours to others in the group.

CASE 1. Bangert Publications, Inc.

It's 7:30 A.M., on Tuesday, March 12. The first shift is returning to the pressroom after the customary Sunday–Monday weekend. Eddy Burk is in the group, slowly waking up in the chill of Akron's rapidly departing cold front. The tension is thick in the ready-room and in the locker area. This is no ordinary first day of the week at Bangert Publications.

The Bangert strike had lasted sixteen weeks and had been a failure for the union, primarily because of the massive violence that marked the strike almost from the beginning. Although only a small minority of pressroom employees had any part in the violence, the pall cast by the acts of sabotage hindered and finally destroyed any hope of successful negotiations. The union signed a new contract, but the management viewpoint was dominant throughout it. The strike had been called because of management's desire to install automated equipment in the pressroom; it would be a move that would ultimately reduce employment in the Akron plant from sixty-two employees to just less than twenty-five. However, management was careful to assure all workers that no present workers would lose their jobs.

Those who could not be placed in other jobs in Akron would be given comparable jobs (and full moving expenses) in one of the five other cities where Bangert owned newspapers. A few dissidents pushed the issue, and the union leadership was forced to call the strike. Two days later, a band of thugs broke into the pressroom and destroyed seven of the nine presses. The guilty individuals were never caught, although their identities were thought to be generally known among the other pressroom employees.

Eddy Burk, a senior supervisor in the pressroom, was the "man on the spot." Because he was a manager, he and a handful of his colleagues had to work with upper management (including the publisher, Sven Bangert) to keep the paper going during the strike. Now, he is huddled in a corner (beside the gas warmer) talking with Bill Ignasinski, another supervisor.

"I can understand how they felt about all this," Bill said. "I never really was sure if supervisors would be secure when the new system was installed. In fact, during the entire strike, I never could figure out all the issues and why the darn thing went on so long. I don't know about you, Eddy, but I don't want the men to confuse me with those guys up in management."

"But you are management," Burk protested, "and right now you—we've—all got a problem. We may not be the cause of it, but we are darn sure going to have to solve it. Nothing in my experience prepared me for this moment, and I'm not sure what to do."

1. Evaluate the discussion between Eddy and Bill. Do you ever find yourself in this sort of position?
2. What is supervision? Is it a part of management, or is it a transition between management and the workers? With whom should a supervisor's loyalty lie?
3. What facts in the case might contribute to Bill's feeling that he is not a part of management?
4. How would you respond to your returning workers if you were faced with similar circumstances?

CASE 2. The Ride Home

"I wish they would make up their minds," Jim Welch said to Mark Howard as they headed home in their old Chevy in the Friday night commuter traffic. Both men were foremen with production responsibilities at the local aerospace plant. "I just can't produce all that paperwork and keep up with production on that experimental model. One minute they call down for a report that's due an hour before, and then they chew you out for not being down on the line when the offset machine went out of calibration and no one knows what to do."

Mark commented on the traffic and stared out the window. "You're right, Jim. I only see my supervisor when something goes wrong. And even then he doesn't come down to help but just gets in my way—asking questions, making demands, and chewing me out while I'm trying to solve the problem he came down to complain about."

Jim nodded his head in agreement. "And what do we do it for? After taxes, a stinking twenty dollars a week more than the men in my shop!"

As traffic began to improve, the men's mood seemed to improve too. "Well," Mark said, "I got by the OSHA inspector. He didn't seem to know much about my job, but he seems thorough." The good mood ended. "By the time he got to me, he must have been poisoned by lunch in the cafeteria because he was all over our area getting in people's way. You know that MK-12 run we had a rush on? He stopped the work four times to check safety equipment. Does he think I would let those men work in an unsafe situation?"

Traffic got worse, and Jim directed his attention to the staff man who won all his first place votes for Mr. Worthless. "That darn production schedule guy was down this morning to give me the schedule for next week. If that simple son-of-a-gun ever had a job in the shop, he wouldn't put those schedules together like he does."

Mark interrupted Jim, saying, "You're right. He does those darn schedules to please the guys upstairs. Whatever they say goes. He knows that he'll never get promoted sticking up for us. He keeps his nose where it counts."

"Lets face it," Jim said, "we're the last line for management, and that's what they think of us."

The car pulled into the driveway of Jim's modest surburban house. "I'll see you Monday, Mark."

"All right, Jim, have a good weekend."

1. If you were the third passenger in the car, what would you have said and why? Consider the entire conversation.

CASE 3. International Society of Supervisors

A letter was addressed to Joe Caggman and was sent to his home. In it was a personal note from the president of the International Society of Supervisors. Joe was being invited to join in what the letter described as a "select group of men and women engaged in the practice of professional supervision." For twenty dollars a year, and a ten-dollar membership fee, Joe could join this select group.

The society was established two years ago by a group of professors and industrial supervisors in California who wanted to create a feeling of professionalism among people engaged in supervision. Part of their plan involved the establishment of a certification program, similar in administration and purpose to other certifications such as Certified Public Accountant (CPA), Chartered Financial Analyst (CFA), Certified Association Executive (CAE), and Certified Life Underwriter (CLU). The founders felt that only by developing a professional self-image could supervisors meet the challenges and problems of the coming years.

This letter went on with a description of the society and some of its prominent members and academic advisors. The close of the letter quoted Professor Fritz Roethlisberger who, forty years ago, noted that supervisors had the most difficult (and thankless) job in organization. According to the letter, the society proposed to do something about this problem by developing supervision as a recognized profession.

1. What is a profession?
2. Is it possible for supervision (and what supervisors do) to come under your definition of a profession?
3. Is an international society the best way to improve supervision?
4. If a certification program were developed by this society, which areas of supervision should be included for study and testing?

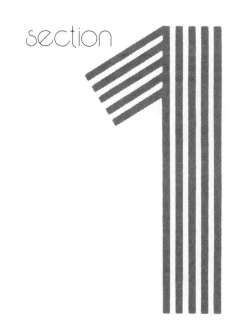

FUNCTIONS OF SUPERVISION

Planning, Controlling, Organizing

Objectives

When you complete your study of this chapter, you will be able to

1. Develop objectives, which should be measurable, realistic, challenging, clearly stated, and reviewed regularly.

2. Understand the need to recognize conflict, and its role in supervision.

3. Take the steps in the planning process.

4. Convert plans into actions.

5. Discuss some of the advantages of planning, including help in problem identification, help in developing alternatives, help in focusing attention on the important parts of a job, improved teamwork, and employee recognition of modern organizations.

6. Describe the elements of control, and discuss the use of standards as a management tool.

7. Demonstrate how to obtain valid information from feedback.

8. Use the "managing by the exception principle."

9. Apply preliminary, concurrent, and feedback control.

10. Measure employee performance effectively.

11. Use counseling for control.

12. Define the meaning of organization.

13. Discuss the basis of organization and its relevance to the satisfaction needs.

14. Discuss the concept of division of labor.

15. Describe the types of departmentalization.

16. Discuss the operational differences between tall and flat organizations.

17. Discuss the principle of span of control.

18. Define the factors affecting span of control.

THE QUESTION "What do supervisors do?" is usually answered "They plan, organize, direct, and control." These are the traditional *four functions of management*. It is through these functions that managers set goals and proceed to reach them.

All managers, at all levels in all organizations, perform these functions. They do so in different ways and in differing amounts of time. For example, a supervisor of assembly workers in an air-conditioning plant may spend little time planning and much time maintaining control. A supervisor in a new retail store may have to organize everything. She or he may not have time to do much controlling.

First-line supervisors usually do much directing, with some planning, organizing and controlling. Middle managers direct and organize more than they plan or control. Top managers are supposed to spend most of their time supervising immediate subordinates.

DIRECTING

The common thread in all manager's activities is *directing*. It is the heart of every manager's job. The most vexing and challenging problems facing today's supervisors usually appear in the area of directing.

Directing includes such supervisory activities as

- Communication
- Decision making
- Problem solving
- Motivation
- Leadership
- Delegation
- Discipline

Because of the importance of these directing activities, each will be discussed in an individual chapter.

In this chapter, we will concentrate on introducing and discussing the other three functions of management: planning, controlling, and organizing.

PLANNING

What is Planning?

Planning is the setting of goals and the establishment of means of reaching those goals. It involves both a supervisor's personal goals and those of her or his department or section. Planning puts the objectives of

25

Photo courtesy of Potlatch Corporation.

A SUPERVISOR'S CONSTANT RESPONSIBILITY IS DIRECTING

top management into a format that helps all employees understand what they are supposed to do. No organization or small work group can reach its goals if these goals are not clearly thought out and stated in advance. Planning brings objectives to reality. They serve as guidelines for supervisory action.

How to Plan

The basic steps in planning are as follows:

1. Set objectives and ensure that these objectives form the basis for planning activities.
2. Develop and state your planning assumptions.
3. Review all possible limitations on planning.
4. Develop action and contingency plans or alternatives.
5. Evaluate the alternatives carefully.
6. Convert plans into actions.

Step 1. The first step in the planning process is to be sure that the objectives, which have already been determined, serve as the basis for planning activities. All planning should help employees reach the agreed-upon objectives. Before planning begins, it is helpful to double-check to be sure that your employees have a clear understanding of the unit's objectives. Poor understanding of objectives will usually result in the employees' failure to understand the reason behind plans being developed. This essential tie between objectives and plans helps the employees develop confidence in the supervisor's ability to manage. In order to create this understanding, many supervisors find it useful to begin each plan or planning session with a brief statement of the objectives to be reached. This, they report, aids in focusing employees' attention on the "why" of the plan.

Step 2.   The second step in the planning process involves stating the assumptions that the planner is making. Each of us makes assumptions for everything we plan. For instance, you bring a lunch box to work, or you bring money to buy lunch, even though you are not hungry when you leave for work. You know that you will be hungry again by lunch time. A plan of action (such as arranging for lunch) is based upon your assumption that you will be hungry by lunch break. Supervisors develop plans based on their assumptions about their work and other factors. When we schedule production, we assume that employees are experienced in handling the specific kind of operations involved. If the regular experienced crew is working, this assumption is accurate. If new employees are on this shift, the assumption may be incorrect, and plans may fail. Careful planning helps supervisors avoid disruptions on the job. Failure to review basic managerial assumptions can undermine all planning efforts.

Step 3.   The third step in planning is a thorough review of all possible limitations. Ask yourself: What could affect the ability of the employees to reach their objectives? Anticipate the conditions that might restrict the smooth operation of the job or the work unit. Key areas for planning anticipation are machinery, inventories of material and parts, and labor availability. Supervisors who draw up a plan involving the use of machinery must allow for maintenance and repair downtime (downtime occurs when machinery is not running). Equipment must be serviced at periodic intervals and unexpected repairs may often be necessary. Wise supervisors also consult vacation schedules before they plan in order to ensure that an adequate number of trained employees will be available. The availability of raw materials is another limitation to be considered in developing a plan.

Step 4.   The fourth step in the planning process is the development of action or contingency plans. Every supervisor quickly learns that "it never happens just the way we planned it." For this reason, we develop contingency plans to smooth out deviations in our original plans. For example, one supervisor's plan was to switch all second-shift employees doing final assembly and rework over to a line completing a rush order on another model. However, the supervisor discovered that the first shift did not assemble enough on each of the other model units to warrant the use of the entire work force from the second shift. The supervisor had a contingency plan put into effect to take the workers not needed in the new model and have them inspect the old model units previously produced. The supervisor in this example took an alternative course of action because forces beyond his control made it impossible to use the entire work force to accomplish the original objective.

The advantage of having this contingency (or alternate) plan is that workers did not sit around idly. They were directed to work that needed doing. Often we must learn to anticipate changes and prepare employees for alternatives.

Step 5.   Step five is evaluating all alternatives. When all alternatives have been evaluated thoroughly, the most feasible plan can then be chosen. The reason for considering many alternatives is to determine which plan offers the greatest chance of success in reaching the supervisor's objectives. Because plans that will not result in reaching stated objectives are worthless, supervisors should concentrate their planning efforts on practical solutions and work assignments.

Step 6.   In the final planning step, plans are converted into action. We develop schedules, targets, standards of performance, and budgets. Expressing a plan in these terms helps employees to focus their efforts on specifics. A schedule, such as the one shown in Figure 2–1, establishes milestones for completion. Each box represents the time in which an

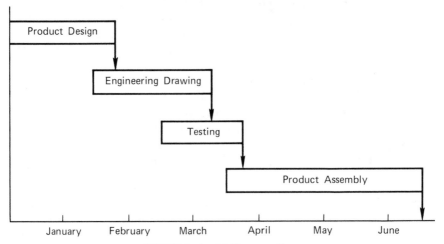

FIGURE 2–1   A Milestone Chart

activity should be completed. Instead of stating that an entire process will begin on January 1 and will be completed by June 1, this type of planning shows when each step of the process will begin and when each is expected to be completed. This sort of chart is used in many industries to improve planning. For example, assume you are the supervisor of the product testing department. You know the work force and equipment limitations of your shop. Your plan should enable you to know well in advance that on February 1 a new project will be given to you for testing. In reality, such plans are agreed upon in advance by all the supervisors involved, and supervisors are asked if their departments can perform the tasks required in the time allotted. This coordination makes possible the conversion of plans into reality.

Rules and Procedures

Every organization tries to operate in an orderly way by establishing rules and procedures that are to be guides to action. *Rules* are specific regulations which must be followed, in contrast to policies which are broad and general. Rules serve as boundaries to behavior, ensuring that work will occur within established limits. For example, rules normally specify when work will begin each day. If there were no such rule, there might never be enough people on the job to start the necessary operations and meet the company's objectives.

Procedures are also guidelines for action in organizations, yet they seldom involve disciplinary action if they are not followed. Procedures are developed over time and, in most cases, are the "best way" that has been found to do a job. After many techniques or methods for performing a task have been experimented with, the one that seems best is designated as a procedure. The steps of the technique or method are then put in writing and distributed to all persons who do a particular job. The purpose of a procedure is to improve efficiency and therefore reduce costs. Many organizations have procedures manuals which specify how all routine problems or situations are to be handled. However, there are probably as many "unwritten" procedures as there are those that have been formalized in writing.

Procedures exist throughout most organizations. Clinical procedures specify which forms are to be used for a particular function and how they are to be routed through the organization. In the factory, procedures specify how materials, parts, or equipment are to be inspected upon receipt, how they are to be stored, and often which parts, materials, or equipment are to be used first. Procedures and rules are ongoing plans that do not need to be written out each time a job is done. They are used to create a stable basis for an operation, and they help to create a normal and smooth work climate.

BOX 1. An Example of Some Unrealistic Rules

Memorandum

To: All Personnel

Subject: New Sick Leave Policy

It has been brought to my attention that the attendance record of this department is a disgrace to our gracious benefactor, who, at your own request, has given you your job. Due to lack of consideration for your jobs with so fine a department, as shown by such absenteeism, it has become necessary for us to revise some of our policies. The following changes are in effect immediately.

1. SICKNESS:

   No excuse . . . We will no longer accept your doctor's statement as proof, because we believe that if you are able to go to the doctor, you are able to come to work.

2. DEATH:

   (Other than your own) . . . This is no excuse. There is nothing you can do for them, and we are sure that someone else with a lesser position can attend to the arrangements. However, if the funeral can be held in the late afternoon, we will be glad to let you off one hour early provided that your share of the work is ahead enough to keep the job going in your absence.

3. LEAVE OF ABSENCE:

   (For an operation) . . . We are no longer allowing this practice. We wish to discourage any thoughts that you may need any operation, because we believe that as long as you are an employee here, you will need all of whatever you have and you should not, under any circumstances, consider having anything removed. We hired you as you are, and to have anything removed would certainly make you less than we bargained for.

4. DEATH:

   (Your own) . . . This will be accepted as an excuse, but we would like two weeks notice because we feel it is your duty to train someone else for your job.

Continued

Also, entirely too much time is being spent in the restroom. In the future we will follow the practice of going in alphabetical order. For instance, those whose names begin with "A" will go from 8:00 to 8:15, "B" will go from 8:15 to 8:30, and so on. If you are unable to go at your time, it will be necessary to wait until the next day when your turn comes again.

Feedback

Every supervisor needs to have a feedback system to tell her or him how well the organization is performing and what changes need to be made. In most living organisms, the nervous system keeps the brain informed about what is happening around the body. For example, if your hand touches an object that is too hot, the nervous system tells the muscle of the hand to release the object. In the same way, there must be a feedback system in planning to tell you if your operations are working correctly. A feedback system should operate in order to help make changes in the operation when they are needed; it should not be used to gather evidence that will be used to punish employees.

Even the best designed and most reliable plans have feedback systems, because plans are rarely perfect. The information needed to make adjustments comes from a feedback system. In most cases the adjustments are minor, as in the case of how the human eye, brain, nervous system, and muscles work in driving a car along a seemingly straight road. Scientists tells us that we only think we are driving straight. In fact, we are making hundreds of small adjustments through the automatic reactions of our body system. The brain is programmed to keep the car inside the boundaries of its lane. When the eye gets signals that the car is heading out of these boundaries the message is sent, via the nervous system, to the brain. The brain then tells the muscles of the hand to make the required corrections to bring the car back to the proper course. This automatic feedback-correction system is so perfect that we often never notice the deviations in the direction of the car. As supervisors, we need to develop and use a similarly sensitive feedback system to check our planning.

Types of Plans

Plans range from very simple to highly sophisticated ones. As we examine some of the many kinds of plans, we begin to see how plans help supervisors direct their actions within their organizations.

Financial Plans. Almost every family runs on a budget or financial plan. Organizations, too, have budgets which are plans for spending financial resources and which direct the financial resources of management toward various organizational activities. In Figure 2–2, we examine a typical flow of financial resources in a production-oriented business. Funds obviously must be available from previous revenues or existing revenues in order to pay the salaries of managers and employees in the various functional areas of the firm. Funds must be available to pay for materials, supplies, equipment, and other items required before any sales are made and new funds are generated. If all the funds are spent for the engineering of the product, there will be no funds left to produce or sell that product. A budget allocates funds in a way that allows each segment of an organization to accomplish its objectives. Every unit in an organization must have a financial plan or budget that ties the financial resources of the organization to the tasks expected of each department.

Production Plans. Production plans involve work scheduling, the arrival and testing of raw materials and inputs, and the assignment of workers to particular shifts or work groups. Production planning can also include the actual mix of models or products to be produced in an assembly situation.

Marketing Plans. Marketing plans usually involve decisions about a company's markets and the products and services that the company sells. These plans may also include distribution, pricing, and other factors (such as models, credit terms, and optional equipment) that can have a direct bearing on production and financial planning as well.

Marketing plans frequently include the allocation of salespeople and the establishment of policies on returning merchandise, refunding to customers, advertising in the media, and the like.

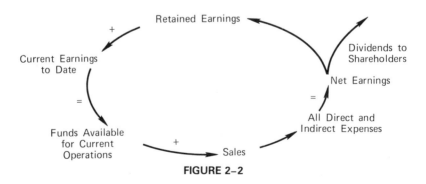

FIGURE 2–2

Forecasting

Inputs and information from supervisors usually form the basic data used in developing forecasts. Budgets are based on the availability of various resources, and forecasts outline what managers assume will happen in the immediate future. Forecasters consider data given them by supervisors throughout the organization. From this data, they develop an idea of where the organization presently stands in terms of operation, goals, and so on. They then review the objectives of the organization and decide where the organization should be going. Only then do they develop plans to reach the firm's objectives.

With the firm's goals in mind, forecasters study various possibilities. Market research may be conducted to determine how new products or services will do in the marketplace. Production alternatives are considered to determine how to produce the best quality at the lowest price. Using "make or buy" analysis, forecasters can predict if it will be feasible to subcontract the production of some parts, subassemblies, or processes. On the financial side, forecasters use economic models to determine the direction of the nation's economy and how it might affect the organization as a whole or in specific departments. If there are indications of rising interest rates, the forecaster may suggest borrowing before funds are actually needed in order to reduce financing costs. Sales forecasts are used to determine how a product or service can best be marketed in the future, and they can tell management what revenues can be expected in the future.

Forecasters take their projections and create an operational plan, combining the present position of the organization with the forecasts. This creates an overall master plan. It guides the organization's management toward its objectives.

Advantages of Planning

There are several benefits and advantages to good planning.

Planning Identifies Problems. When supervisors are involved in planning, they tend to identify potential problems in time to avert them. Planning forces a supervisor to think into the future and evaluate alternatives. It also forces supervisors to face up to potential problems and take action to resolve problems before they get out of control. One supervisor commented that since she had started spending more time planning, she had significantly reduced the number of operational problems that used to plague her. "I simply began to see the source of our difficulties and was able to take actions to eliminate the problems before they could affect our work."

Planning Develops Alternatives.   All too often, supervisors continue to do whatever they have done before. Consequently, they take actions that are no longer appropriate. Planning forces supervisors to explore alternative solutions and to look at the merits of other approaches to doing their jobs. It is easy to fall into a rut, creating our own routines or failing to look for alternatives. Planning forces the development of alternatives so that decision making includes as many options as possible. "There is always an alternative," one supervisor told us, "and often you find a half dozen more. In most jobs, a yearly review of progress points out where changes should occur to make the job a good deal more productive."

Photo courtesy of Diamond International Corporation.

Planning Improves Productivity. When the organization produces plans that involve the employees and then communicates those plans to each employee, productivity usually improves. Employees feel that they have a greater knowledge of what is happening. When employees can follow the progress of their work, completion dates are more easily reached and work is done within budget. Their efforts can be measured by themselves in terms of how their work leads in completed objectives.

Planning Improves Teamwork. When an employee sees that other employees depend on his or her work in order to perform their own jobs, an increased feeling of responsibility develops. Plans demonstrate to employees that their company depends on them to work together to get a job done. Plans can help each employee see his or her role in the overall operation. Teamwork requires coordination, and plans serve as the catalyst for bringing work groups together. The more that employees appreciate the responsibilities and duties of others, the better will be the chance that they will want to work together. Supervisors are often amazed at the lack of knowledge that exists among workers in a single organization. Top management assumes that each group of employees knows what the others do. Yet all too often, poor coordination results because work groups distrust each other or have no real idea how they are interrelated. Planning that shows actual interrelationships helps employees realize how their work group depends on others. By recognizing mutual interdependence, coordination can be measurably improved.

Why Does Planning Fail?

There are a number of reasons why planning fails.

Plans that are based on inaccurate or irrelevant information are not only useless but detrimental to the organization. Plans must be based on facts. Supervisors are the major source of the information used by management in developing plans. Many of the reports which supervisors complete in their daily activities form the basis for future planning. Supervisors often do not realize that the data they provide is critical, and they often do a sloppy job of putting it together.

Planning fails if management does not relate planning to the organization's objectives. The actual task performed by employees must be coordinated with the supervisors involved, or plans will be ineffective.

Planning also fails when plans are not designed to show employees how their individual goals can be obtained by accomplishing the objectives of the organization. Plans must show each employee his or her role in the organization. Plans, such as budgets, are often viewed by many employees as "negative" controls rather than helpful guides to aid the group in reaching their goals.

CONTROLLING

Control is the sequence of activities and tasks that compares *actual operations and results* to the *plans and standards previously established.* If you have ever assembled a child's bicycle on Christmas Eve, only to find at the end of the job that you had five bolts left over, you know the meaning of lack of control. The plans for the bike specify what "ought" to be, and your handful of bolts tells you "what is." If the two don't match, you could have problems. Control involves matching actual and planned operations, discovering the reasons for mismatches, and making whatever corrections are necessary to complete a job properly.

The plans of an organization are like blueprints or guides to action. For these plans to be converted into reality, every process and operation involved must be monitored and controlled. Control usually involves a comparison of the time estimates in the original plan with the actual time required to do a job. It also involves monitoring the money and effort used to complete a project. If your department met all its objectives, but spent far too much money doing so, you would not likely feel that the effort was a total success. All standards were not met. Thus, there is an economic dimension to control as well as time and quality dimensions.

Elements of Control

Control is the responsibility of every supervisor at every level of the organization. Just walking through the work area, talking with people at their desks, work stations, or machines, is part of the supervisor's control responsibility. You may not even ask specifically, "How's it going?" The fact that you are available and keeping watch over a department is an exercise of control. The problem is that many supervisors view control as a responsibility of top management and ignore their own control responsibilities.

To help you avoid this problem, let's look at some of the elements of supervisory control.

Setting Standards. The first part of the control process involves setting standards and communicating those standards to those who must meet them. When you assembled a bicycle, you had a set of plans spread out on the floor. Those plans were your standards or objectives for the project, and your bicycle should have come out looking like the one pictured in the plans. In organizations, standards are developed from the overall goals and objectives of top management. From these overall standards, more specific standards are developed for each department. For example, if the overall goal of the company is to increase total revenues by 12 percent over the next fiscal year, it may be difficult to use this as a standard for measuring the effectiveness of your own department. However, a standard developed from this overall goal might be something like "the Department B production target is 275 units per month." Now we have a standard that can be used to measure actual performance.

Standards must be set up and agreed to before any of the other elements in control come into play. Children often get themselves into arguments by "changing the rules" after the game has started. If you set your sales or production quota after the selling or production period had ended, you would obviously be able to meet your quota; however, you would not be controlling, because you would then have no way to determine if the actual performance was adequate. "Because we completed 208 this year, let's just set the standard at 208 and tell the boss we met our goal." That sounds ridiculous, and it is. Standards must be set in advance, before any action is taken.

Gathering Feedback Information. Feedback is the technical name given for information about the progress of a job which is communicated back to management for corrective action. This information allows managers to determine whether the activity and output of a department match the plan for that department. In the Ace Washing Machine Company, the production plan may indicate that the assembly process, from the beginning to the final test, should take ten minutes. To control the critical variable of manufacturing time, management may identify a washer when it begins assembly and measure how long it takes to reach the final testing. This feedback gives management information necessary to maintain smooth and profitable operations. If the time between assembly and final test is thirty minutes instead of the expected twenty minutes, management would take action to find the specific cause of the extra time. Supervisors who take action only when performance fails to meet predetermined standards are applying the exception principle of management.

Using the Exception Principle. When using the exception principle, no managerial action is taken when feedback indicates that all is well. When a problem is indicated, control actions are taken to identify the cause of the problem and to return the system to normal. Through these techniques the business is kept flowing smoothly.

In some companies, controls are built into an automatic-action system. Inventory (that is, the material used to produce a product) is normally measured to ensure that a shortage of inventory never takes place. If the Ace Washing Machine Company failed to have an adequate supply of a simple item such as a doorhinge, production could come to a standstill.

Some controls work best with graphic tools. Sales forecasts are often compared with actual sales by plotting both on a common chart. This technique allows a fast and easily understood comparison to be made. When the managers responsible for sales observe that sales are less than those forecast, managerial action can be taken to bring sales to the proper and projected level. This information gives supervisors information necessary to make changes in the operations of their departments.

Taking Corrective Actions.   The third and final phase in the control process directly involves the supervisor. Once standards for performance evaluation have been established and information about the actual operations has been gathered, the supervisor must take action.

If information shows that the actual operations are deviating from planned standards, corrective actions become necessary. These corrective actions involve adjustments to bring the department's activities into line with the standards. The bowler who continually leaves the rear corner pins standing will probably make some adjustments in the delivery of the ball and then closely watch the result of these adjustments. If the adjustments result in the corner pins falling down, no further adjustments are needed. If the pins still remain standing, more (or better) adjustments are needed. The same is true about tuning the engine of your car. You make adjustments to the timing or carburation until the engine's performance matches the performance standards of that model.

Not meeting standards in a particular department or section often occurs because of a poor or substandard performance from one or two employees. When this happens, a simple, "machine-like" adjustment is not enough. As a supervisor, it is your responsibility to discover the reasons for the substandard performance. Perhaps the unproductive behavior can be corrected by talking with the employee or by steering that employee toward professional counseling. But, if your adjustment efforts fail, it may become necessary to transfer or fire the offending employee and replace that person with another willing and able to do the job according to the preset standards. Many supervisors feel that the most difficult part of their jobs is telling people to change or be fired. Yet, the productivity of the entire group must not be allowed to suffer unnecessarily because of the substandard performance of one or two members of the group.

Group Control

Because supervisors almost unanimously agree that disciplinary control is their most unwelcome and unappealing responsibility, many have experimented with alternatives. In Chapter 12, we will discuss in far more detail some ideas for keeping order and discipline, which are essential parts of control. However, many supervisors have been successful in establishing and maintaining control by using group processes. People want to be accepted by other members of their work groups, even if those same employees feel little or no loyalty to the department or to the organization. As a supervisor, you can command people to follow the rules and perform according to standards. However, people will also respond to pressures from other group members to comply, when they feel that compliance is best for the group.

One supervisor faced a potential crisis when two of his employees challenged his authority by refusing to produce at the rate set as a standard for the department. Because of these two substandard performances, the entire department was falling behind on its delivery schedule, and the supervisor was taking a lot of "heat" from his superiors. He realized that, although he had the right to control the situation by firing the two offending employees, such a solution would cause other problems. The two offending workers were well liked by others in the department, and in many ways, they were good employees. This supervisor tackled the problem in two ways. First, he called together the three persons in the group who were generally recognized as the informal leaders. Together, the four reviewed all the production and performance standards imposed on the department. The supervisor promised the others that he would personally take all the group's recommendations to higher management and fight for their implementation. However, he cautioned that, once the group's leadership made the suggested new standards, they would be responsible for living up to them. Wisely, he followed up on his promise and was successful in having about 75 percent of the suggested standards adopted by the management. (Some of these suggested standards were, naturally, below those previously imposed. However, other suggested standards were above those previously imposed.)

The supervisor's second move toward group control was to refrain from taking any direct action in efforts to maintain compliance with the new standards. He changed his role so that he merely received information and passed it on (with comments where standards were not being met) to the three informal group leaders. They, in turn, were given full authority to maintain the standards. After about a month of getting used to the new standards, the supervisor reported that all standards were being met (barring the usual, unforeseen difficulties). An added side benefit was that the morale in the group was better than ever before, and the two substandard producers were once again producing at the required level. The pressures that group members can bring to bear on other members is far more powerful than any controls used directly by the supervisor. This strategy of group control requires that the supervisor be completely honest with the group membership. Also, the group's informal leadership must recognize that meeting their standards is in their best interests. By using the natural forces of the group, the supervisor was able to permit his employees to have some direct control over the setting of standards and to improve productivity while he simplified his control responsibilities.

Types of Control

Next, let's look briefly at three kinds of control: preliminary control, concurrent control, and feedback control.

Preliminary Control.   Control follows an actual happening or event: Something is done (a job is performed or a sale is made), and information can be available to the supervisor to be used for control. However, control also has a "pre-action" dimension as well as a "re-action" dimension.

Preliminary control involves monitoring the quality and nature of the inputs of a process. Companies manufacturing products are very careful about the quality of the materials from which they make their products. By eliminating substandard inputs, management can more effectively control the quality of the output.

Preliminary control also involves monitoring the quality of the people who do the work in the department. Many organizations use performance standards to help in selecting and hiring individuals who will perform at the proper level on the job. These preliminary control standards might include education level, skills, training, background, or previous experience. By controlling the quality of personnel at the time they are hired, we reduce the need for control after the product or service is produced.

Orientation as Preliminary Control.   Orientation is often considered part of the staffing function of supervisors. However, when it is viewed from the vantage point of control, it takes on a very different meaning. Orientation can be very useful as a control device. Even if the organization provides a general orientation for all new employees, supervisors should hold some sort of informal orientation in the department as well. In this way, the new employee gets "off on the right foot" with other employees. Often supervisors assume full responsibility for an informal orientation; they hold a short conversation with the new employee and introduce the new employee to the others in the department. The new employee meets each of her or his new coworkers, and (while not remembering many names) gets a feeling of belonging to the group.

Some supervisors delegate the informal departmental orientation to a senior worker or to the leader of the informal work group. This is a good strategy if the informal leadership is cooperative with the management. However, if there is hostility between the supervisor and the informal leader, such an orientation could turn the new employee against the supervisor, creating more problems than necessary.

Concurrent Control. Concurrent control is the control exercised by a supervisor while the actual operations are underway. It is useful in spotting practices and actions that could cause production slowdowns, quality-control problems, delivery foul-ups, and so on. Concurrent control is exercised simply by having a supervisor available while work is going on. The presence of a supervisor will prevent many discipline problems and safety violations as well.

Another part of concurrent control is the reassurance that employees can feel by having their supervisor present while operations are under way. This is especially important when a job is new or potentially dangerous. The presence of a "steady hand," while perhaps not physically necessary, can be psychologically very useful.

Concurrent control should not appear to be a supervisor's mistrust of employees. By maintaining a watch over operations, the supervisor may appear to have little trust in the ability of the employees to perform as required. Thus, concurrent control must be done with tact. World War II General George Patton was revered by his troops because he made it a practice to be with the troops during every engagement. He was not, like many military "supervisors," behind the lines during battle. Patton's presence could be an example of concurrent control. As a supervisor, he was in a position to get critical information first-hand and to act upon it immediately, without waiting for such information to come to him "through channels." This, in itself, was important. However, more important was the effect of Patton's presence on the morale of the troops. Knowing that the supervisor cares and is willing to share the risks (or the boredom) can contribute to the productivity of the group.

Counseling as Concurrent Control. Counseling is another form of concurrent control. Often, an employee's poor performance on the job is related to personal problems. Supervisors should not take the place of trained psychologists or the clergy. However, supervisors who take an active interest in their employee problems (without violating the employee's privacy) will be able to establish and maintain a good rapport. This, in turn, can promote good work relationships within a department and can substantially reduce turnover, absenteeism, and quality-control problems.

In Chapter 10, we will discuss performance appraisal and employee counseling in more detail. It is important that, as a supervisor, you view orientation and counseling as vital parts of your control responsibility.

Feedback Control.   In several sections of this book, we have discussed and defined the nature of feedback and feedback control. Feedback is perhaps the most critical element in proper supervisory control. Without feedback, the supervisor is helpless to make changes or correct situations that get out of balance. Examine your feedback system and the ways you receive feedback from your employees and from your superiors. If you find that there are areas where that feedback may be subject to distortion, begin to make changes immediately. Your success as a supervisor is directly related to the quality (and timeliness) of the feedback you receive.

Characteristics of Good Control

To be effective, controls should be simple and understandable by all employees. Although it may be necessary for legal or commercial reasons to put rules and procedures into complex and difficult-to-understand language, such language makes effective control difficult. Whenever it is necessary, translate such language into the terms that your employees will understand.

Controls should be practical. It does little good to have a control system that fits some textbook description but cannot be put to use. The information required for a control system should be readily available, and such information should not be so expensive to obtain that its cost exceeds the value of the information.

Controls should be timely. It does no good to learn late that corrective action should have been taken. When information indicates that something is "out of control," action should be taken immediately. In addition to timeliness, control information must show devisations quickly. Relying on the "grapevine" is useful for "filling in the gaps," but it is a poor source of control information. To hear three days later that Charlie is having trouble closing the Vishinski contract or that the number 2 machine is leaking oil is little comfort to the supervisor. With timely and accurate information, and with timely action, effective control is possible with a minimum of effort and disruption.

Controls should be flexible. Although fairness is a standard that must be followed whenever controls are applied to people, situations can cause some controls to be less effective. When this happens, the control system should be flexible enough to permit a change in procedures or methods.

Finally, controls should be appropriate, adequate, and economical. Supervisors and managers must continuously monitor their control to be sure that they are controlling what they want to control, and getting good information is only half the battle. Getting information when it is

Photo courtesy of Pitney Bowes, Inc.

A TEAM OF INTERNAL AUDITORS EXAMINE THE COMPANY RECORDS

needed and from the proper sources is the other part of the control equation. When it is properly utilized, control helps to avoid problems and reduce the damage done when problems develop.

ORGANIZING

An organization is a collection of people arranged into groups who work together to achieve a common objective. A group is usually distinguished from an organization on the basis of size. A group is a small number of individuals, usually with full face-to-face contact. Organizations, which are composed of groups, do not usually permit full face-to-face contact among all members, and this limitation is usually due to size.

What Is Involved in Organizing?

Once plans, policies, and strategies have been established, managers must assemble the resources necessary to reach their objectives. Organizing means establishing an appropriate structure for the goal-seeking activities of a firm or department. The internal structure of any organization is often shown on an organization chart or a job-task pyramid. It displays the authority and responsibility relationships among the various functions in the organization by showing who reports to whom. Organizing means establishing the functions or activities to be performed and their sequence of completion. Once this is done, job classifications can be established and the best grouping of jobs can be decided. Supervisors must know how each job in a department relates to other jobs and responsibilities. Organization begins with the most basic job done in a department. If even one activity is omitted from the "organization plan," the final objectives of the organization will likely not be fully reached.

Some Principles of Organizing

Authority and Responsibility.   Delegation of authority and responsibility is important in all organizations. Authority is the right or power to make decisions and give orders. Responsibility is the obligation to perform assigned tasks. Each person in an organization is responsible to one other person, that is, his or her supervisor. These superiors, in turn, report to one individual at the next higher level. This "reporting chain" results in what we commonly call the organization chart or job-task pyramid. (See Figure 2–3.)

Starting with the lowest level of the organization, the jobs being done are divided into as many segments as necessary. The activities of people in these various jobs are coordinated at the next highest level by supervisors. Each worker reports to one supervisor who has authority over a particular department or group. The people on one level report to one individual on the next higher level. Those on the higher level are also responsible for the actions of their subordinates. Authority and responsibility bring order to the many functions and people in the organization.

The authority that every supervisor has to make decisions and to meet responsibilities comes through the chain of command in the organization. Even the person in the top operating position in a business has

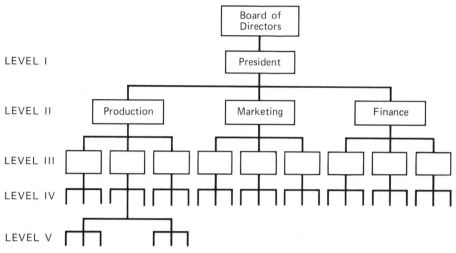

FIGURE 2-3 The Organization Chart or Job-Task Pyramid

a source of authority. In business, the highest policy-making authority is the owner or the board of directors. In a government organization, the highest policy-making authority is the elected representative of the people.

Chain of Command. The chain of command is a principle of organization that supervisors and employees at each level have some authority to carry out policies and procedures within a specific area of responsibility. They are also responsible for the activities of their subordinates. They must be sure that jobs are performed properly and that division or section goals are reached. The chain of command is used to report information up and down the organization chart. Through the chain of command, messages about policy decisions are transmitted to the supervisors who convert policy into on-the-job actions. Supervisors use the upward chain of command to report their activities so that others can coordinate the overall operations of the organization. The chain of command helps to ensure that each person who needs to know what is going on gets informed. Use of the chain-of-command principle usually results in one of two organizing patterns: centralized or decentralized organization.

Centralized and Decentralized Organizations. Your organization's structure is either centralized or decentralized. In a centralized organization, all decisions are made by a limited number of persons at the top. In a decentralized organization, operating decisions are made throughout the organization. Obviously, the key feature that distinguishes the structure of an organization is where the decisions are made. Supervisors who prefer a centralized organization believe that if the most successful and experienced executives are at the top of the organization, important decisions should be made there. Executives at the top of an organization have facts and related knowledge that the lower-level managers may not have. With the introduction of computer-based information systems into business, more and better data can be processed, analyzed, and made available to top management. This can result in more effective decisions.

Factors in Decentralization. Advocates of decentralization suggest that no one can actually understand a problem better than can the manager or supervisor who is directly involved with the situation. Therefore, the manager closest to a problem should make the decisions about the problem. Decentralization advocates ask, "How can supervisors learn to make decisions and demonstrate top management potential if they are not given opportunities to make decisions?" Decentralized management is thus often seen as a training device. Usually, the decision to decentralize is based on such factors as

1. Are the department's (or firm's) operations geographically spread out? The more the physical separation between related activities, the greater will be the need to decentralize authority and decision making.

2. Can the supervisors make good decisions? If the company or department has a history of successful decision making at lower levels, there is a greater chance for successful decentralization. But if centralized organization has been successful for a company, this may retard attempts to decentralize.

3. Is the company committed to developing decision makers? In a fast-growing dynamic organization, the key to continued growth may be the development of future decision makers. A decentralized company will need more decision makers than will one that is centralized.

4. How much financial profit or loss is at stake in a decision being made? The more costly the consequences of a decision, the more likely the decision will be made by the top management.

5. How large (in terms of personnel or dollar volume of sales) is the company or organization? The size of the organization has much to do with decentralization. Small organizations or departments are usually centralized. As growth occurs, decentralization often becomes both necessary and desirable.

6. How fast is the company or the department growing? Fast-growing firms often must decentralize in order to respond to market forces. Decisions must be made quickly and frequently, and a procedure must exist for permitting this. Decentralization becomes a necessity in meeting expanding growth opportunities and pressures.

Division of Labor. In most organizations, the activities of departments are divided into individual jobs in which each person is assigned to a certain task. The results of each job are combined to form a finished product or service. This division of labor makes it possible for individual jobs to be simple enough so that even the most unskilled workers can do them. It also allows supervisors to fix responsibility clearly for each small step or phase in an overall manufacturing, sales, or service operation. When the work each person in the organization does is divided, individuals can become expert in a particular activity.

Division of labor works because of the operating rules and regulations that are set for each different job. All jobs must be performed in a uniform way. If an organization had a division of labor but no work rules, it would be almost impossible for managers to coordinate the various activities. The organizing job of supervisors is to make the activities of individuals in their departments as uniform and productive as possible. This can only be done if each employee is working with the same work standards and rules.

Departmentalization. Similar jobs are usually grouped together by function. Departmentalization stems from an organization's efforts to put together employees who are doing similar jobs. For example, if all tasks performed by a group of people involved accounting, their jobs would usually be put in the accounting department. This is considered functional departmentalization. On the other hand, if all functions involving the West Coast operation of a company were included in one group, it would be an example of geographic departmentalization. If persons or functions were grouped by the product they produced or sold, product departmentalization would exist. Similarly, organizations can also be departmentalized on the basis of time (that is, long-running jobs versus short-time jobs), clients, or customers served (that is, military sales, institutional sales, and general consumer sales). We will examine briefly each of the three major forms of departmentalization.

Functional departmentalization permits people with common tasks to work together to achieve common goals and to share information about the best methods for doing a job. Functional departmentalization also allows for better supervision, because one manager can be responsible for all company work of a similar nature.

Geographic departmentalization is useful for companies operating in many parts of the country. Often, company problems in the South may be different from problems in the North or West. When functions are grouped according to location, these differences can be better handled. It would be difficult to manage all accounting people using functional departmentalization if employees worked in all parts of the country. Geographic departmentalization is the only sensible way to organize in that situation.

Product departmentalization occurs when an organization is arranged according to its various products. The General Motors Corporation has five new-car divisions plus divisions for various other products such as appliances, locomotives, road construction equipment, jet engines, and auto parts. The rationale for such departmentalization is that each of these products (or product groupings in some organizations) requires different kinds of thinking in its design, manufacture, sale, and distribution. Thus, one department or division might have needs that are found in no other division. By allowing functional overlap (such as many sales staffs or many production facilities with duplicate facilities), each department is better able to deal with its market or complete its mission.

All forms of departmentalization are common to public administration as well as private or business administration. Naturally, there are many examples of government agencies departmentalized by geographic area or by the function they perform (such as the various Cabinet departments at the federal level, including the Department of Defense, the Department of Agriculture, and so on). However, many city administrations are departmentalized on the basis of the services that they provide for the public (such as police protection, fire protection, licenses, zoning, and so on).

Unity of Command.   Under the unity-of-command principle, productivity is maximized when an employee receives her or his instructions from only *one boss*. When an employee has more than one boss giving instructions, it would be difficult to tell whose instructions should be followed first. A worse situation would be when instructions are in conflict with one another, whose instructions should the employee follow? Conflicts between supervisors' orders creates a work climate where the subordinates can become confused and unproductive. The morale of the work group can decline because workers believe that the organization's management is confused. When doubts about a supervisor's ability to handle a situation arise, it takes a major effort to reassure subordinates that management knows what it is doing. Unity of command gives management strength and control by having only one person in authority to make decisions at each level or department. When it is properly applied, unity of command strengthens the role of the supervisor because it establishes the sole and final decision-maker for a work group.

Unity of Command and Project Management.   One of the most significant changes in organizational structure in the last thirty years has been the development of project management. In a project management organization, employees are assembled from various departments and functions to work toward completing a specific project. When the project is completed, each person returns to his or her previous functional area (or to a new project group). While the project is going on, the employees who are assigned to it have two or more bosses. These supervisors usually are the boss from the functional group of the employee and the boss of the entire project. (See Figure 2–4.) In order to avoid

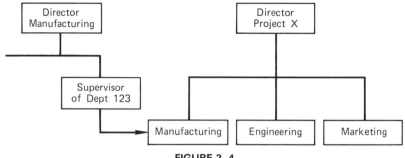

FIGURE 2-4

problems, both supervisors in the project must determine the exact authority and responsibility each will have during the project's life. With such an arrangement, employees will be receiving orders about a specific subject from only one boss. Both supervisors and their subordinates can operate smoothly if problems are solved early. Most of the criticism of project management stems from the many human problems that arise when the initial agreement on authority and responsibility is not clearly determined and followed.

Span of Control.   How many people can one supervisor manage? This question cannot be answered with a specific number. The concept of span of control or span of supervision reminds management that each situation must be studied to determine the *best number* of subordinates for a supervisor and situation.

Factors in Span of Control:

The Employees.   How much experience do employees have at a particular job? What is their present attitude about the organization and the supervisor? The more willing the employees are to perform tasks, the less supervision they will need. The same is true with experience. The more experienced employees will have more confidence and therefore will usually need less direct supervision. With new employees, supervisors must take time for training. The type of employee to be managed is the single most important determinant of how much time must be spent in direct supervision.

The Experience and Competence of the Supervisor.   Not all supervisors have the same talents and abilities. In some cases, supervisors are more efficient because of previous job experience. In other cases, the supervisor must learn the job while attempting to supervise. With experience and through trial and error, supervisors learn many time savers which produce cost savings and greater efficiency.

Some supervisors are not effective with certain types of employees.

They do not like assignments in which their jobs or responsibilities are not clearly defined. Some work assignments may be new and have no "track record" on what should be done. In these situations supervisors must make decisions where the outcome is actually in doubt. This can create tensions among members of the work group and reduce efficiency. The other extreme occurs when the supervisor has a "maintenance" role. The task has been performed one way for some time, and the problems have all been "ironed out." Procedures have been established and few new decisions must be made. In this case, more employees can be supervised by one individual because less time is taken up with decision making. Some supervisors do not work well in this sort of situation because they view the job as being boring. They prefer a job with greater challenge.

The Type of Work Involved (The Situation).   The work being done influences the span of supervision. This includes simple-function tasks or complex ones. In assignments in which the work is simple and the employees have done the job before, the span of control can be significantly broader. In complex jobs, in which the employees have had no previous experience, the relationship between the supervisor and each employee must be closer, and the span of control is much narrower. For example, consider the span of control of a supervisor in manufacturing, where all employees are working on familiar machines and on jobs they have done for years. In this instance, one supervisor can supervise as many as thirty to thirty-five people. On the other hand, consider an intensive care unit in a hospital. New problems, with no specific procedure established and little or no experience to rely on, are constantly coming in the door. These cases usually require the direct involvement of the supervisor. In such situations, a supervisor's control span may not include more than four or five employees.

Other Factors.   A wide variety of other factors will influence the span of control of a supervisor, including the full-time or part-time distinction. The less time spent directly involved in supervision, the more narrow (smaller) the span of control must be. Another significant factor influencing the span of control is the degree of coordination that is required between work groups. If the supervisor is active in coordinating with other work groups, the amount of time required for person-to-person supervision can be reduced. This will reduce the span of control. With better defined and better understood work standards, a wider span of control can be used. Detailed standards enable employees to work on their own with less need for direct supervision.

The distance between members of the work group also influences the span of control. The more time that is used in travelling between employees, the less will be available for supervision. If supervisors are

Photo courtesy of Diamond International Corporation.

A LARGE SPAN OF CONTROL IS MORE POSSIBLE HERE

physically removed from employees, supervisory efficiency is reduced. In some situations, this problem cannot be avoided. Sales supervisors may have salespeople spread across the entire region, and they are forced to depend on telephone and mail communications for personal contact. In these situations, it is extremely difficult to discuss problems with subordinates, and the individual in the field is pretty much alone.

A final factor that can influence the span of control of a supervisor is the amount of teamwork existing in the work group. Most supervisors rank teamwork as the key to their success in managing their employees. Employees who work well together often solve problems before they even come to the attention of the supervisor. One supervisor in a Canadian department store chain, when asked why she thought she was a good supervisor, responded by saying that her group can get their work done on time with or without her being around. This may, at first, sound like she doesn't do anything. In reality, she has developed a work team that has learned to do the job and have confidence in their decisions and actions.

Line and Staff.   In any formal organization, those employees who are directly involved with the production, distribution, or financing of the products or services of the organization are called line employees. Employees who serve the line functions are considered staff employees. There are no specific rules for all organizations that indicate which employees are line and which are staff. This determination depends on the structure of the organization. The organization chart in Figure 2–5 gives a typical example of a line and staff relationship. The manufacturing and engineering departments are considered line employees, and the personnel and industrial relations departments are considered staff. The manufacturing and engineering departments are directly involved with the design and production of the company's product. In a bank, the

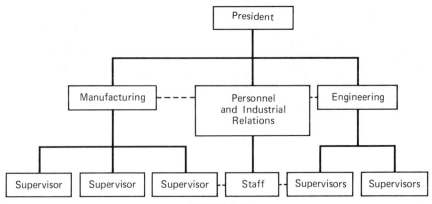

FIGURE 2–5

tellers, cashiers, and the loan, trust, and customer service department employees would likely be considered line, while the personnel, building maintenance, and public relations department employees would likely be considered staff. Because the personnel, industrial relations, public relations, and maintenance department employees help the line departments by providing them with services, their roles are supportive in nature.

ACTION GUIDELINES FOR PLANNING

1. Be sure that your plans are based on and in agreement with the organization's objectives.
2. For best results, work to obtain commitment from your employees. Commitment to the organization's objectives requires you to demonstrate to your employees that their personal objectives can be best achieved through the attainment of organizational objectives. Remember, action speaks louder than words.
3. Every plan should be related to job performance. Be as specific as possible. Don't forget to demonstrate how individual job performance relates to the overall job plan. Show how a total effort results in accomplishing group and individual goals.
4. Employees will begin to understand the use of plans better if they see that plans become working documents. A plan should be used to create action in the work place.
5. Whenever possible, formulate plans in concrete terms, such as units of production, dollars of sales, units of product sold, letters typed, percentage reduction in units rejected by inspection, and so on. The more specific and concrete the targets, the better will employees relate to them.
6. Supervisors should develop a workable and timely feedback system. This will provide their employees with useful knowledge about how they are doing in reaching their established goals.
7. Planning means participation. Supervisors who involve their employees in the planning process find that their employees show greater commitment to achieving the planned results. Planning gives the work group a look into the future. It is the first step in making the future happen.
8. Never accept a plan without giving it a thorough and complete review. Spot areas for improvement. This review procedure will help develop a reputation for thoroughness and creativity. Involve your employees in the review. Ask for (and use) employee comments on the plan.
9. Never use a plan as a weapon to coerce productivity. A plan is a guide that should help organizations reach their goals; it should not be used as a tool to threaten employees. Employee attitudes can quickly deteriorate if employees feel their supervisor has been trying to "trap" them with the plan.

10. A plan must be flexible, or capable of change when circumstances change. A plan is a working document that should reflect the changes taking place in the work environment. Don't make the planning document a semishrine locked up in your desk. Keep it available. Write on it; let others write on it. Convert a piece of paper into a set of working ideas. A plan will not become a viable working document if it is locked away.

ACTION GUIDELINES FOR CONTROLLING

Control is an ongoing activity and a major responsibility of every member of the management team. Control functions are performed all the time, often without the supervisor knowing or being aware that they are taking place. Control can, and most frequently is, performed after actions have occurred. However, in recent years, supervisors have enlarged their view of control to include precontrol. This means that supervisors are taking a more active role in preventing unfortunate or unproductive situations from getting out of hand and affecting productivity or performance. When thinking about control, consider these ideas:

1. Develop standards before attempting to control. Without having standards to act as guides, supervisory actions become arbitrary and are often seen by employees as unfair and dictatorial.

2. Control requires coordination between supervisors and employees in their departments. Your department can't do its job if others don't do their jobs, and all supervisors must have a clear understanding of the overall objective. Working at cross-purposes will defeat any control efforts.

3. Be alert to feedback from many sources. Shutting off information can damage your efforts for better control.

4. Evaluate your information before acting. Don't react immediately when you hear bad news or when questionable sources bring you information. Evaluate the source, decide on the importance of the information, and then act.

5. Rely on the exception principle. If you try to control and stay involved in every job in your department, you will never have time for your other responsibilities. Once proper standards are communicated to employees, you should be able to control by paying attention only to those things that deviate from the plan.

6. When control is necessary, take action immediately. Once a situation is clear and all information has been evaluated, unnecessary delay will only compound the problem.

7. Remember that discipline is an important form of control, and that discipline can be performed before as well as after other actions have taken place. By the wise use of orientation and counseling, supervisors

can avoid problems before they reach the crisis stage, where discipline and control measures may be harsh and counterproductive.

ACTION GUIDELINES FOR ORGANIZING

1. Organization does not just mean the entity to which you belong. It includes your responsibility as a supervisor to establish the activities to be performed and the sequence in which they should be performed in order to reach your group's or department's goals.
2. The elements of organizations should be interrelated in order to attain organizational and group goals and to satisfy human needs.
3. In order for supervisors to be effective, authority and responsibility must be equal.
4. Organization charts can help employees by outlining the formal organization and by providing proper paths for reporting and communicating.
5. The chain of command should be represented by the organization chart.
6. Individuals in a work environment should develop special skills to allow for division of labor to be used to increase productivity.
7. Unity of command can be used as a principle of organizing which stresses that a worker can and should have only one boss or one superior to whom he or she reports, from whom that worker takes orders and direction.
8. The number of subordinates that a supervisor can effectively manage should determine the span of control. This number will be influenced by the nature of the job, the skill and experience of the supervisor, and the nature of the employees involved.
9. Supervision must operate within a work environment which is composed of an informal as well as a formal structure. Learn to use the informal organization if you plan to bring about change and reach organizational goals.

DISCUSSION QUESTIONS FOR PLANNING, CONTROLLING, AND ORGANIZING

1. Discuss how supervisors can make objectives more measurable, realistic, and challenging.
2. Why should a supervisor expect there to be any conflict among goals?
3. Is it important to follow each step in the planning process, or can some of the steps be short-cut to improve speed in planning?
4. What are some of the ways that plans are converted into actions?
5. Why should supervisors spend time reviewing plans with participants?

6. Identify the elements of control and discuss how they relate to the environment of the supervisor.

7. How do standards help supervisors maintain control?

8. Discuss the use of the exception principle and how it can be used to improve supervision.

9. How is the group used by supervisors to control performance?

10. What is dissatisfaction compensation, and how is it used for control?

11. Is counseling the proper activity for supervisors? Should it be used for control purposes?

12. What is organization, and how does it relate to the satisfaction of needs?

13. How can we distinguish between authority and responsibility?

14. Is there any practical use for the chain of command?

15. Under what conditions is decentralization useful?

16. What is the principle of unity of command, and how is it violated?

17. What factors affect the supervisor's span of control?

ACTION EXERCISES FOR PLANNING, CONTROLLING, AND ORGANIZING

1. Describe (and discuss with your colleagues) the major activity for which you must plan.

2. Develop a list of areas or activities in which you feel planning has been lax over the last few years. Again, discuss your list with others. This should help you discover how your planning has been done in the past.

3. Develop a detailed plan for one of the following:
   (a) building your own home
   (b) taking a vacation trip across the country
   (c) reducing (or increasing) your weight to a healthier level
   (d) selecting a new car for your family
   (e) putting yourself in contention for the next promotion

   Be sure to identify objectives, subobjectives, priorities, and so on, and to identify points where your plan should be checked for progress. This exercise can give you some valuable insight into how you actually plan.

4. Because control involves preliminary control, concurrent control, and feedback control, identifying each of these elements can be a useful exercise for any supervisor. Organize in small groups, or as individuals, and examine two different situations and see if you can identify examples of each of the three types of control in those situations. For example, in the school setting, what would serve as an example of preliminary control? Perhaps it would be the admissions standards that screen applicants. Can you identify other kinds of preliminary control? Concurrent control? Feedback control?

Next, drawing on experience from your present job or from a job that you have recently held, identify examples of each of the three kinds of control.

While this exercise is basically one of listing, it is useful occasionally to go through such an exercise, because it can help you to become more aware of the control function and the various dimensions as they relate to you and your supervisory responsibilities.

5. Draw (or get a copy of) the organization chart for an organization. Use either a chart from a company you now work for or another chart with which you are familiar. Draw dotted lines connecting your position on this chart (or the position of an individual of your choosing) with the other positions that a person would have contact with on a frequent basis. In doing so, you will be drawing the "informal" organization chart, or the network of acquaintances and friends that permits each supervisor to have wider latitude and power than would be possible using just the formal (solid) lines of authority shown on most organization charts. Next, see how many different formal organization networks you can identify using just this one chart.

CASE 4.   The Special Job

A large California manufacturer set up a special assembly operation to manufacture a sizeable order of a modified model of his product for a very large and important customer. Specifications had been written, material contracts let, and about 40 percent of the material had already arrived, when the customer wired a change in specifications. The change was completed prior to the delivery deadline two months away. The job looked impossible, but the manufacturer could not afford to lose the order. The assembly foremen were called together by the general supervisor and told what had happened and what the effect of a failure to meet the new modifications might mean to jobs and profits. He then told the foremen exactly how the modifications were to be made. He then reemphasized the importance of the job and dismissed the group.

1. How would you feel as a foreman in this situation?
2. If you would have been the general supervisor, how would you have handled the situation?
3. Is there any way to plan for the unexpected and still do a good job on routine matters?

CASE 5. The Annual Report

The police chief was about thirty-five minutes into his annual report to the city manager and the council. The members were seated at the council desk in a large semicircle, with the manager on the end. Dennis Garza, the veteran police chief, was just finishing with his review of the work-force statistics and was getting into a review of performance measures when he was interrupted by Martha Donovan, the city manager. She was holding a copy of last Sunday's newspaper, with the front page feature on crime statistics. "Dennis, this article just doesn't square with your report. They say that robberies in our town increased 12 percent last year. During the same period, we increased your department's budget 15 percent. I get calls from parents about the rash of bicycle thefts at the high school, and that doesn't even begin to lay out the problems. Traffic accidents are increasing to the point where you can't even drive across town without getting your fender dented. As far as I'm concerned, your performance measures don't reflect any of this. Instead, you're telling us about calls answered and miles driven on the police cars. Just what in blazes does that have to do with crime? After all, the citizens are paying you to stop crime, and so far, you haven't done much of that!"

Garza responded to the questions (which were clearly on the minds of other council members as well), by noting that "... it's just a matter of priorities. This year alone our population rose 18 percent. Read the statistics closely. You'll see that major crimes remained constant. Now, I'm not happy with that, but we've all got to be realistic. The opinion of the professionals in my department is that these crimes, which physically hurt our citizens, are where we should put our emphasis. The trouble is, you can't measure effort or dedication or perseverance. Law enforcement is just not measurable the way patronage at the playground, or use of the boat ramp is."

1. Are the city manager and the chief of police using the same standards for measuring performance? Can they?
2. When crime statistics are compared, what problems of interpretation can get in the way of meaningful analysis?
3. Does the population increase have any bearing on the problems of measurement?
4. Is the chief right? Is it possible to measure dedication, perseverance, and effort, since these things have a lot to do with the results the public does see?

CASE 6. Idaho First Fidelity Insurance Company (IFFI)

IFFI is a major insurer of homes and automobiles. Its headquarters are in Twin Falls, and it has a legislative office in Boise. Gladys Richards is the manager of the Storm and Flood Insurance Division. She is directly responsible to the company vice president and supervises five departments. These departments, each with about thirty-five employees, perform a variety of functions, including claim checking, filing and retrieval, and adjusting.

Today, as in the past, she has given her secretary, Joan Christian, instructions to contact three of the department heads and work with them on a number of important problems. Some of these problems involve changes in personnel. Joan has also been told to go to the mailing department and reprimand an employee that Gladys personally observed being rude to a visiting legislator. For years, Joan Christian has done these jobs for her boss, and Gladys has a great deal of confidence in Joan's ability and judgment. She has encouraged her to apply for a position as supervisor in one of the departments, but for personal reasons Joan has always declined. She prefers to remain Gladys Richards' secretary.

Two of the younger department managers usually deal directly with Joan on most matters, while the other department heads resent her activities and go directly to Gladys on important business. Gladys' administrative assistant, Herb Stenerude, is a nephew of the company president. Gladys views Herb as a potential rival, and usually gives him only menial jobs to do. Just last week, the performance ratings for Gladys' department for the last month were announced. They were down again, this time by 12 percent.

1. What major supervision problems do you see in the activities of Gladys Richards' department?
2. What principles of management are apparently being violated? Why? By whom?
3. What would you do to remedy the situation, if your opinion were asked as an outside consultant?

4. Does the fact that performance ratings for the division are declining have any relationship to the problems of Gladys Richards?

CASE 7.   Marine Electronics

"It's not my responsibility."
"You'd better check with Dave. I had nothing to do with it!"
"If you'll remember, I was on vacation when this all came up."
"Doesn't anybody here know what's happening?"
"We would *never* put out something like that . . . No way, it can't be my guys!"

Dan Willingham was getting steamed. The meeting was going nowhere, and something had to be done. Management was waiting, and the order was already three weeks late—not to mention its being way off specifications when it was first delivered. Yet these five people (supposed to be the best project managers in the company) were passing the buck like a bunch of schoolkids.

The five supervisors in the meeting all report to Dan. They were pulled from other operating departments and organized under a project management structure to work on a custom marine electronics package for the Navy.

Dan finally spoke: "Start over, fellows, and see if we can get somewhere. First, who was in charge of the design for the original package?"

Howard Thompson shifted in his seat, but Al Soames spoke first. "My guys had the original responsibility, I guess. But—and let me make this clear—the other departments were involved right from the start. I'm not gonna be the fall guy for the project's failures to perform in the sea tests."

Howard got the floor. "The changes had to be made or this thing would never even have passed our own inspection department. For almost two years we've been hearing the same nonsense about responsibility."

Paul Kraus jumped in. "Speaking for manufacturing, I can tell you that we only did what we were told. No one pays my people to think . . . or at least it doesn't seem that way. We do what we're told, nothing more. If you'd asked me, I could have told you that metal just can't be bent that way without serious damage to its conducting properties. Seems we just get the same old. . . ."

"Come off it, Paul," Al interrupted. "You're just trying to throw it back to my department again."

Dan Willingham's face was crossed with lines. He was bewildered. When the project management structure was first considered, the management consultant assured the company's top planners that such problems would never occur. One consultant on the team even went so far as to say that "Project management is the best thing to ever hit business. Control and management are improved 1000 percent. You can kiss your buck-passing problems goodbye. "I sure wish that turkey was here now to hear this meeting," thought Dan. "It might change his mind."

1. What seems to be the basic problem here?
2. Assuming Dan Willingham was involved with these five managers from the start of the project, what could he have done to avoid this problem?
3. What can he do now? Is it too late to get proper control of the responsibility system in the project?

Management
by
Objectives

Objectives

After studying this chapter on management by and with objectives, you will be able to

1. Better describe what employees want to know about their jobs.

2. Discuss the key elements of an M.B.O. system.

3. Describe the type of manager who will succeed using M.B.O., and know how to avoid being the manager who fails.

4. Describe the characteristics of good objectives.

5. Describe the steps in making M.B.O. work for you.

ONE OF THE most used management techniques is management by objectives (M.B.O.). The concept of M.B.O. was developed by Peter Drucker and is widely used in management today.

M.B.O. is a process in which the superior and subordinates in an organization jointly identify common goals, define each individual's major areas of responsibility in terms of results expected of him or her, and use these measures as guides for operating the unit and assessing the contribution of each of its members. The real value of an M.B.O. system is that all employees who participate in the system gain control over their jobs. This self-control over the work tends to be a source of motivation for many employees. More than a management system, M.B.O. is a philosophy based on open communication.

As a supervisor, you may well be involved with the M.B.O. management technique. M.B.O. succeeds in an environment in which workers are respected. Some people see M.B.O. as "management by trust," since it forces managers and subordinates to assume that everyone really wants to make meaningful contributions to the goals of their organization. M.B.O. assumes that if employees know what is expected of them, they will be willing to work toward common goals. Management, in effect, trusts that employees will actively work towards the goals of the organization. All supervisors can, and should, manage with objectives. In a growing number of firms, managing with objectives is formalized into M.B.O.—management by objectives.

WHY SHOULD SUPERVISORS LEARN
ABOUT M.B.O.?

Management by objectives is a program that must be operating at all levels of an organization in order to be successful. Clearly, a supervisor in one part of the organization cannot be responsible for an M.B.O. program if it does not have the full support of higher management.

More organizations each year adopt some form of M.B.O., and the responsibility increasingly falls on supervisors to work with their people to ensure the success of an M.B.O. program. If an M.B.O. program is now (or will be) in your organization, your management will inform you about the philosophies and mechanisms that make their version of M.B.O effective. However, even if your organization does not have an M.B.O. program, you can still profit personally from the philosophies and action plans of management by objectives.

In many organizations an M.B.O. approach is not used at all. This may be because managers and supervisors know little about M.B.O. and its benefits. They may even feel that such a system threatens their jobs or weakens their ability to supervise their employees. Neither case is true. In practice, M.B.O. is only a tool. It permits you and other supervisors to do a better job of motivating, managing, and evaluating your people. It can also give people a more productive environment, one that results in real improvements in productivity and morale.

HOW DOES M.B.O. BENEFIT EMPLOYEES?

Most employees want to know what their job really is. "What is really expected of me?"and "What are the work criteria against which I will be judged?" are questions often asked. There is often a lot of miscommunication between supervisor and employee as to what one expects from the other. Beyond this, employees want to know how their job "fits" into the overall organization. "Am I a simple cog in a big outfit, or is what I do really important?" Today, with mass production and automation, many workers feel that the world, and their organization, is passing them by. M.B.O. helps put employees back into the center of their worlds. M.B.O. helps relate a person's job to the total organizational effort, and it details the major responsibilities of a job and what performance is expected from persons doing these jobs.

THE KEY ELEMENTS OF AN M.B.O. SYSTEM

M.B.O. is a system that depends on the actions of top management to support effective goal setting throughout the organization.

(a) In order to succeed, M.B.O. must have the active support of top management, and it requires that the long-range goals of the firm be made known to employees throughout the organization.

(b) Management at all levels must truly believe in a managerial philosophy based on employee trust and respect. In order for M.B.O. to be truly effective, all members of the organization will need to direct their efforts toward the organizational goals.

(c) There must be mutual goal-settings. Through mutual goal-setting, supervisors and subordinates agree in advance on the work requirements for the upcoming period. Talking and discussing will lead to some agreement as to what employees believe their output for the work period should be and how their output should be measured.

(d) In order to reinforce appropriate behavior, reward those employees who reach their goals, and redirect performance for those who do not, regular performance reviews are necessary. Reviews of performance focus on the predetermined goals of each employee and each work group. This enables employees to feel secure in the fact that they know in advance the criteria for success. No longer is the reward system based on personal likes or dislikes, but it is based instead on performance. Standards are mutually set and agreed to in advance of performance. It is the performance review and related rewards which will ultimately demonstrate to employees the value of an M.B.O. system.

(e) Another element of an M. B. O. system is the amount of freedom given to each employee to develop the means necessary to achieve both organizational and personal goals. This freedom (hopefully) will result in a greater degree of voluntary energy and creative thought toward the employee's work group. Why limit a person's performance? If people can find a better way to do a job, encourage their initiative. Each person's natural abilities and interest allow them to perceive a work situation differently. The time has passed when supervisors should try to force all persons into the same mold.

THE UNSUCCESSFUL M.B.O. SUPERVISOR

The potentially unsuccessful M.B.O. manager holds many or most of the assumptions about human nature that the late Douglas McGregor identified as "theory X" managers. These assumptions are negative views about people.

Theory X Assumptions in M.B.O.

1. Most employees are not self-motivated; they are lazy and take no real interest in the goals of the organization. If you want the employees to give you a "fair day's work for a fair day's pay," you had better keep a close eye on their performance. The only way to ensure performance toward work goals is to closely supervise and tighten controls.
2. Most employees are lacking in any real initiative to get the work done or to improve the work situation. It is the supervisor's job to "get those people off their duffs and back to work." Because employees lack initiative, you cannot trust them to work toward the goals of the organization; they are only interested in taking care of themselves. If they have any opportunity to slack off, they will take it. "It's us against them; I had the initiative to move up and they don't."
3. You cannot expect much from employees today because they don't have the mental equipment to adjust to change. That's why they are not supervisors. There is little creativity among the rank-and-file employee, and subsequently you cannot expect them to become involved with their job. "I would be happy if they would just take orders well; I will do the thinking and they can do the work."

Supervisors who hold the views expressed above are not going to be successful in an M.B.O. program. They are unwilling to trust their employees. These supervisors will tend to react to all managerial situations by imposing their will on others by autocratic commands and the establishment of detail control to ensure that everything is "done correctly." No room exists for employees to have freedom to control their jobs.

THE SUCCESSFUL M.B.O. SUPERVISOR

The successful manager is usually one who shares McGregor's theory Y assumptions, which take a positive approach to human nature.

Theory Y Assumptions in M.B.O.

1. Supervisors can honestly respect and trust the employees in their group. People today are generally well-educated and trained and have the ability to accomplish the tasks required and assigned. Employees are able to exercise self-control without being led through each step of their job like robots. Employees are willing to work toward the goals of the organization without direction. They will exercise self-direction and self-motivation toward their work goals and do not need minute-to-minute directions by the supervisor.
2. Employees want to help their organization reach both its short- and long-run goals. This will happen if they are convinced that reaching these organizational goals will result in specific rewards and attainment of their personal goals. Each of us has individual goals which we feel are as important as the goals of the organization. No one lives only to serve the organization. But most people have learned that if they want to reach their personal goals, they need to make the organization which employs them successful. This mature attitude is reinforced by the fact that the work situations present an opportunity for employees to demonstrate to themselves and to others their skills and abilities. Such an opportunity for display of skill is essential to the psychological well-being of each person.

Supervisors who hold these attitudes tend to manage by recognizing each employee as an individual who has a unique set of individual values and skills. These supervisors recognize that employees can be developed and can grow into increasingly more productive resources for the organization. They tend to aid and encourage this development through the delegation of authority to employees whenever possible.

The successful manager using objectives communicates well and lets every employee know what is happening in order to focus all of the employee's energies on the attainment of goals which must be reached. Frequent and effective downward communications from the supervisor can bring the work group closer together.

The supervisor must also recognize that M.B.O. implies that each employee will have the resources necessary to do the work. M.B.O. is not a magic technique which allows supervisors or employees to "spin straw into gold." M.B.O. does help the supervisor clarify what the needs of the work group will be in the future.

THE CHARACTERISTICS OF GOOD OBJECTIVES

A. Objectives Should Relate to the Job

Written or implied objectives should be related to the goals of the organization or department. If you want employees to respect an M.B.O. approach, they must see that what they are being asked to do relates to the organizational goals. Be sure that the objectives for each person are ambitious. Each person should have different specific objectives due to their experience, skills, or training. Objectives should allow each employee to stretch and reach out, but they should not be set too far beyond the range that an employee can realistically attain. If employees do not believe the objectives are reasonable, they will discard them as impractical. Realistic goals should require that for each period the employee should try a little harder and work more skillfully.

B. Objectives Should Be Written

Goals or objectives should be stated in writing, as clearly and concisely as possible. Both parties should have a copy of the objectives, and both should know what they are agreeing to. The supervisor should ask questions or restate each objective in order to ensure that the employee understands the goals.

C. Objectives Must Be Measurable

Objectives should be measurable and stated in numerical terms if possible. When it is time to review the accomplishments for a period, there should be no disagreement about what or how much was actually accomplished. For example, in a production situation, the number of items produced in a specific time period can be counted and considered when evaluating accomplishments. A vague goal such as "increase production," is not nearly so effective as one that asks employees to "increase production output of completed and inspected units by 5 percent."

In the second goal statement, the supervisor and the employee are both being more specific. In a service industry, many measurable goals—such as the number of sales calls, new customers contacted, and dollars of expenses, sales, or profits—are also possible.

The measurement of some goals is not as simple as counting the units produced, sales made, or profits produced. Quality, new skills, and worker morale are all examples of work factors that are difficult to measure accurately, yet are extremely important to a supervisor's success.

D. Objectives Must Consider All Organizational Variables

Objectives should account for factors, both within and outside the organization, which will influence the output of the work group. Internal constraints or variables include the equipment employees work with, the top management of the firm, and the rules of the union. All of these internal constraints will affect the success any supervisor can have with an M.B.O. system. External constraints or variables can also alter the results of M.B.O. These include economic trends which may result in increased sales and profits when actual productivity is falling. On the other hand, even well-managed organizations can, in periods of recession, have declining sales and employee layoff when productivity is increasing. Goals should not be used in a vacuum. They must relate rewards to actual manager and employee performance.

E. Objectives Should Serve as Guides to Action

Once targets are established, the planning process allows supervisors to sharpen their managerial tools in order to take the necessary steps to reach the goals. Specific action plans should stress how goals are going to be accomplished. Goals should contain a statement of the things a supervisor plans to do to attain her or his department's goals. Thus, the actions planned become actions taken.

BOX 1. Sample Action Plan

GOAL—Improve Parts Inventory As Follows:	*MEASUREMENTS*
1. Reduce back orders by 40 percent.	1. Back order list—e.g., down from 50 to 30.

Continued

2. Reduce interim orders by 50 percent.	2. Record of interim orders—e.g., down from 4 a month to 2 a month.
3. Reduce parts-picking time by 15 percent.	3. Results of time study of parts picking now versus October 1 of previous year.
4. Remove overstock.	4. Inventory records now versus records of October 1 of previous year.
5. Increase stock space by 10 percent.	5. Cubic feet of stock space open now as compared with October 1 of previous year.

Completion Date: October 1, 198_

ACTION STEPS	WHEN	EXPECTED RESULTS
1. Accumulate data to measure where we are now.	7/1	1. A base from which to measure progress will be established.
2. Review order points and parts usage.	7/15	2. Overstock will be identified and shortages causing backlogs will be located.
3. Ship excess parts to regional warehouse and scrap those damaged.	8/1	3. Clearing of stocking space.
4. Rearrange and identify parts.	10/1	4. Reduced parts-picking time.
5. Check records to measure where we are now.	10/1	5. We can see how close we are to the goal.

SUMMARY: CHARACTERISTICS OF GOOD OBJECTIVES

Good objectives

1. Are related to the organization's goals.
2. Are ambitious for each employee. (Remember individual difference.)
3. Don't allow employees to set goals that are too low or too high. The key lies with objectives that are realistic.

4. Are easy to understand. They are concise and complete.
5. Are in writing. Be sure that all parties have a copy of the objectives.
6. Are measurable. Both the employee and supervisor should agree on how they are to be measured and evaluated.
7. Should be responsive to changes that take place in the system.

MAKING M.B.O. WORK FOR YOU

As a supervisor, you should have a good working knowledge of what each employee is doing. But do you know a good job from a "snow" job? It's not always necessary that you be able to do any job better than your employees. Rather, you must be able to analyze the requirements of each job and be able to measure results accurately. When supervisors get caught up in the notion that they must be able to perform each task better than anyone who works for them, they make a serious error. Supervisors are being paid to manage, not to do the actual tasks in their departments.

Begin to formulate objectives by listing the key work outputs for each job under your control. Next, determine the various ways you can tell when each job is being done properly. Find a happy medium between stopping work every few minutes to inspect the results and waiting until a job is finished. You need to judge accomplishments in order to recognize when things are going smoothly, and you should make "midcourse corrections" when errors are discovered. The best way of determining which criteria to choose is to use those that you have found are the most accurate measures of performance.

Photo courtesy of Pullman, Inc.

GOOD OBJECTIVES MAKE FOR BETTER PERFORMANCE

After doing this, talk with each person in your department to determine if they agree with your thinking about the best measures of job performance. They may have valuable suggestions that can be incorporated into your plan. At this point, you have started employees participating in setting work goals and are asking each employee to participate in making the operation a success. Employees can now begin to see that through the attainment of work goals that they have helped to set they can reach their personal goals. Department goals and employee goals do not have to conflict; they can and should be in agreement. An M.B.O. approach can help shift the employees' goals in the direction of the organizational goals. Employees want to know how their output is going to be measured. Knowing (and having a part in setting) department goals can be a big step toward better management.

THE STEPS IN MANAGEMENT BY OBJECTIVES

The process normally followed to implement management by objectives is

1. Top management determines what the overall objectives for the organization will be for the next period. They also decide the goals for each of the major components of the organization.
2. The overall goals are divided for each level of the organization to coordinate the efforts of all departments or divisions within the organization. At each level, managers agree with their bosses on the specific goals of their groups.
3. Supervisors meet with their superiors to discuss the objectives for the work group. Supervisors then decide what their groups will be able to do in order to reach the broader objectives. The supervisor and boss then must agree on the plan submitted by the supervisor. This plan must include the means by which accomplishment will be measured.
4. The supervisor in turn meets with employees and repeats the procedure above.
5. During the performance period the supervisor takes a "performance reading" in order to identify possible deviations from the goal. If either internal or external variables alter the work relationships, the supervisor must reevaluate the goals of the group and make adjustment with each employee.
6. Supervisors meet individually with employees to review their performance during the previous period. During the meeting the emphasis should be based primarily on the measured results. "How did you do compared with what we agreed you would do?" The more performance evaluation is based on facts, the more confident the employees become that salary increases and promotion will be based on performance.
7. Goals for the next period are set.

This cycle is repeated after evaluation is made of each group performance.

THE GOALS OF MANAGEMENT BY OBJECTIVES

The goal of a management by objectives approach is to improve the total managerial performance throughout the organization. It is also designed specifically to give supervisors a managerial tool that will enable them to operate on a performance base. Supervisory planning with M.B.O. is improved because the entire emphasis is based on goals and objectives. Coordination is improved because the system begins with a set of overall objectives and works down through the organization. At each level, more detailed goals are established that tie the various departments' work groups together. Control is also improved through the establishment of both goals and measurement criteria. Supervisors are free to monitor the results as they happen, and they can also retain the flexibility to make some changes in the operation as the need arises. The result is an improved superior-subordinate relationship based on trust, respect, and productivity.

ACTION GUIDELINES FOR M.B.O.

1. M.B.O. is a managerial technique developed from the behavioral sciences. If you believe that it might improve the management of your group, you may wish to read further on the topic.

2. M.B.O. stresses the process of mutual goal setting between superiors and subordinates at all levels of the organization. This technique brings superiors and subordinates closer together in understanding what must be accomplished.

3. The goal of an M.B.O. system is to improve productivity and goal attainment in an organization by encouraging the participation of employees in setting the goals for their jobs. If your employees are committed to reaching their goals as they see best, productivity and morale should improve.

4. M.B.O. is based on a managerial philosophy that recognizes the positive and productive nature of human beings. As a supervisor you must be in agreement with that philosophy if you expect M.B.O. to work for you.

5. M.B.O. managers recognize that employees want to know what is expected of them and how their work will be measured. Employees feel isolated in large organizations, and the involvement in goal-setting makes them a real and productive part of the organization. Become the type of supervisor who encourages this involvement.

6. Objectives, in order to be effective, should be goal related. This is an ambitious, highly personal undertaking. Goals must be realistic, clearly stated, measurable, and responsible to change. They form the basis for supervisory action. Check the objectives that you are agreeing to, and see if they pass all the tests.

7. The M.B.O. process is person-to-person management based on the work to be performed, rather than on personality characteristics. As

a supervisor you will find this system more challenging and a great deal more rewarding.

8. Performance must be related to reward. Agreement is reached in advance as to goals and how results will be measured. Supervisors must reward performance in order to motivate their employees.

9. M.B.O. improves planning, coordination, control, flexibility, and superior-subordinate working relationships. M.B.O. helps the supervisor become a better manager.

10. M.B.O. can be used by any organization and can be adjusted to fit the specific needs of your organization. You are in control. M.B.O. is a tool for the supervisor to use. If done well and if supported from the top of the organization, results can be exceptional. Use your specific skills to make necessary modification in the M.B.O. techniques which will help you to manage your subordinates better.

DISCUSSION QUESTIONS FOR M.B.O.

1. Why is mutual goal setting important in an M.B.O. process?

2. Are there any steps in the M.B.O. process that can be omitted without destroying or significantly altering the basic process?

3. Is M.B.O. based on any particular management philosophy?

4. Should personal objectives of an employee (that is, objectives relating to off-the-job activities or aspirations) or those of the supervisor be considered in an M.B.O. system?

ACTION EXERCISE FOR M.B.O.

This action exercise is designed to focus your thinking toward the goals and objectives that you have and use. There are really two parts to this exercise. First, answer each of the questions as honestly and completely as possible. Second, compare and discuss your answers with those of your classmates or fellow supervisors. You should come away from the discussion with a better understanding of the difficulty (and importance) of setting objectives and helping others to do likewise.

1. What are the three major objectives of your work group or class?

2. As a supervisor or class leader how can you communicate these objectives to employees or classmates?

3. How could setting objectives help you be recognized by your boss or teacher as an outstanding performer?

4. Do you encourage classmates and employees to participate and contribute their ideas toward common problems with the hope that such

participation will result in a sense of accomplishment? If yes, how? If no, why not?

5. Can you identify an employee or student who does not contribute to discussion at work or in class? If yes, how can that employee or student be communicated with to encourage participation?

6. How does the class outline relate to the objectives of the class?

7. If you were responsible for developing a new set of objectives for this supervision class, what would those objectives be?

 CASES

CASE 8. The Introduction of the Problem Identification and Solution (PIAS) Plan

"Well, I knew it would happen sooner or later," remarked Joan Jackson as she and five other lab supervisors walked toward the conference room on level 3. "I knew they would finally ask the people on the line to solve the problems."

After coffee and a small talk, Howard Horowitz, the Director of Laboratories at General Research and Development Corporation, got right to the point. "I have asked you six people here this morning in order to explain to you a new plan by top management. The plan is PIAS (Problem Identification and Solution). PIAS will be instituted in all sections of our operation. Its goal is to form groups, like us, to identify problems that we have presently or situations that may soon become problems. Once identified, we will pool our ideas to determine solutions which fit into our situation."

Jeff Keeler nudged Joan Jackson and whispered, "It's the old find the problem and solution and tell Horowitz the answer trick."

Horowitz was continuing, "The format of our procedure will be as follows. . . . " He produced a small flip chart. "First, as you can see, we will define the problems. Second, we will consider all factors which might affect the problem and limit the range of alternative solutions. Third, we will collect and analyze all facts relevant to the problem."

"Somehow this all sounds familiar," Joan whispered to Jeff Keeler.

"Fourth, we will list and discuss alternatives to the problem. The evaluation of each suggestion will be done in order to identify the strengths and weakness of each proposal. Fifth, we will agree on the best solution, and, finally, we will suggest ways of putting the plan into action," Horowitz concluded. He looked to the group for a response, but none came. "Well, what do you think?" Still no comments were made. Horowitz was getting obviously upset. "Well, what do you think?" he repeated.

Walter Cox finally spoke up, "It sounds like a fine idea, Howard. I am sure it will help us a lot." "That's what I like to hear—enthusiasm," replied Horowitz. "How about the rest of you guys?"

To a man, each indicated his approval.

"O.K., let's meet next week at this same time to get under way." The group broke up and headed back to their labs in a group, leaving Horowitz to collect his flip chart.

1. Did Horowitz ever clearly set the objectives of PIAS?
2. Do you feel that Horowitz honestly solicited the cooperation of supervisors at the meeting?
3. What follow-up could you expect on the PIAS program?

CASE 9. Regional International Airlines

It was the monthly supervisor's meeting for Regional International Airlines, and the men and women who managed the Salt Lake City facility were beginning to file to their seats to begin their meeting. John Runningbrook was one of the supervisors who had been with Regional International Airlines since it established its operations in Salt Lake City eight years ago. The son of a tribal chief, John had learned aviation mechanics while in the Air Force. Regional International was a small western freight carrier which, because of its size and competition, was always operating close to the breakeven point. The operation's director was Hank Subiashi, one of the three original founders of the airline. It seemed to many observers that the management of Regional International was always "drawing for straws" trying to find a new gimmick to improve profits. It was for this reason that John was not surprised when Hank announced that Regional International was about to institute "management objectives" throughout its entire organization.

Hank began by distributing to the supervisors a revised list of Regional International's new yearly objectives.

"This is what the company must do if we wish to be in the black by January 1."

The objectives were quickly reviewed and for the most part seemed similar to what had been distributed last year. Next, Hank produced a detailed list of objectives for each supervisor present, which he announced would be implemented immediately.

"You and I are going to work together to reach these goals. If you have any questions call me in San Francisco on our Wats Line. If there are no further questions, I'll see you all again next month."

John glanced at his objectives quickly, and got up and walked to the door, thinking to himself as he went how he planned to announce to his department what their new objectives were. Stopping to talk with the flight line supervisor, Marv Morallas, John said, "You know Marv, these objectives are just what we needed in aircraft maintenance. Now the men will know what is expected of them in the future."

1. How would you evaluate the management of objectives program at Regional International Airlines?
2. How successful would you expect John to be in obtaining commitments from his mechanics to carry out the objectives on the list obtained during the meeting?
3. Is Subiashi's approach to management by objectives in line with your understanding of the process?

section

2

PROCESSES
OF
SUPERVISION

Solving Problems and Making Decisions

Objectives

In this chapter we will study the various elements of problem solving and decision making. After your study and discussion of the concepts and ideas in this chapter you will be able to

1. Recognize the best sequence of steps for making good decisions.

2. Define in concrete terms the decision problems facing you.

3. Identify your expectations for your decisions.

4. Recognize where to gather and how to use the best data for making decisions.

5. Develop realistic alternatives, which is an essential step in making good decisions.

6. Identify and begin overcoming goal conflicts.

MANAGERS AT ALL levels in all organizations are constantly solving problems and making decisions. Some are routine and take little time or effort to handle. Others, involving much money or time, require managers to be careful and cautious. Regardless of the importance of any one decision or how many people the decision affects, each of us will be affected by decisions made by today's managers and supervisors—and others around us will be affected by *our* decisions.

Everyone in an organization makes some decisions. The kind of decisions made and the impact of the decisions on the operation of an organization vary greatly depending on an individual's job and responsibilities.

Operating employees usually make rather routine decisions. They are given standards which they apply to determine if they are doing the right job. A clerk in a department store is given certain tasks to perform when "ringing up" a customer's purchase. The actions of the clerk are based on the decision reached as to how this particular order should be handled. Is this a credit purchase? Does the customer prefer a "layaway" plan? Is the customer planning to pay by personal check? Each of these questions requires an answer, and the clerk then decides what actions to take to complete the sale. These decisions are made over and over again.

Supervisory decisions usually have greater impact on the operation of a department or the organization. Supervisors' decisions affect how policies are implemented and how objectives are reached.

WHAT'S YOUR DECISION-MAKING STYLE?

Each of us makes decisions in her or his own way. As long as the decisions we make are generally sound, there is no problem. However, few supervisors are satisfied with all of the decisions they make, and when decisions go wrong, they begin to question their decision-making style. Take a few minutes and test your decisions by answering the following questions. For each of the twelve questions, circle the number in the column that indicates if you "strongly agree," "agree," "agree on occasion," "agree, but that it happens rarely," or "disagree." Then total the numbers you circled, and use your total score as a guide to your decision-making style.

Generally there are three styles of decision maker: reflexive, consistent, and reflective. If you scored high on this test (between 32 and 48), you lean toward a *reflexive* decision maker. You like to make decisions quickly, with only a quick look at goals, alternatives, and conse-

STRONGLY AGREE	AGREE	AGREE ON OCCASION	AGREE—HAPPENS RARELY	DISAGREE	DECISION-MAKING SCALE
0	1	2	3	4	1. When making a decision, I recheck my work more than once.
4	3	2	1	0	2. I tend to interrupt people when they are talking.
4	3	2	1	0	3. I try to take control of conversations.
4	3	2	1	0	4. I make decisions by going with the option that first pops into my mind.
0	1	2	3	4	5. I try to use the most precise, correct word to describe or illustrate whatever it is I'm discussing.
4	3	2	1	0	6. I answer questions almost before they are asked.
0	1	2	3	4	7. I am concerned about having made an error after a decision is reached.
0	1	2	3	4	8. I review alternatives before finally deciding on a course of action.
4	3	2	1	0	9. I like to find the right choice quickly.
4	3	2	1	0	10. I "shop" for other alternatives after making my decision, regretting that I made the decision so quickly.
4	3	2	1	0	11. I complete sentences for other people.
0	1	2	3	4	12. I take more time to consider a difficult question before expressing my answer.

quences. Although you do make decisions, your tally of "good" decisions will likely better if you take more time to carefully consider more options and the consequences of choosing those options.

If your score is low (between 0 and 20), you are a *reflective* decision maker. You like to take plenty of time to make a decision. You do so only after considering all of the options and their consequences carefully. You search for more information and find it easy to "put off" making a decision. Of course, you can point to the fact that the decisions you reach are generally good ones, but if you find decision making hard, or unsatisfying, you might want to try narrowing down your search for alternatives, perhaps by setting a time limit for yourself. Tell yourself, "Tomorrow by noon, I *will* decide."

Consistent decision makers (scoring in the middle of this test, between 21 and 31 points) are likely to make the best decisions, with the most consistent record of "good" decisions. They follow the basic steps in the decision-making process. If you feel your score is too high or too low, think carefully about the following steps in making a decision.

STEP 1: PROBLEM IDENTIFICATION AND DEFINITION

Before we can begin to solve a problem we must identify what the problem really is and define all the aspects of the problem. While managing people, we may believe that a problem of lack of motivation exists because of a failure of employees to direct their work toward the objectives of the job. Poor employee performance which seems to come from lack of motivation may be caused by other factors. The problem *may* be poor understanding of work objectives. It may be that the employees want to work, but they may not know how much is expected of them. The same result could be caused by poorly trained employees who lack the skills to do the job. Motivation cannot overcome a lack of skill. If you think it can, ask yourself if you would rather receive medical treatment by a person highly motivated to perform operations or by a trained doctor. This, of course, is an exaggerated example. But people can fail to achieve due to a lack of training and still possess ample motivation. Thus, the *real* problem may be difficult to get to, and we must get to it *before* we can begin to solve it.

Continually "scanning" the situation for problems is the best way to identify small problems before they surface as larger ones. The identification of problems early by means of scanning helps the supervisor stay on top of current problems. In many instances, supervisors act surprised when problems arise. Most problems, even those which seem to erupt suddenly, are usually related to previous problem situations. The best way to solve problems is to short-circuit them before they become major in nature. An accurate definition of the problem often leads to quick, decisive actions that get at the root of the problem and not just at the symptoms.

The first and most crucial step in the problem-solving sequence is to accurately identify the real problem and define it. Some supervisors overreact to problems before they get this first step completed. Management by substitution is very expensive and will seldom cure the problem.

In order to get an accurate definition of the problem, get a variety of views. Your perception of the problem is limited to your perspective of what is happening. In order to define the problem, ask others how they see it. Why are we not achieving results? What do you think the obstacles are to completing this project on time? The open-ended question technique reduces the bias you may have concerning the source of the problem. Don't do as one supervisor did. He went down the line and asked one of the men, "Which one of these guys is causing the foul-up on this project?" He demonstrated that he had already made up his mind that it was caused by an employee problem. If you were the employee he asked, what could you have said?

Seek the advice of other managers and appropriate staff people. People who are not directly involved in the problem can often provide useful and sometimes unbiased insights. Even when their views are biased by their positions in the organization or personal attitudes toward the problem, they may provide clues about the problem that you may have overlooked. Supervisors can become so involved with their work that they suffer from the classic "failure to see the forest for the trees" syndrome.

Recognize that not all persons can tell you the truth when you ask them a question. They are often embarrassed admitting that they don't know how to perform a specific task or that they are scared to do a job. In one instance a supervisor was having real productivity problems from a group putting up a tower needed for a communications network. He finally told one of the men to "get up there and get the wires connected." The man refused to do it and the supervisor was about to fire him for refusing to follow a direct order when he realized that the men on this crew had never worked at heights before. The employee in question was afraid of heights, yet would rather be fired than admit his fear in front of fellow workers. The cause of the delays was not deliberate and intentional, but was instead one which derived from some employee's fear of doing this specific job. In this case, the supervisor assumed that this job was like others, but to some of his employees, it definitely was not.

Problems Are Interrelated

The problems which supervisors face are seldom, if ever, as simple as we may first believe. Most of them involve other aspects of the job which may initially be hidden from view. The seemingly simple problem of rearranging employees on an assembly line for the purpose of increasing productivity or accommodating the installation of a new piece of equipment will generally result in the disruption of people's work habits and social relations on the job, especially if the supervisor decides simply to move the people around to make a change in their work environment. A simple change in work structure may fail to solve the problem of productivity. It may, in fact, result in lower productivity than before the change. For the problem to be effectively dealt with, all interrelated factors must be considered. A solution that is aimed at only part of the problem is likely doomed to fail.

STEP 2: SEARCHING FOR THE CRITICAL FACTOR

When a problem is identified you must then identify the critical factor. Is there one part of a problem that will affect the other parts of the problem? Who is affected by and who is involved with the problem? Is a decision necessary immediately, or can the decision wait for a few days? How critical is the speed of decision making in this case?

Another problem concern is cost. A supervisor must learn what time and dollar costs are involved with each problem in order to establish the relative importance of one problem over others. For example, if a problem could lead to a general strike by the employees in the department, the dollar cost would be far greater than the cost involved in replacing a machine or transferring an employee. By looking at the costs involved, you will be better able to calculate and weigh the risks involved in making your decision.

STEP 3: GATHERING DATA

Data are the vital ingredients in decision making. Once you are reasonably sure of the real problem, and once you have a feel for the effects of the decision, you are ready to gather data. There are two kinds of data used in decision making: primary data and secondary data.

Primary Data

Primary data are gathered from original sources. Examples include personal interviews with employees, questionnaires sent to people involved in a problem, and experiments. In some problem-solving efforts, information gathered by various departments of government is considered primary data. In solving any problem, the more primary information a decision maker has available, the more likely he or she is to reach a good decision. Primary data are less likely to be altered. There are few interpretations added by people outside the problem. However, primary data alone do not usually supply enough information for most managers to reach a decision. Managers need background material, and they should also have some idea of how others in similar situations might go about reaching decisions. For this background, they turn to secondary data sources.

Secondary Data

Secondary data come from sources that use primary data. Books, journals, periodicals, yearbooks, and other similar publications all rely on primary sources of information in developing their articles, stories, and commentaries. Secondary source data are useful because they usually give more information on a problem than would be available just from the primary data.

By using both primary and secondary data, the decision maker is always in the best position when the total information becomes available; he or she can draw from primary sources and use the secondary information as backup. The real difficulty with using secondary information in decision making is that the decision maker can never really be sure just how accurate the information is. Primary data give more of that assurance, because the original sources are known and can be evaluated.

STEP 4: GENERATING CREATIVE ALTERNATIVES

After you have unearthed the real problem and have gathered data, the next step is to develop alternatives to solving the problem. Here another common pitfall is encountered; the temptation to find only one alternative for a problem. This temptation is called "tunnel vision." It happens when a person looks at the problem with a very narrow perspective. Often supervisors who have dealt exclusively with one kind of work situation will be unable or unwilling to look at that problem in any other way.

Successful supervisors are willing to look at problems in many ways. The development of creative alternatives demands a wide open search for ways of solving the problems. No suggestion should be automatically rejected.

When the search for alternatives is done in a group, it is called "brainstorming." All ideas or suggestions are written down as they are given, and they are analyzed later. Often the idea or suggestion of one participant will spur another idea by someone else in the group. The goal is for each member to feed on the ideas of every other member. Each participant is sharing ideas based on her or his view of the situation. Through this technique and others like it, supervisors can use the knowledge and experience of one another to develop alternatives to common problems. For example, one supervisor may be having a problem with employee turnover. A group of others may be having similar problems, so it would be beneficial for them to share their views for the purpose of finding alternatives. Supervisors who have successfully developed ways of dealing with the problem can share their solutions with those who now have the problem. The result of such a meeting might be the development of a better list of alternatives than any supervisor could create on his or her own.

Ask employees for their opinions. Listen carefully without being critical. Write down what you hear. It represents a new and possibly important point of view concerning your problem. The employees' opinions may not always be used, but just by asking for opinions can help to motivate them.

Developing Alternatives

When making decisions, there should be several alternatives open to the decision maker. However, it is unrealistic to assume that all of these available alternatives be feasible. An alternative is an option, one of two or more available to solve a problem or deal with a particular situation. Some alternatives, which are technically possible, are not realistically feasible. In fact, it may be impossible for the decision maker to select some alternatives. For example, for a merchant deciding how to react to increased competition, one alternative might be for the store to go out of business. Usually, this alternative is unrealistic, except as a last resort. Other alternatives might be unreasonable, and easily forgotten. Within the wide range of available alternatives, the decision maker is usually able to narrow down the realistic alternatives to a few.

Characteristics for Realistic Alternatives

Realistic alternatives are those alternatives that the decision maker could use to satisfy the requirements in a situation. They must be based on the information available to the decision maker and should represent a workable solution to the problems being decided. Realistic alternatives must satisfy all constraints (such as time, money, law and union requirements, and basic human concerns) within which the decision maker and the organization operate. Because the two final steps in the decision-making process are implementing and following through on the decision, realistic alternatives must allow for smooth implementation and proper control after implementation. It does little good for a supervisor to consider seriously a decision alternative that cannot be implemented or monitored.

STEP 5: SELECTING THE BEST ALTERNATIVE AND PUTTING IT INTO ACTION

From the realistic alternatives the decision maker should be able to select one that solves the problem.

When supervisors develop problem solutions, they must consider many alternatives. They must also know when enough alternatives are available and then go forward with a decision—no matter how difficult it is. Experienced decision makers realize that decision making involves risk. They can never be sure about all of their information or even about whether they have all the information available. Rather than search endlessly for more alternatives, they make the decision.

At some point the decision has to be reached, and the alternative which seems best must be put into action. Too often, supervisors think that because a decision was reached, it will automatically go into action. A fatal error in problem solving is to assume that all decisions will be accepted because "you are the boss." Without a plan of implementation and a good job of selling your decision, your problem may never be solved. Not everyone will understand why changes are needed, and they will try to resist. Others may think you made a wrong decision and will be opposed.

When the solution is in any way complex, it must be accompanied by a plan of action. The plan should explain where changes will be made, how they will be made, and in what sequence, over what time period, and by whom they will be made. Specific assignments should be made. Involve the employees in the decision, and show them using the plan how they will be involved in the process. Set times when the progress of the new decision can be tested and the results checked to be sure that the plan has some control point. The goals of this phase of problem solving are to explain and sell the decision, thus obtaining participation and commitments from the employees.

Review with the employees how this decision fits the organization's policies and how it will result in the group's better reaching its goals.

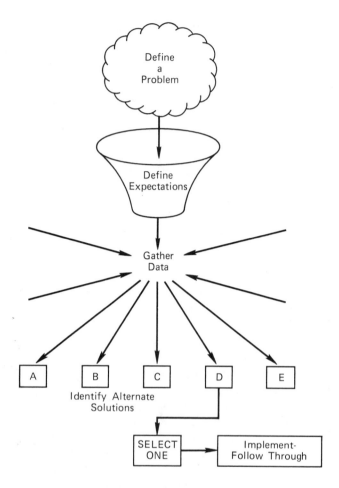

FIGURE 4–1 Making a Decision

STEP 6: EVALUATING YOUR DECISION

All decisions we make do not turn out to be effective. Therefore, set aside a time to review your decisions to determine in an objective manner whether your decision really solved a problem. It is important to wait a reasonable time for evidence of results. Don't be overly optimistic or pessimistic. If you are, you may scrap a good decision before all results are in.

Once the timetable is set, establish an objective review process which asks the question, "Has this decision solved the problem?" If not, it may be necessary to reevaluate the problem.

THE ESSENTIAL STEPS FOR MAKING
GOOD DECISIONS

All management problem solving involves some form of decision making. Decision making is the ability to identify and choose between alternatives and then to accept responsibility for the results of making that choice. It is this activity that distinguishes the supervisors from the operating employees.

To make a decision, supervisors must first identify a problem. Once the problem has been recognized, it must be defined and analyzed by breaking it down into its various parts. Once the problem has been identified, defined, and analyzed, the decision maker must gather data and begin finding alternative solutions. Next the decision maker must select the best alternative. Decision making, however, is not complete until the chosen alternative has been implemented by the supervisor, who issues orders to convert the decisions into action, and then monitors the results.

The results of most supervisory decisions must be measurable. Some results can be measured in specific units or in a short time period; other results may be general or ill-defined and may require weeks or even years to evaluate. The success of a decision of a first line supervisor to set a weekly production quota can be measured at the end of the week. If the quota was 10,000 units and 10,500 were produced, the goal was successfully reached. By contrast, the president of a major aircraft manufacturing firm must wait three to five years to see whether a decision to design and build a new airplane was correct. With the longer time period required to evaluate results in the latter type of situation, other factors may make the original decision incorrect by current standards. The factors affecting the success or failure of a project may not have existed when the original decision was made.

Many managers and supervisors use a haphazard approach to making decisions. When they are faced with a situation requiring a decision and a commitment of resources, managers must resolve in their own minds a number of important questions: Which condition (of many) is most likely to occur? How will that condition affect a particular course of action? A buyer, facing a shift in economic conditions that could affect price, must intuitively account for this *state of nature* before making the actual "buy-no buy" decision. A merchant must assume that the competition will behave in a certain way before setting prices for products. Both the buyer and the merchant are making decisions in essentially a "win-lose" situation. If the decision maker is right about the economic conditions or the competitor's behavior and if the assumptions about the state of nature are correct, he or she will "win." If not, the decision maker will lose—that is, he or she will suffer from an actual loss of income or an opportunity loss—and he or she will not make as much money as might have been possible.

These examples of guesswork decision making are very typical of supervisors today. In a realistic situation, a decision maker seldom faces just two possible states of nature and two alternative courses of action. Usually, there are many things that could happen, and a variety of potential alternatives or decisions may be available. In such a maze, guesswork simply won't do. A better approach to this dilemma is *Bayesian Decision Making*—the use of probability analysis.

The "Bayesian" Approach

Suppose you are faced with an important decision about which of two production lines to convert to a new process.[1] Your state of nature* is the availability of a newly developed raw material, that is now in the final test stages. After the conversion, both lines will continue to operate. However, the overall profitability of the lines will vary depending on whether you can use the new raw material or must instead rely on existing raw materials. The monthly profits from running both lines, under both states of nature, and assuming that either line A or line B is converted, are shown in Figure 4–2. If the new raw materials were available, the conversion of line B would generate a total profit of $2 million per year. If the old raw materials were used, the conversion of line B would result in an overhead on unused capacity and a loss of $500,000. The conversion of line A would fare better if the new raw material weren't available, by producing a $100,000 total profit. However, with the new raw material, the total profit contribution would not exceed $1 million.

FIGURE 4–2. Decisions

STATES OF NATURE	CONVERT LINE A	CONVERT LINE B
New raw material not available	100,000	(500,000)
New raw material available	1,000,000	2,000,000

Values in each cell represent the profits (losses) resulting from a given decision under given states of nature.

*A state of nature is a condition which affects the outcome of a decision, over which the decision maker has no real direct control.

If you knew for certain whether new raw materials would be available, your decision would be simple—take the option with the best payoff under those conditions.

Without the luxury of such certainty, many decision makers use one of two approaches: They either assume one or the other of the economic conditions will occur, or worse, they decide not to decide at all, that is, to do nothing. This latter course of action sounds quite irresponsible, but the former isn't much better. It assumes that the probability of each economic condition occurring is 100 percent or 0 percent, and it fails to take into account the payoffs of the two decisions.

Supervisors can avoid pure "shot-in-the-dark" decision making by following the simple logic of the *Bayesian approach*. It takes into account the various alternative payoffs of a decision, together with the probabilities of the states of nature. It produces a series of statistical or expected profits (or losses) that can be compared for a better decision.

The first step is the determination of probabilities for the states of nature. Probabilities may be found by actual reference to historical data or physical quantities (objective probabilities) or by an intuitive estimate of the chances of given events occurring (subjective probabilities). Either way, the system of Bayesian analysis (and, indeed, the entire concept of statistical decision making) rests on the "reliability" of the probabilities used. Good decisions will result only if probabilities are thoughtfully and consistently developed. The important concern with these probabilities is that they best reflect the actual conditions prevalent at the time of the decision.

In the production line conversion decision mentioned before, the relevant states of nature involve the availability of the new raw material. Probabilities for each state of nature should take into account the various public data available on the new material, the economic history (objective data) of it, the assessment of possible government moves that could affect it, statements of business and government leaders, and consumer behavior (subjective data).

Once the probabilities have been determined (for this example, let us assume that there is a 60 percent probability of the new raw material not being available, and a 40 percent probability of it being available), it is possible to calculate the expected values or weighted average payoffs for each of the options or decisions open to you as the decision maker.

The expected values (EVs) of the decisions in this example are:

EV conversion of line A = $100,000(.60) + $1,000,000(.40)
                         = $460,000
EV conversion of line B = $500,000(.60) + $2,000,000(.40)
                         = $500,000

These expected values for the two alternative decisions represent the long-run average outcome of our option, that is, the average payoff if the process is repeated often with the same probabilities and payoffs. By using the expected value (in this case, the expected profit or loss), the decision making can compare options on an objective basis.

Because the Bayes approach states that we choose the alternative with the largest expected value payoff, in our example the decision would be to convert to line B, because its expected profit is $500,000 as compared to the $460,000 expected profit for converting line A.

If the probabilities were 70 percent for no new raw material available, and 30 percent for new raw material available, the expected values would be:

$$\text{EV conversion of line A} = \$1,000,000(.7) + \$1,000,000(.3)$$
$$= \$370,000$$

$$\text{EV conversion of line B} = \$-5,000,000(.7) + \$2,000,000(.3)$$
$$= \$250,000$$

Under these conditions, the best decision would be to convert line A, because it provides here the largest expected value ($370,000).

Naturally, not all decisions facing a supervisor can be easily converted into Bayesian analysis. However, many supervisors find that the use of such methods improves even their "nonquantitative" decision making. Although we often make a decision by using the experience of similar situations, we can benefit by taking an exacting and professional approach to all our decisions.

Remember that decision making is a personal activity. No two supervisors will approach the decision-making process in the same way, and no two supervisors will make exactly the same decisions, even with the same set of facts and objectives. Perhaps the best first step toward improving your decision-making ability is to do some self-analysis. How do you make decisions on the job and off? Do you like to make a quick decision in order to have the decision making behind you, or do you take a long time before deciding? Do you prefer to have someone else give you so many facts or standards or constraints that the decision almost "makes itself?" Do you hope secretly that if you wait long enough, no decision will be necessary at all because the problem will just go away? What facts do you consider when you make a decision? Because it's often difficult to isolate any one decision that we make on the job, and because decisions are usually tied into so many other situations and factors, do your self-analysis of your decision making with a non-work situation that most of us face—buying a car.

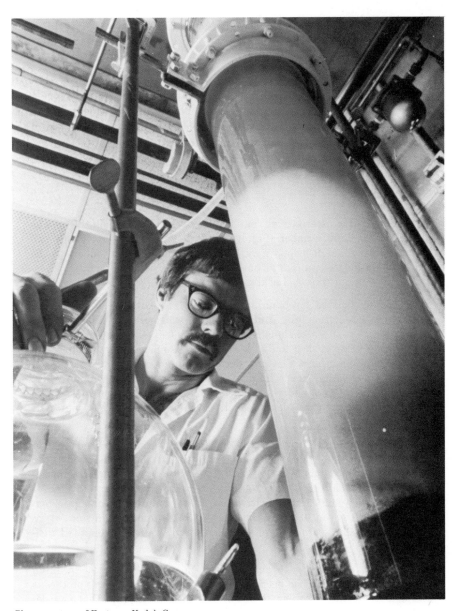

Photo courtesy of Eastman Kodak Company.

ACTION GUIDELINES FOR PROBLEM
SOLVING AND DECISION MAKING

Think back to the last time you bought a car. Did you follow the steps outlined for good decision making? Did you skip steps? Why? Were you satisfied with the outcome of your decision? Perhaps the most important question for your self-analysis is, "Have you made all your car-buying decisions in the same way, or do you often change the way you make decisions?" This self-analysis can give you some valuable insights into your own thought processes. Try it, and consider also some of these ideas.

1. Search for alternatives, but set a realistic cut-off point. There is never just the right number of alternatives. Some decisions have only two alternatives; other decisions may have hundreds. The key idea is to be realistic. Gather as many alternatives as you realistically feel are necessary to give you a good feel of the entire problem.

2. Define the real problem and not merely a symptom. We can take medical steps to cure a fever, but often the fever is not the sickness; it may merely be a symptom of something more seriously wrong with the body. The same is true in decision making. Don't be misled into defining as a problem something for which easy decisions can be made, but which is not the real problem that needs solving. Often we confuse the symptom with the real problem. Your success as a decision maker depends on your ability to identify the correct problems as well as your ability to decide what to do about them.

3. Use information you can rely on. Remember that "garbage in-garbage out" means that your results and decisions will be only as good as the information used to get those results. You cannot ignore rumor, supposition, and second- or third-person accounts. A wise supervisor never ignores any information and communication that might contain valuable information. However, if you use only these less reliable information sources instead of reputable primary and secondary data, your decisions will ultimately suffer.

4. Follow selection with action. Don't fall into the trap of thinking that once the selection has been made that the decision-making process is completed. You must follow step #6—implement. Imagine that you decided on which car to buy, but you never went back to the dealer to pick it up. All your decision-making efforts would have been wasted.

5. Be prepared for the unexpected, and remain flexible. Some supervisors get very upset, and thus become ineffective, when the rules of the game change in midplay. Yet in most organizations it is impossible to control all the variables that influence decision making. When your bosses change the rules, you can usually assume that the changes were

made to make a current situation more realistic. Your decision-making process is never a "set-in-concrete" proposition. Instead, decisions are constantly being made. Often, supervisors become demoralized when a decision that seems at the time to be the best one turns out to be a bad decision because the facts or the situation changed after the decision was made and implemented. Don't be discouraged by this. You can't reasonably be held responsible for things that happen beyond your control, and realistic decision makers at all levels of all organizations base their evaluations of other decision makers on "batting averages," rather than on the occasional error.

6. Use logic in evaluating alternatives. Don't be swayed by subjective and emotional pressures. We are all human, but the scientific approach to decision making is designed to minimize subjectivity. Develop a professional approach to your decision-making responsibilities.

7. Whenever possible, involve the group in the decision. This is not done specifically to aid in making decisions. Instead, it becomes a useful way for supervisors to gain more commitment from their people, while at the same time it broadens the decision-making base and helps to gather more useful information. If you are responsible for a decision, hiding behind a group won't solve anything. However, by asking your employees to give their thoughts and opinions, you can often turn up alternatives, facts, and options that you might not otherwise have considered. Another viewpoint is always a valuable resource, regardless of who ultimately makes the final decision.

DISCUSSION QUESTIONS FOR DECISION MAKING

1. Do supervisors really make decisions?

2. What are the most common kinds of decisions supervisors make?

3. Discuss how the six steps in decision making are related.

4. Examine a current problem in your organization. Did the people making the decisions on the problem use all the steps in the decision-making process?

5. When would a supervisor use primary and secondary data?

6. What are some of the standards supervisors use for developing alternatives?

ACTION EXERCISES FOR DECISION MAKING

1. Develop a decision tree of the steps you would follow in deciding which of three employees you will recommend for the next promotion.

2. In the "Action Exercises" following Chapter 2, you were asked to develop a detailed plan for one of five events. Using that plan, construct a decision tree of all the decision points in your plan.

CASE 10. What's the Answer? Quick!

Tom Koprowski had the answer, right off the top of his head. In fact, Tom always had an answer. He took great pride in his ability to look at a problem, make a few brief inquiries, sum up what was needed, and move on to the answer without looking for more and more alternatives. To Tom, people who took too long to make a decision were insecure. They were hoping that something or someone would come along and make the decision for them.

The most recent example of Tom's decision-making ability was the previous night. Following an emergency meeting with the security committee, Tom was given the responsibility for coming up with the company's response on a case involving shoplifting and the wife of a prominent citizen and a major customer of the company.

The problem began when a woman was picked up for attempted shoplifting in the company's north side store. The woman refused to identify herself to the security officer, and she was detained in the office of the store manager while the police were called. Just as the police officer arrived, one of the salespeople happened to come by the store manager's office, and he recognized the suspect as the wife of a prominent and important client. This changed the situation somewhat, and the police officer was sent away. (Actually, he was told it was a false alarm.) The matter was immediately referred to the security committee, which met in an emergency session at 8:30 P.M. Tom listened to the facts and announced that since this was his responsibility, he would take action, and that for the good of the company no further charges should be pressed. No mention was to be made of the incident, and all other supervisors should consider the case closed. However, Tom failed to contact the store executives and the husband of the suspect. The woman was released on Tom's instructions.

At 10:00 A.M., the company's vice president came into Tom's office with disturbing news. The woman detained last night was indeed the wife of a good customer. She was just found, dead, the victim of an auto accident. Her husband had informed the police of her unstable mental condition and of the fact that she had been missing for several days. Because he was a good friend of the store manager, the husband had called Tom's boss the morning of the incident to inform him that the woman was mentally unstable and that she might return to the store, because it was one of her favorite places to shop. The good customer asked that if his wife was seen, the police be notified and that she be held until either the police or himself could arrive. After hearing about Tom's decision and the subsequent action, the husband began a suit against the company for damages, and the store's lawyer felt that the husband had a good case.

1. What went wrong here?
2. What steps did Tom omit in the decision-making process?
3. Is there a way this problem could have been avoided?

CASE 11. The New Car

You are planning to buy a new car. In fact, the decision to buy a car has already been made for you. Your old car just died last week, and several mechanics have indicated that it is hopeless to try to rebuild it or to repair it. Thus, you face a decision about what kind of car to buy.

If your basic need is for transportation, and you must have some type of automobile, what are the questions you would ask yourself in reaching the decision? In your discussion, see who can come up with the longest list of possible concerns in the decision process for this situation. Are all of your considerations realistic? Do you really think about those things when you go out to buy a car? Finally, once you have assembled a list of data to make a decision, how do you actually make a decision? Do you

1. Like to decide quickly to get the decision making over with?
2. Prefer to stall and look for more information, hoping that the decision will make itself?
3. Decide simply to buy this time what you bought the last time? Compare your personal style of decision making and those of others. Is there a "best way" to make decisions?

CASE 12. Hijack!!

Captain Marty Schuh is an experienced airline pilot for Empire Airlines. He has been flying for the company for seventeen years. He flew transports and bombers in the U.S. Air Force, and he has a distinguished combat record as a pilot.

Last night on a scheduled flight from Atlanta to Ft. Lauderdale, a passenger attempted to hijack the plane with a bottle of "gasoline." Threatening to blow up the plane in flight, the passenger ordered the crew to fly to Havana, Cuba.

The airline's policies on hijacking are very specific. The crew is to comply with all reasonable demands of the hijacker(s), and to avoid doing or saying anything that might anger the hijacker and result in harm to the passengers. No attempt is to be made to stop the hijackers or to change their minds. Marty knew this policy well.

He radioed to the Ft. Lauderdale tower, telling them of the situation, and he received the necessary clearances. He then calmly flew the plane to Ft. Lauderdale. He was counting on the darkness, general confusion, and the hijacker's unfamiliarity with Ft. Lauderdale and Havana from the air. His gamble paid off. The plane stopped, the steps were rolled up, and the hijacker jumped off the plane—right into the waiting arms of the Broward County Sheriff's Department. No one was injured or inconvenienced in any way. The authorities determined that the liquid in the bottle *was* gasoline.

Marty's boss has a problem. Should Marty be fired for disobeying policy and endangering the passengers' lives? The plan could have backfired and the plane blown to smithereens. Or should the airline reward or recognize Marty, because his bravery and quick thinking worked out so well?

1. If you were Marty's boss, what would you decide to do with him?
2. Why?
3. What are the possible effects of your decision on other employees who might face similar situations?

Leadership and Delegation

Objectives

After studying the chapter on leadership and delegation, you should be able to

1. Lead more effectively.

2. Analyze yourself in terms of your leadership traits.

3. Discuss the various patterns of leadership: autocratic, consultative, democratic, free reign, manipulative, and expert.

4. Understand the emotional reactions of subordinates in various leadership patterns.

5. Discuss the situations where particular leadership patterns are most appropriate and least appropriate.

6. Discuss the limitations of delegation.

7. Delegate better.

LEADERSHIP IS A process of influencing others to act in a way that will accomplish the objectives of the leader or the organization. This process involves some form of interpersonal influence in a specific situation toward the attainment of a specific goal. The various elements of a leadership situation are

1. leader
2. follower(s)
3. specific goal or objectives
4. situation
5. contact between the leader and the follower(s)
6. communication of what is wanted
7. feedback

Effective leadership is a function of the leader's style, the nature of the followers, and the characteristics of the situation. All of these factors of leadership place emphasis on the interaction of many elements that determine leadership effectiveness in a specific situation. Thus, you can be effective in one situation with one type of follower and ineffective in other situations or with other types of followers.

DOES BEING A SUPERVISOR MAKE YOU A LEADER?

If you are assigned to the job of supervisor, you are assumed to have the qualities of leadership. This is reasonable, given the nature and theory of organization and management.

Today we recognize that some employees are concerned not only with their supervisor's authority, but also with the supervisor's knowledge and experience. Being a leader depends on acceptance of your leadership by your employees. In other words, leadership is influenced by your employees' willingness to follow you. Cases of insubordination and failure to follow orders during the United States involvement in Viet Nam bear this out. Soldiers in the field were often unwilling to accept traditional rank authority automatically. In a similar situation, supervisors are now finding that their employees do not look to them for unquestioned leadership. Leadership, like respect, is seen as being earned by performance and by the reaction of those who are led. This is unlike the situation of supervisors in an earlier time whose employees gave unquestioning respect to managerial authority and decisions. They are now less willing to accept orders until they can accept the legitimacy of the order given.

Leadership Traits

Is it possible to isolate a few key characteristics or traits that are associated with leadership? Early leadership theories focused on the obvious physical traits. Were all successful leaders tall, with light hair, blue eyes, and good speaking voices? As you might expect, none of these traits, nor any other specific physical traits, were useful in predicting a person's potential for leadership. However, there are still many managers today who believe that it is possible to relate physical characteristics to leadership success. Many military managers use height or size as a guide when choosing leaders during basic training. It is not unusual to find otherwise intelligent corporate, hospital, or public managers discussing how they always select a certain physical type for promotion to the supervisory ranks. Such invalid assumptions about leadership have been used for years to exclude women or minorities from leadership positions. Yet history shows that prominent leaders appear in all shapes, sizes, sexes, and colors, and with all kinds of physical attributes and handicaps.

There are some personality traits that seem to have some relevance to leadership success. Intelligence is one of these traits. This does not mean that the most intelligent persons will automatically emerge as leaders. However, supervisors who have the mental ability to seek out solutions to complex problems will usually be able to put themselves in positions where their leadership potential can be seen and appreciated.

Leadership Skills

Effective leaders can usually communicate better than nonleaders. They are able to verbalize what needs to be done and how it should be done.

Successful leaders also differ from nonleaders in their desire to influence others. Successful supervisors have a desire to be in charge—to make things happen. In some situations, this drive for power is harmonized with the needs of the members of the group and is directed toward the attainment of group goals. All too often, however, new supervisors extend their desire for power to the point where they become autocrats. Successful supervisors find that working with their employees can be more satisfying and productive than trying to work over or around them. A drive for power does not have to rule out the use of participative techniques in reaching goals.

Successful supervisors are self-confident, and seem to be able to make decisions more easily. Subordinates accept their decisions more readily and seem to have less difficulty implementing those decisions.

Successful leaders are able to handle uncertainty and they usually have a positive attitude toward change. Supervisors willing to accept change are more likely to maintain a position of leadership and reach the goals assigned to them. Effective leaders recognize and can find areas for improvement and encourage employees to make the necessary changes.

Within a work group, a leader gets involved in participation and discussion. The effective leader encourages inputs and suggestions to make a group's performance more productive.

Successful leaders are in control of themselves. They have confidence in their ability and can effectively plan and organize to reach their goals. One supervision expert describes the successful supervisor as an "active, striving, aggressive individual." The person who displays these leadership traits is likely to be looked to by others as a leader. Subordinates will believe that their supervisor can make things happen, because she or he is a leader.

LEADERSHIP STYLES

Autocratic Leadership

The *autocratic leader* is work centered. He or she wants to get the work done and to reach the firm's goals. The autocrat believes that his or her leadership is based on authority granted by the supervisory position. The autocrat usually feels that this power automatically forces followers to obey orders and follow instructions without question. This also implies that the leader is the source of knowledge for the group, and that the leader has the ability to expect obedience. There are two different types of autocrats: the "tough" autocrat and the "benevolent" autocrat. Let's look briefly at these two forms of autocratic leadership.

The *tough autocrat* views leadership as a means of giving orders. The follower's role is to take orders and obey without question. Often, tough leaders are insecure. They lack confidence in their employees or in themselves. This quality prompts close supervision and swift punishment for failure to perform as directed. The motto of the tough autocrat is "pay for performance and praise sparingly." The tough autocrat relies on money as enough of a reward and as a lever for punishment or for changing behavior.

The *benevolent autocrat,* or paternalistic leader, sees her or his role in the work group as that of a "parent figure." The paternalistic leader would never agree that this style is in any way related to autocratic leadership. Quite the contrary. The benevolent autocrat praises employ-

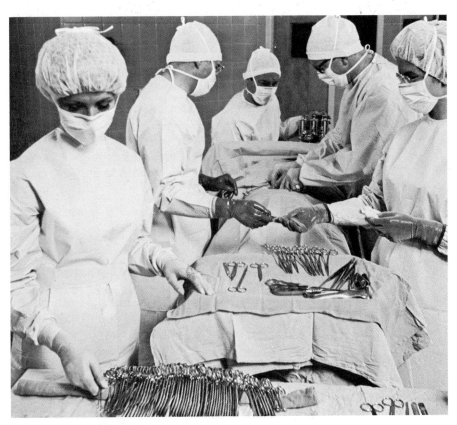

Photo courtesy of FMC Corporation.

AN EXAMPLE OF EFFECTIVE AUTOCRATIC LEADERSHIP

ees for work well done, and encourages (even demands) employees to consult her or him for solutions to their work problems. "Father or Mother knows best" is perhaps the phrase most descriptive of this kind of leader. The benevolent autocrat tries to create a climate where employees can take no actions without the prior approval of the boss. The apparent kindness here is a form of subversion that may result in a climate where employees do not feel secure in taking any action; they will prefer to rely on the leader for approval and acceptance. Nonconformists in this situation are treated in the way misbehaving children would be scolded by a parent. The benevolent autocrat is the dispenser of knowledge and approval. Loyalty by subordinates is highly valued, even more than performance. Disloyalty is the "capital crime" in the eyes of the benevolent autocrat. Initiative, change, and independent action are not permitted. All such traits are viewed as being the prerogative of the leader.

Tough autocrats usually have the following characteristics:

1. The leader makes all of the decisions.
2. The leader's right to lead is derived from positional authority.
3. The leader rewards and punishes.
4. Often the leader will hide information from followers in order to maintain the position as the "source of knowledge."
5. All work is described in detail and rigid work standards are imposed on the performance of followers.

The emotional reactions to the tough autocrat by followers are

1. Resentment of the leader and his or her methods.
2. Resistance to the orders given.
3. Fear and dependence.
4. Frustration with the lack of opportunity to demonstrate ability and perform actions without prior approval and constant supervision.
5. A sense of security, gained from the knowledge that acceptance of the individual by the autocrat is earned simply by following orders.

Tough autocratic leadership is useful when

1. Subordinates are new on the job and have no experience.
2. Decisions must be made immediately, such as in an emergency.
3. The work group becomes complacent and needs shaking up.
4. Disciplinary action is required.

Obviously, there are many situations where an autocratic pattern of leadership is not desirable. Some of these are

1. When the employees are very knowledgeable about their jobs and have considerable experience with the tasks they are doing.
2. Where an established and successful work group has already been formed and is successfully working to reach its objectives.
3. When the job requires the development of teamwork and cooperation among employees.
4. When the supervisor is interested in improving morale and group attitudes about management.

The benevolent autocrat has many of the following characteristics.

1. Makes all the decisions.
2. Stifles creativity and innovation by employees, and resents those who are disloyal or who openly display positive attitudes toward change.

3. Becomes concerned with details. He or she tends to play the role of the "all knowing," thereby becoming the source of subordinate information.
4. Requires that group members come to him or her for advice and approval before taking action.

The emotional reactions of subordinates to the benevolent autocrat are

1. Frustration over the inability to act without supervision.
2. Disrespect, under the guise of friendship or artificial respect.
3. Dependency based on the leader's attention to family details of the subordinate. In fact, the family image is central to this type of leadership.
4. An atmosphere of trust, often felt by all members of the group, even those who do not necessarily respect the superior or his or her actions.

The benevolent autocrat is appropriate in many situations. Among them

1. When subordinates are not interested in seeking more responsibility, or when they enjoy strong and friendly leadership.
2. When subordinates are immature and must be closely managed.

In many situations, the benevolent autocrat is not appropriate. These include

1. Dealing with strong, independent, and mature employees who want to participate in the decision making of their group.
2. When the development of leadership for future years is necessary. Often, a family-founded business is managed in a paternalistic fashion. This usually leaves a leadership vacuum when the founders die. New leaders were not permitted to develop, and therefore managerial succession is difficult.

Consultative Leadership

Consultative leaders involve group members in decisions that affect the group. However, there is no question that the final responsibility for making decisions still rests with the leader. The consultative leader believes that cooperation in reaching the goals of the group can only be achieved if employees are committed to certain goals and actions. Commitment can be gained only by honest and open consideration of employees' suggestions and comments. A consultative leader usually has the following characteristics:

1. Delegates as much responsibility to members of the work team as their experience and knowledge will permit.
2. Emphasizes results instead of actions. The philosophy is that "it's not always *how* the job gets done that's important, but that the job gets done." The consultative leader does not require the follower to do it "by the book" or "my way" so long as the goals set are reached.
3. Demonstrates concern for the employees in the group and, in doing so, generates respect for the leader and the followers as human beings.
4. Encourages cooperation when it will lead to greater productivity and creativity.
5. Defines the objectives for the group and gives them some freedom for performance within the standards.
6. Makes all the final decisions and accepts full responsibility.

Some of the emotional reactions of subordinates to this consultative pattern of leadership include

1. A feeling of cooperation with the boss.
2. Respect for the boss as a person.
3. Warm and friendly relationships between superior and subordinates in the work environment.

Situations where the consultative leadership style is least effective are

1. When the employees lack both experience and training.
2. In groups where employees do not wish to work as a team, or where they are unable to do so because of the nature of the work or the geographic distance between employees.

The ideal situation for the application of the consultative leadership style is

1. When the work force is well trained and experienced.
2. When the work group has a proven record of cooperation and performance.
3. Where employees are able to work independently, with little or no direct contact with the supervisor.

Democratic or Free-Reign Leadership

The democratic or free-reign leadership is often described as no leadership at all. Some supervisors have very little ability to make decisions. They depend on employees to make decisions and take action.

Discipline and control are not enforced because it is hoped that employees will act in a mature manner by themselves. In this situation, group goals are often not clearly stated or understood, and confusion develops among employees. The free-reign leader believes that "one who leads least leads best."

Some of the major characteristics of the democratic or free-reign leadership style are

1. Maximum concern for the individuals who make up the work group.
2. Open discussions and creativity, with respect for all views.
3. Majority rule for making decisions.

The emotional reactions of participants in a democratic situation are

1. A feeling of a free and informal work environment, where each individual can seek his or her own answers to problems on the job.
2. Insecurity and frequent frustration because of the lack of specific decision-making authority and responsibility.
3. Lack of cohesive behavior. Cliques will often form, to the detriment of the group's goal directed actions.

The democratic leadership pattern can be effective in situations such as

1. Where the participants are truly experts and are willing to make decisions on their own.
2. When the group is small and enjoys the opportunity to interact in problem solving.
3. Where there is plenty of time to make a decision.

Democratic leadership has some severe limitations, such as

1. The work group will have some members who refuse to cooperate.
2. The work group will be unable or unwilling to reach a decision.
3. The group will be either too large to work effectively together or it will lack the necessary information to reach a decision.

Manipulative Leadership

Manipulative leadership exploits the aspirations of each employee by trading-off performance for rewards (or promises of rewards). Under this kind of leadership, employees who recognize that they are being manipulated can become bitter and resentful of the leader. The manipulative leader is usually very sensitive to the needs and desires of the employees as individuals. However, this sensitivity is not used for the well-being of the employees unless the leader is able to find some personal "profit" in using it.

The dominant characteristics of the manipulator are that

1. Personal goals are reached by using the employees.
2. Employee needs and desires are viewed as "tools" to extract performance (a sort of carrot-and-stick approach).

The emotional reactions of subordinates to the manipulator include

1. A high degree of motivation in the work group, because they believe that they've found a manager who understands their needs and will help them attain them.
2. Distrust, formed when the manipulative nature of the leader becomes evident and when the employees find that they have been "used."

The manipulator's leadership style can be effective in a limited number of situations, including

1. Where coordination and cooperation must be achieved on a project and previous supervisors were unable to motivate the group. The success of the manipulator in this situation is limited to the time it takes the group members to discover (and begin to resent) the manipulation.
2. Where highly motivated employees are needed for short duration projects. Through the illusion of reward, employees can be motivated for short periods.

Manipulative leadership is not effective where

1. A long relationship is involved.
2. The structure of the organization is so controlled that the ability of the manipulator to "wheel and deal" is severely restricted.

Expert Leadership

Expert leadership is based on the individual leader's knowledge and ability and the leader's ability to use her or his expertise.

If a passenger cruise ship sinks in mid-ocean, the passengers are put into lifeboats and put out to sea. In that unusual situation, the pilot with experience and training in ocean survival may become the group's leader. This leadership role is assumed regardless of the person's age, sex, physical stature, or other attributes. Expert leadership depends on the appropriate mix of individual skills and the needs of the others in a problem situation. Once the situation changes, another person with expertise for that challenge would become the leader. In the expert leadership situation, the person looked to by the group members as the expert must continually demonstrate the expertise to maintain the leadership position. Organizations often make the mistake of promoting to a formal leadership position a person who demonstrates expert leadership in only one situation. Evidence indicates that such leadership is not transferable. An individual can be the finest hospital intensive care unit supervisor, or the best sales manager, or the most competent manager during any sort of crisis, but he or she will not automatically continue to be the leader in another situation.

The most common characteristics of expert leadership are

1. The perceptions of group members permits the joining of the individual's talents and expertise with the needs of the situation.
2. Leadership skills are not usually transferable. The expert leader who's effective in one situation may really "bomb" in another.

The emotional reaction of subordinates to the expert leader can be

1. Relief and confidence that the person in charge knows how to get the job done.
2. Confusion about why the specialist was chosen to be the leader and lack of respect for his or her supervisory ability, especially when the "expert" situation has passed, and things are back to routine.

An expert can be a successful leader in situations where

1. Group members are convinced that they can reach their goals by following the advice and guidance of the expert.
2. A situation develops where specific expertise is necessary for the survival or performance of the group.

The expert leadership style will fail when

1. The individual is no longer recognized as an expert.
2. The situation changes, either to routine or to one requiring a different kind of expertise.

None of these leadership patterns and styles are recipes for success or failure. The style of leadership you use should be determined by many factors in the situation, such as the maturity of your staff, the experience and the dedication of your employees; and your own traits and abilities. It is important to recognize that leadership styles must adjust to fit new situations, new challenges, and new people. A static style of leadership may be worse for you than showing no leadership at all.

WHAT CAN WE GENERALIZE
ABOUT LEADERSHIP?

It's always difficult to generalize about anything in supervision because of the variations in supervisors, in persons supervised, and in situations that supervisors find themselves facing. However, it might be useful to look briefly at some observations about supervision.

D.G. Bowers and S.E. Seashore looked closely at leadership, and concluded that there are four dimensions to leadership.[1] They include

1. Support. The supervisor's behavior should be supportive of the group members. Group members should be able to feel their personal worth and importance.
2. Interaction. All actions taken by the supervisor should be aimed at increasing interaction and mutual respect among group members, thereby bringing group members closer together.
3. Goal Emphasis. Supervisors set challenging goals and should encourage high level performance.
4. Work Facilitation. Supervisors should have the technical and managerial experience to assist group members in reaching their work goals. This is done by scheduling, coordinating, planning, and resource gathering.

Another approach to leadership involves three critical situations which determine the most suitable leadership style.[2] These factors are the nature of the personal relations that exist between the leader and the subordinates, the degree of structure of the task, and the power and authority the leader has because of the supervisory position. The two best leadership patterns are control of employees and high task orientation, or permissiveness, with good interpersonal relations among group members. In other words, the effective leader should "read" the situation before deciding upon a leadership pattern.

Robert Blake and Jane Mouton in *The Managerial Grid* suggest that a supervisor's concern for the job requirements and production will not necessarily get in the way of his or her concern for employees. Using a grid diagram (see Figure 5–1), they have examined the various combinations of a manager's concern for job and concern for people. The managerial grid can help you develop a greater sensitivity for others in the organization by promoting an understanding of the way your leader-

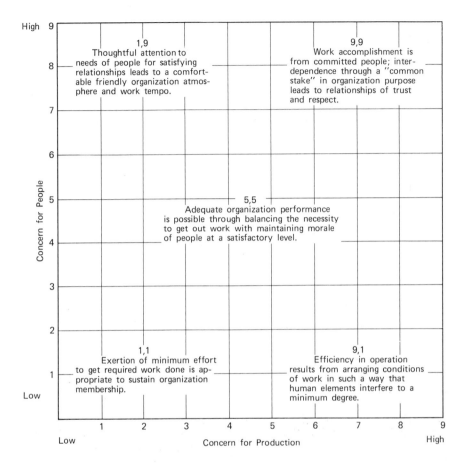

FIGURE 5-1 The Managerial Grid*

*The Managerial Grid figure from *The Managerial Grid*," by Robert R. Blake and Jane Srygley Mouton. Houston: Gulf Publishing Company, Copyright © 1978, page 11. Reproduced with permission.

ship tendencies look. Each of the leader styles in one grid is characterized by a number, where the first digit is "concern for task" and the second number is "concern for people." A high number shows high concern, a low number, low concern. Where do you fit?

Possible results of your grid could be as follows:

Task Management (9,1). The supervisor with this style is an autocrat, with a high concern for production and no concern for people. This type of leader is interested only in meeting schedules, getting production out, and telling people what to do.

Country Club (1,1). This style is the opposite of (9,1), and is characterized by a high concern for people. This supervisor wants a happy and harmonious work force, even though the organization's goals and objectives may not be met.

Impoverished (1,L). This shows up in the lower left corner of the grid chart. It represents a supervisor who does not act at all like a leader. This supervisor has low concern for both people and production. This means no management is present at all. Rather, this supervisor tries to not "rock the boat," and he or she accomplishes just enough to avoid pressure from superiors. This is often called "retired on the job."

Middle of the Road (5,5). This leadership pattern shows up at the center of the grid chart. The supervisor shows moderate concern for both people and production. She or he may push for both but really strive for compromise. The result is often neither the best for people nor for production.

Team Management (9,9). Team management or "leadership through commitment" combines high concern for production with high concern for people and their needs. This is close to an ideal leadership style because the leader accomplishes objectives, while permitting people freedom to reach their personal goals.

The managerial grid is a useful analysis to help you tool your leadership style, because it shows a variety of styles. Think about your style, and then ask: Is it appropriate for my people and department?

DELEGATION: AN IMPORTANT LEADERSHIP TOOL

Supervisors must delegate. Delegation does not mean giving up leadership. Rather, it means that you get the most from each employee. Delegation is a process entrusting certain employees with responsibility for tasks they can do on their own. Employees are made responsible for reaching certain objectives, and they must also be given enough authority to perform well. They are then held accountable for their actions and for successful completion of delegated tasks.

Many new supervisors are reluctant to delegate responsibility. They incorrectly assume that "if you want something done, and done right, then do it yourself." This is a negative attitude about employees and does not lead to maximum productivity.

Why Some Supervisors Do Not Delegate

There are good and poor reasons for not delegating responsibility. If you have a group of employees who are new to the job and do not have the skills or training necessary to do certain tasks, or if your employees do not have enough time or resources to do delegated tasks, or if you are delegating just to get an unpleasant job off your back, you'll likely experience delegation failure. For all these reasons, you should avoid delegation.

There are some poor reasons for not delegating responsibility. There is the "only I can do it" syndrome. Insecure supervisors often try to make their job into a mystery. They build up their jobs to make them sound as if only one person (themselves) can perform certain tasks. With this excuse, no employee has enough training or work experience to accept these "great responsibilities." This builds an artificial wall between the supervisor and employees. With an "only me" attitude, employees never became qualified, and they often don't know what they need to do to *become* qualified.

Some supervisors don't like risk and are unwilling to trust any employee with delegated tasks. Lack of trust in your employees is difficult to overcome. There are, of course, situations where employees may not be qualified or where they are untrustworthy. The fear of being held responsible for a subordinate's error can be a crippling fear that blocks delegation. Frightened that "something might go wrong," the supervisor retreats into a behavior pattern of "play it by the book" or "don't rock the boat." Employees hoping for promotion into supervision will find little opportunity for receiving delegated tasks from this leader. Because there's an employee feeling in this situation that there's no where to go, good employees leave. Consequently, the supervisor's feelings of distrust deepen. This vicious cycle is often started by higher upper management that does not support employee development; they are unwilling to delegate real responsibility to their own subordinates.

Supervisors who have not established a means for ensuring accountability are unlikely to delegate. When you delegate, you must establish *how* and *when* your subordinates will report on their progress. If you are not familiar with accountability and its demands, you will likely not delegate.

Some supervisors are unwilling to share credit for a job well done. The attitude here is: If you keep employees out of the spotlight, you will get full credit for your group's performance. This attitude is usually obvious to employees, and it can build resentment and an unwillingness to accept responsibility.

Why Subordinates Don't Respond to Delegation

Some employees are unwilling to be involved in the delegation process for a variety of reasons. Perhaps it is because there is a lack of trust in management. Employees who do not trust their supervisor may have previously been in situations where they were poorly delegated or managed. Because they became resentful from past experiences, these subordinates need to see that your delegation is not a trick or a gimmick. After you have proven yourself by your actions and delegation skill, most employees will come around.

New employees may lack confidence in their skills. They may fear failure and criticism. If they believe they will fail, they will choose not to accept delegation. This reluctance may be due to the supervisor's failure to evaluate the employee's performance or failure to praise the employee's growth on the job. Without positive messages from the boss, employees may feel they are not making progress in their work. Build employees' confidence if you want them to accept greater responsibility.

Employees who feel that the big rewards go to employees that follow orders are unlikely to accept delegation. If they believe that delegation is "just words" and that, in time, you will tell them what to do and when to do it, they will hold back from accepting delegated responsibility. New supervisors often get frustrated when they try to delegate and find no takers among those who seem most qualified. They feel rejected and angry. In time, they give up and return to giving direct orders. They don't realize that they are being *evaluated* by their employees who want to see how to get along with the new boss. Keep in mind that some resistance to accepting delegation comes from the fact your new employees are probably judging you the way they did their old boss. It takes time for employees to recognize your new—and sincere—approaches to delegation.

Why Should We Delegate?

1. You can't do everyone's job. Even if you are the most productive employee in the organization, it is not possible to work as efficiently as a group of employees working together.
2. Your job is to manage. Inexperienced supervisors often continue to do what they did before being promoted to supervision. The operational activities of a job must instead be left to the employees. Supervisors are responsible for management functions, and they should do them.
3. Those close to a problem often make better decisions than those farther removed from it. Employees have first-hand information available. No matter how closely you supervise, it's just not possible for you to be closer than employees to a situation. This is especially true when the span of supervision is broad, or when the functions performed are highly specialized. Untimely communications can interfere with decision making as well. Often, immediate action is needed to solve a problem. Without delegation of the authority to make decisions, employees have to wait for the supervisor to appear. Meanwhile, the problem gets out of hand, and a crisis develops.
4. Delegation demonstrates a trust of and respect for the individual. You show your employees that you respect their judgment and trust them to make correct decisions. This creates an atmosphere of participation

and commitment to the organization or departmental goals. Subordinates can take pride in their association with the organization, which in turn leads to a better product, a better service, or a better performance on all jobs. Even those employees who have not been delegated authority by the supervisor feel the effects of delegation. By observing that the supervisor trusts employees with independent action, all employees share in the respect and trust.

5. Delegation is a step toward employee development. Employees permitted and encouraged to act on their own have an opportunity to explore their own abilities. This is valuable training, especially when the supervisor is supportive when mistakes are made. If you trust the judgment and dedication of your employees, and delegate responsibility to them, you must be willing to accept errors and mistakes. By making mistakes and having supervisory support and instruction, employees learn. Confidence is built. This results in an easier and more rewarding job of supervision.

The Limits of Delegation

You, as a supervisor, can delegate the authority and responsibility for performing certain tasks. This does not, however, relieve you of full responsibility for all the actions taken by your people. Trust, backed by the knowledge that your employees are capable and deserving of trust, must be present. Since supervisors cannot delegate tasks to employees who are unable to do what is required, delegation must be preceded by adequate training. Also, employees must be willing to accept the responsibility for performance that is at the heart of delegation. You cannot delegate to an individual who is unwilling to accept responsibility. Some employees refuse to make decisions, preferring to rely solely on direct instruction from the supervisor. These employees will work well in an autocratic situation, where rules and procedures are clearly stated and understood. In this situation, delegation probably will be a failure.

Delegation is also not possible when there are poor communications between the supervisor and employees. If an employee is unable to understand what responsibilities you are delegating, delegation will not work. There must be full and complete understanding between boss and employee about all expectations, standards, limitations, and exceptions being delegated.

When to Delegate

The following conditions are likely to be favorable for delegation. They include

1. When there's not enough time to complete all the supervisory tasks assigned to you. This is often a good sign that you need to delegate some of your responsibilities.
2. When the quality of the decision making would be improved by having the people who are closer to the actual problem become directly involved in the decision.
3. When the supervisor is serious about the development of subordinates.
4. When the work group is willing to accept the obligations of the organization, and where a harmonious relationship exists between supervisor and employees.

ACTION GUIDELINES FOR LEADERSHIP AND DELEGATION

1. Recognize that a leader possesses many personality traits but no individual leader can have them all. There is not a formula equating leadership traits with successful supervision.
2. Leadership patterns reveal that every leadership style can be effective in some situations and with certain kinds of employees.
3. Some generalizations can be made about leadership style in organizations. However, it is usually the situational variables that determine the most appropriate leadership style.
4. The most important thing a supervisor can learn is to become more sensitive to all the factors that influence leadership effectiveness in the work environment.
5. Delegation is not a sign of weakness. It is a way of managing that is based on the opportunity for each employee to develop maximum commitment to the organization. Delegation is an important form of motivational leadership.

DISCUSSION QUESTIONS FOR LEADERSHIP AND DELEGATION

1. Discuss why the supervisor's role may not make an individual the leader.
2. What are some of the psychological traits of successful leaders?
3. Compare and contrast the characteristics of the various patterns of leadership.
4. When would these various leadership patterns be successful, and when would they be inappropriate?
5. Discuss your employees' reactions if you decided to change your leadership style over a short period of time.

ACTION EXERCISES FOR LEADERSHIP AND DELEGATION

In the chart below, identify four persons from any area of activity whom you consider to be leaders.

After identifying the individuals, complete the other categories in the chart. When you've finished the chart, you will have a summary of the leadership profile of the individuals you've chosen. Compare your chart with those of your colleagues. Where you have identified the same individual, contrast your comments about a particular leader with the comments of your colleagues about the same leader. List three contrasting comments. Why is there a disparity? From your chart and those of your colleagues does it seem that certain styles of leadership are commonly found in particular activity areas (such as government, politics, business, sales, production, entertainment, and religion)? Are there any traits of leadership that seem to appear in the profile of most of the individuals you've cited? What conclusions can be drawn from this "leadership profile"?

Name	His/Her Leadership Style	Types of Followers	Situation in which Leadership takes Place

In order to analyze your leadership style

1. Describe what you see as your leadership style, and consider the strengths and weaknesses of the approach.

2. List the types of people you find you can most influence.

3. Describe the situation in which you have been most successful.

CASES

CASE 13. Eternal Rest Monuments

The Eternal Rest Monument Company is a large, family-owned organization with sales offices in five cities in a three-state area. They also have a small sales office in a major city in Canada. The company has two construction/production yards and half–ownership of a concrete company and a quarry. It employees seventeen salespeople, plus a resident manager who also does sales for the Canadian office.

Eric Reinhardt is the sales manager. He is not a member of the family, but was recognized early in his sales career as an expert salesman and company representative. He exceeded all his quotas during every one of the five years he actively sold for the company, and he was rewarded last spring with the job of sales manager. He is responsible for supervising the work of the seventeen salespeople, and he maintains informal contact with the Canadian branch manager as well.

Since Eric took over, three of the best sales people have left the company. They were all supporters of Eric's selection as the sales manager, and the promotion did not seem to be a factor in their individual decisions to leave. The other salespeople (including the three new people hired to fill the vacancies) are grumbling about Eric's performance. They feel that he should be doing more to help them develop as sellers. Instead, Eric seems to want to prove that he's still the best salesman in the company.

Esther Lancaster's experience with him is typical. "Last week, I was having difficulty closing on a big account. I knew that my client was just about ready to sign, but I couldn't find 'the handle.' I went to Eric for help, and we talked. Next thing I find, he's out there talking with the client. Sure, sure, we closed the sale, and I'll get the commission, but I'm steamed. That was my customer, and he practically stole the account out from under me. If this keeps up, I'm gonna quit."

Evans McBride was listening to Esther, and came over just as she finished talking. "That's not all about Eric," Evans began. "I had real high hopes for that boy. Despite the fact that he's about fifteen years younger than me, I was the first to agree that his selection as the manager was a natural. And one reason I was all in favor of Eric's selection was that I thought that because he was a salesman, and not tied emotionally into the family, he'd be able to do something about the stupid arrangement of territories that we salesmen serve. The way they're laid out, it's just not equal. It goes back to the days when the family did all the sales as well as run the company. Eric knows how we salespeople feel, and we all figured he'd finally do something about it. I don't know what's with that 'kid,' but if he doesn't get on with it, and quick, there's going to be real trouble in this outfit."

1. What particular form of leadership is Eric using, if any?
2. What problems seem to be evident, and why did they come about?
3. As a supervisor, what can Eric do to resolve some of the problems in the organization?

CASE 14. Olde Berlin Brewery

"Listen, now it's us or them. You know I've always been straight with you. As your boss, I am going to take care of you. Remember when you didn't listen to me, and botched up the Clarendon deal? I didn't hang you out to dry. I covered up the whole thing for you. I run this operation as if you and the others were family. A family member wouldn't go against the others. Now, on your idea about the changes in the record-keeping procedure, let's not make any waves about it. If changes are needed, I will get the word from up top. Then I will assign you to the job. Anyway, I never told you to do that work. What have you *not* been doing while you were working on this? What should I know about?"

Bill Dixon was stunned. He had come to Jack Logan with the best idea he ever developed. It would revolutionize record keeping in the brewery, and would increase profits as well. Bill liked Jack, and Jack always looked after him, as he did for the rest of the staff. But Bill figured that this new procedure he was recommending was his big chance to be recognized by the top management, and he couldn't understand why Jack would stand in his way.

1. What is the leadership style being displayed by Bill's boss, Jack Logan?
2. If you were Bill, and truly felt that your new procedure was a good idea, what would you do next?
3. If you choose to go over Jack's head with your innovation, what would you expect his (Jack's) reaction to be?

CASE 15. Randy Walton

Randy Walton always had an angle. In fact, the other day Paul Howard and Vivian Colter were discussing a recent incident where Randy, their immediate supervisor, was reportedly promising a new employee a chance at "real recognition."

"I overheard the whole conversation and it was 'typical Randy.' In listening to Randy you always have the feeling that you are watching a reincarnation of Tom Sawyer convincing the kids in his neighborhood to pay him to paint the picket fence."

"Vivian, you may be right, but consider all the special favors that Randy has been able to get our group. Remember the time he worked the deal with the guys in personnel and got us those extra days off for the time we had put in on the X-7 Project? If it wasn't for Randy's contacts, we wouldn't be able to have the well-stocked inventory of supplies we have."

"You're right about that, Paul, but when you look at it objectively, you have to ask yourself if when we all enjoy watching Randy work with others in the organization, do we realize that he is probably doing the same thing to us?"

"I don't think so, Vivian, we work for Randy. . . ."

About this time Randy joined Paul and Vivian at the water cooler and began to talk about his plan to get the plant's facilities engineer to give them some additional space.

"I think I've got him going our way. I found that he really likes to play tennis, and I have invited him and his wife to join my wife and me for some mixed doubles this weekend. I figure that if he wins a couple of sets of tennis and then comes by our place for some of my wife's prime ribs and a few drinks, then on Monday he will be about ready to see the expansion our way."

1. How would you evaluate Randy Walton's leadership style?
2. Would you like to be an employee of his?
3. Is it possible that this style of leadership can be effective over the long run?

Motivation

Objectives

After studying the subject of motivation, you will be able to

1. Discuss the importance of the work climate.

2. Describe the role of individual differences in motivation.

3. Describe why it is important that rewards be based on performance, and begin using those rewards.

4. Explain the importance of a supervisor's personal loyalty to employees.

5. Communicate to improve motivation.

6. Become more employee oriented.

7. Apply the concept of work teams to your work group.

8. Relate the concepts of job enrichment and motivation.

MOTIVATION IS THE key factor in the making of a work climate in which employees work willingly to reach the goals of the organization, because they feel that in doing so they will be acting in their best interests. In other words, we don't motivate people, our people motivate themselves. As a supervisor, you give employees an environment in which motivation is possible.

A motivating work climate is influenced by many things. Some of the most important parts of this "climate" are

1. The supervisor's willingness and ability to recognize individual differences in employees and to treat each employee as an individual.
2. The employee's view of her or his chances for success or failure.
3. The actual opportunities that employees have to achieve personal goals.

Supervisors must continuously try to provide opportunities for improving an individual employee's sense of motivation. This means communicating meaningful feedback to employees and maintaining an atmosphere where each employee can feel good about herself or himself.

Supervisors must recognize that individuals are motivated by different factors. Effective motivation involves helping each employee to satisfy some dominant needs. Abraham Maslow described this need of satisfaction as a hierarchy of needs. Frederick Herzberg suggests that individuals are motivated by those things that make the work itself meaningful. Herzberg also proposes that such things as money, good supervision, and good work relationships don't really motivate people to perform better. Rather, they can help overcome an employee's demotivation. Both of these approaches to motivation are useful for supervisors. Later in this chapter, we'll look at them in more detail.

FACTORS THAT FORM
THE "MOTIVATING CLIMATE"

Figure 6–1 shows some of the many forces that form a work climate that can motivate employees to greater productivity. Each of these factors can be influenced to some extent by a supervisor. No two people are ever alike. The supervisor who tells you "all my people are alike" or "one's no different from another on this job" is sure to have motivation problems. People are different, and any discussion of motivation must begin with a look at these individual differences.

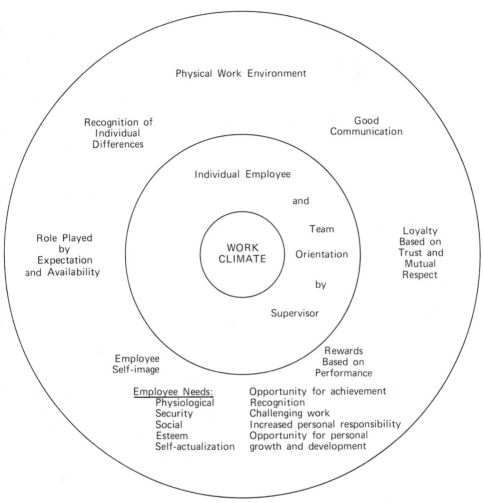

FIGURE 6–1 Factors That Affect the Supervisor's Ability to Motivate through the Creation of a Motivating Work Climate.

INDIVIDUAL DIFFERENCES

Each person has unique qualities which make them different from others. Some of these qualities include physical characteristics, intellectual and manual skills, drive, desire, and ambition. If intellectual and manual skills are not present, you cannot motivate a person to do a job. However, without a proper motivational climate, none of the other characteristics will be nurtured nor will motivation ever take place.

Supervisors must not simply accept the individual skills and characteristics of their employees. Employee skills can be improved. Employee desire, drive, and ambition can be stimulated by creating a work environment that demonstrates in a concrete manner the fact that employees can achieve more than their present accomplishments.

A "climate" of motivation cannot be created haphazardly. It depends upon a supervisor dealing daily with employees. It also depends on the supervisor treating employees as people. This may seem obvious, but unfortunately, it is not. In a seminar for first line supervisors, we were discussing motivation problems. One participant said "Paul, I'm really having trouble motivating my human factor productive components." He was talking about his people, his employees as though they were interchangeable machinery components. He showed me no more personal concern for their needs, desires, and concerns than the rest of us show for our car's spark plugs. This supervisor's sad attitude is all too common. And then we wonder why employees have a poor self-image and resist motivation.

SELF-IMAGE

Motivation experts agree that a motivating environment is one where feedback to the individual reinforces, or confirms, her or his positive self-image. Poor or negative feedback can damage an individual's self-image. When this happens, that person is not likely to perform properly to reach management's goals. By providing positive feedback you can help create a good motivational climate. Failure to recognize the signals when "self-image repair" is necessary will usually contribute to a demotivating environment. It is important to note that a supervisor must not only provide positive feedback to reinforce a positive self-image. He or she must also recognize that some employees have negative self-images. For them negative feedback will provide damaging reinforcement. Thus, feedback can be a two-edged sword.

Let's look at the example in Figure 6–2. Bill, an employee, is reflecting on his chances of being promoted to a supervisory position. Because he is aware that there will be some openings for new supervisors in the next six months, Bill has enrolled in supervision courses at the local community college. He is motivated by a desire for self-improvement, convinced that he can advance beyond where he is now. His incentive for becoming a supervisor may be the increased money he believes he will earn, or it may be the recognition he wants for his accomplishments. Bill's behavior reflects these goals. He has applied for a job as supervisor and has attempted to demonstrate his good work record so that those who evaluate candidates will recognize his desire

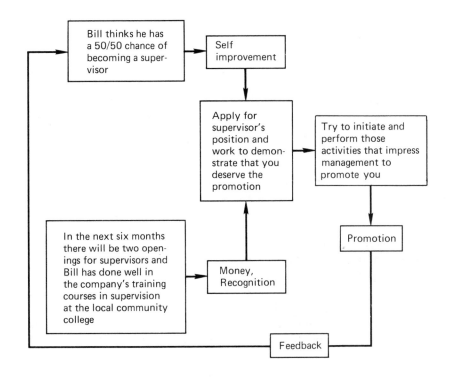

FIGURE 6-2

for promotion. If Bill is successful, the promotion should encourage him to continue striving to develop himself further, with the hope of even more rewards. But if he is rejected, how will he deal with the frustration? He may simply reapply for another supervision job, or he may see if another firm will give him a job as a supervisor. However, he may simply accept the rejection of his application as a reflection of his worth and lose interest in becoming a supervisor.

Supervisors must work hard to determine what their employees really want from their jobs, what their abilities and limitations really are, and how recognition can help them establish a climate where they feel they can satisfy those needs. Many employees are unable or unwilling to express their real needs. Some needs are subconscious. But, even conscious needs are often difficult to communicate. In many work situations, employees may not feel open or comfortable about asking their supervisor for more "meaningful work," so they have learned to ask for more money. A supervisor who is not sensitive to employees' real needs will then end up by simply paying more money—and not addressing real needs. As a supervisor you must be able to determine (by listening and observing) the needs of each of your employees.

THE HIERARCHY OF NEEDS

Abraham Maslow's *Hierarchy of Needs* concept[1] helps us to begin to understand our employees' needs (see Figure 6–3). According to Maslow, there is a natural set of priorities for all people's needs.

For each of us, certain group of needs must be satisfied before we are motivated by other levels of need. The basic needs are the *physiological needs:* the need for food, water, air, warmth, and shelter. If these needs are not satisfied, we will die. To satisfy these needs, people will set aside any consideration of security or social or emotional satisfaction. If you need money to support yourself and your family and have no skills, you may take work that you dislike or that you know to be very dangerous in order to just survive. Many immigrants who came to America went to work in coal mines or in sweat shops, not because they wanted to, but because they had no alternatives for keeping themselves and their families alive.

Once all physiological needs are satisfied, the dominant needs are those called *security needs.* They involve desires for some assurance that one's home, family, and job are secure, and that despite illness or disability, money will be able to meet other basic needs. In our society, the government guarantees some of these security needs. Other security needs are provided by unemployment compensation, workmen's compensation, social security, and medicare. Most businesses have retirement programs, medical insurance, disability insurance, and accident and death insurance—all of which are designed to satisfy workers' needs for security. Union contracts always stress an individual's "right" to a job, which is a concept based on the desire to satisfy the employee's need for security.

Studies indicate that employees want to know what their boss and the organization expect of their performance. By clarifying work expectations, supervisors can help employees reduce job insecurity. Through performance appraisal and managing by objectives, we can reduce insecurity by letting our employees know how they measure up to previously communicated criteria.

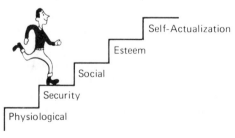

FIGURE 6–3 Maslow's Hierarchy of Needs

Social needs stem from people's desire to identify with others. This need for belonging can be seen in the value workers place on their relationship with their coworkers and supervisors. Most people are not loners; they need the companionship and acceptance of others, and they readily seek membership in informal work groups. Being a part of a social group helps employees feel that they are able to influence others and thus exercise some modest control over their work environment. The natural formation of informal or voluntary work groups satisfies a need, one that every supervisor must recognize. Workers need social relationships on the job in order to form a personal identification with their jobs. As employees develop friendships, their work environment becomes warmer and more acceptable. It becomes more of a motivating environment.

Esteem needs emerge once a person's social needs are satisfied. Employees then attempt to get recognition from their supervisor and their coworkers. Attempts at satisfaction of esteem needs can be seen in the self-confidence, self-respect, and sense of independence that employees demonstrate while working smoothly within established work groups. Failure to satisfy esteem needs often results in complex forms of psychological frustration. For example, if a person believes himself or herself deserving of a promotion, and he or she is passed over, that person may find it difficult to handle the feelings of loss of respect. Such persons may change from being good producers to being problem workers. They may show everyone that they don't care or they may try to get even with the boss or the company for their loss of esteem.

Self-actualization needs involve personal fulfillment. Satisfying self-actualization needs requires reaching goals we have set for ourselves. When a worker begins to study or learn a craft or a skill in the first year of apprenticeship, his or her eventual goal may be to become a master in that skill. It may take years to accomplish, but when it is attained, the worker will set new goals. Reaching self-fulfilling goals can result in tremendous positive rewards to employees. Professors and teachers report that one of the biggest thrills in any graduation is the emotional "high" reached by students who have given so much of themselves for years, just to reach the day when they would be awarded their diploma. The challenge for supervisors is to develop similar "self-actualizing challenges" in the workplace.

Use of Employee Needs

Identifying employee needs is important for all supervisors. Use of the employees needs in motivation can be summarized in three maxims or rules:

Rule 1: The need which is most critical at any given time is the need that the individual wants satisfied. Any attempt to satisfy an employee's higher level need at that time will be a waste of time. For example, if an employee is concerned about losing his or her job with no prospect of getting a new job, efforts to satisfy esteem needs are wasted. The employee is probably operating at the security or physiological need level. To expend effort to motivate using social or esteem need satisfaction would be foolish.

Rule 2: A need, once satisfied, is no longer a motivator. Supervisors often attempt to get greater productivity from employees by offering more money when the employees are operating at a need level where money does little to encourage motivation.

Rule 3: The need level of an individual will change due to changes in the individual or in the environment. It takes a skillful manager to determine the level of motivation that each employee is on, and then develop appropriate ways of motivating by serving those needs.

THE MOTIVATION-HYGIENE CONCEPT

Motivation-hygiene theory suggests that true motivation is not the same as lack of "demotivation".[2]

The hygiene theory is so named because certain things in a work situation are important even though they do not create motivation. These factors—money, status, and security; interpersonal relationships; working conditions; supervision; and company policies and administration—when positive, prevent employees from being dissatisfied. Water purification and personal cleanliness don't make you healthy, but they sure keep you from getting unhealthy. In the same way, Herzberg's hygiene factors are essential in removing or reducing employee dissatisfaction. As a supervisor, you can't successfully motivate employees if they are dissatisfied with their work environment. Thus, you can see the importance of paying attention to employees' "hygiene."

Motivators are what really "turn on" employees, causing them to

FIGURE 6-4   Herzberg Motivation-Hygiene Theory

HYGIENE FACTORS	MOTIVATORS
Working conditions	Opportunity for achievement
Money, status, security	Recognition
Interpersonal relationships	Challenging work
Supervision	Responsibility for work
Company policies and administration	Opportunity for growth and advancement

Photo courtesy of Eastman Kodak Company.

be motivated. Motivators include (1) an opportunity for achievement, (2) recognition by supervisors (and fellow workers) of the individual's work accomplishments, (3) challenging work to do, (4) increased responsibility for the work produced, and (5) the opportunity for personal growth and development. All of these "motivators" should be within an employee's job. Herzberg believes that *true motivation* comes from within the employees. Supervisors can create a climate that will support employee efforts to be more productive, and thereby achieve greater satisfaction, using the motivators as a guide.

Figure 6–5 compares the hierarchy of needs of Maslow with the motivation-hygiene theory of Herzberg. Both emphasize that in our present society, workers have passed the lower level needs, and yet they may not find their *current needs* satisfied by the rewards offered in most organizations. Supervisors today deal with employees who expect more than money and fringe benefits, and more than status and a friendly

FIGURE 6–5 Comparison of Maslow and Herzberg

MASLOW	HERZBERG
Physiological needs	Money
Security needs	Security, working conditions
Social needs	Status, interpersonal relationships, supervision, company policies, and administration
Esteem needs	Recognition; challenging work; responsibilty for work; opportunity for growth, advancement, and development
Self-actualization	

supervisor. Employees want to be recognized for what they contribute. Employees and supervisor alike want an opportunity to advance in order to feel involved, to do something meaningful, and to be treated as mature individuals. The days are long past when rewards could be counted solely in dollars and cents. Today, a supervisor must deal with a more complex employee, one with new demands on the organization and the supervisors.

OTHER FACTORS IN MOTIVATION

Rewards Based on Performance

When employees work toward the goals of the organization and reach those goals, they expect to be rewarded for their efforts. Failure to provide rewards for performance is a sure-fire way to discourage later performance in later times.

The management, through supervisors, attempts to produce, provide, or deliver as many products or services as possible. Supervisors are responsible for encouraging each worker to produce or sell as much as possible. The basic rule, whether written or unwritten, spoken or unspoken, is that high performance brings high rewards. The only way that supervisors can continue to successfully encourage high performance is to provide employees with the rewards they feel they deserve. It should also be restated here that these rewards are not necessarily monetary. Money and fringe benefits are not necessarily what the employees want, but they may be the only things employees know how to ask for. It is very difficult for a person to request greater recognition. One of the most difficult jobs a supervisor must do is to identify which needs are not being met for each individual and then decide what can be done to satisfy those needs when employee performance merits it.

Personal Loyalty to Employees

Managers are always searching for the elusive "loyal employees." Seldom do we see the reverse. However loyal supervisors can be a strong motivating force for employees. Employees like to know that their supervisor represents them "up the line" as well as being just part of management. This "dual role" of the supervisor can help to create employee feelings of security and trust. Employees will respect a supervisor who will "go to bat" for them. In one instance, when interviewing the workers in a manufacturing plant, the authors became suspicious that the employees were "putting us on" about their work attitudes. Just then, one of the senior workers stepped forward and explained the situation quite clearly. "Down here in assembly, we may not know how those guys in management come up with all their ideas. What we do know is that Bill is the kind of guy you can trust when things ain't right. Last year management came up with a procedure that must've looked good on paper, but it just wouldn't work out here. When we went to Bill about the problem, he didn't give us the old management hard line about 'make it work' or 'do the best you can'. Not Bill. He got the facts and went right to the production manager with our complaints. In two days we rearranged the system. Now it works even better than before. That's what we call a supervisor."

This incident dramatizes the fact that employees will put out extra effort for a supervisor who is honest and "straight" with them. You might call it "paying a psychological debt." Employees feel they should repay their boss for his or her loyalty to them. This is far more motivating than a situation where the boss *uses* employee loyalty as just another "motivation tool." Supervisors should work to develop a bond with their employees. Respect does not come easily, and it is not earned overnight. In some cases, where employees have held very negative opinions about management, it may take years for a group of employees to show that they feel you are the kind of supervisor who can be trusted, that is, one who deserves their respect.

Communication within the Organization

Today, it is more important than ever for employees to feel that they know what is going on in the organization. With the exception of personnel matters, employees have a right to know the plans and objectives of the organization or at least those that directly relate to the work situation. Good communication helps employees feel that they are part of the organization. However, if a supervisor (from higher management) fails to communicate with employees, they will still be gathering information. What employees don't know from the facts given them they will assume. They will act on their inferences as if they were facts. When you fail to communicate with your employees, you create mistrust. You cause employees to rely on the "grapevine" to get information that they want. When employees guess what is happening, they tend to be pessimistic, and they often severely overstate problems. Open communication, on the other hand, moves messages quickly and accurately to employees. It can reinforce other motivation efforts.

When you communicate, be honest. If you lose your credibility, you may never be trusted again. A good supervisor quickly learns to communicate with his or her employees frequently and honestly. The chairman of the board of Montgomery Ward recently expressed just such a view, saying that "the most powerful tool of any manager is *open communication.* [Italics added.] You cannot constantly surprise your employees and expect to retain their confidence, respect, or trust." This is good advice about motivation.

Employee Orientation

Rensis Likert has observed that supervisors of high-producing work groups are perceived by their employees as being *employee-centered.*[3] Supervisors of lower-producing groups are often perceived as being *work-centered.* As a supervisor, you should take a personal interest in the problems of each employee up to the point where you feel you might lose your objectivity. At this point, an employee's problem should be taken, in strictest confidence, to someone who is better equipped to handle the situation. Employees will bring problems to their supervisors if they feel that their supervisor is someone who can help them. Psychologists see this occurring in every organization. Because you are in a position of authority, employees look to you for guidance. If they respect you as a person, they hold your opinion in high esteem. Because of this relationship between employees and their supervisors, supervisors have a great responsibility to become employee oriented and to approach employees' problems in a serious and professional way.

Supervisors who are employee oriented have a great opportunity to create a positive and motivating work environment. The employee-oriented supervisor is one who is interested in all aspects of the jobs being performed in the department and who is interested in and concerned about those people who perform the jobs. This attitude builds trust and respect that will help the work group reach its peak potential.

We should clarify that being employee oriented does not mean a "soft" or "give-in" managerial style. On the contrary, supervisors who wish to manage high-producing work groups must set challenging, yet reasonable, work goals. Beyond this, supervisors must manage in such a way as to create a sincere "union of trust" between themselves and their employees. It is not by your words that you will be judged, but by your actions. As an aid to developing rapport with your employees, commit to memory (and then put into practice) the Ten Commandments of Human Relations:

1. Speak to people. There is nothing as nice as a cheerful word of greeting.
2. Smile at people. It takes 72 muscles to frown, only 14 to smile.
3. Call people by name. The sweetest music to anyone's ear is the sound of his or her own name.
4. Be friendly and helpful. If you would have friends, be a friend.
5. Be cordial. Speak and act as if everything you do is a genuine pleasure.
6. Be genuinely interested in people. You can like almost everybody if you try.
7. Be generous with praise and cautious with criticism.
8. Be considerate of the feelings of others. There are usually three sides to a controversy: your side, the other fellow's side, and the right side.
9. Be alert to giving service. What counts most in life is what we do for others.
10. Add to this a good sense of humor, a big dose of patience, and a dash of humility, and you will be rewarded many times.

Development of Work Teams Based on Individuals

One of the most successful ways to improve productivity is by team building. Each member of a work team is an individual who shares his or her needs and objectives with other members of the team. Individuals within the group are encouraged to share honestly with fellow team members their perceptions of how the group can reach its goals and why it may not be as successful as it may wish to be. With this technique, employees begin to bring themselves fully into the work problems. The aim of team building is not to accuse or to blame employees. Rather, it is to alter human relationships which may be standing in the way of the employees' reaching personal organizational goals. Many people feel that the success of Japanese management has been through the use of "team effort" and group involvement.

Effective supervisors can develop motivated employees by investing time and energy in team-building exercises. One successful supervisor found that honest and open communication resulted in a new view of her supervisory methods. She thought she was effective, but her employees revealed that her methods were causing them to develop negative feelings about work projects because of their feelings about her style.

Through the development of open communication with her team, both the supervisor and employees learned how to better work together.

The work-team concept is based on bringing each employee "into" a group rather than just assigning a person to a group. In this way employees will come to feel that they belong to the group. They will find that mutual participation in reaching goals is more advantageous than not being a part of the organization. The team-building technique is the opposite of the classic "divide and conquer" tactic designed to "keep the workers in their place." The team-building approach requires that the supervisor focus the attention of group members on the work goals and that each member is rewarded as part of the team.

Employee commitment to the attainment of organizational goals evolves through good supervision. Team members find satisfaction in the work they do, and in turn, they respect the supervisor for the role he or she plays. The role of team leader is one which is earned, not imposed.

TEAM BUILDING[4]

Today's management problems are too complex for one person to handle alone. Sure, there are many times when a supervisor should make decisions alone. There are many other times when a group's involvement can help the quality of the decision being reached—or when the group's commitment to the decision is necessary for successful implementation.

Team spirit and team work is valuable beyond decision making. Many experts feel that the key to Japanese industrial success is their use of team feeling and a team effort. Even under the most autocratic, crisis-type conditions, managers are finding a considerable payoff from team building.

Yet, there is resistance. Some managers feel that "only managers should have a say in management." It may be said out of habit, "after all we've never operated with a team approach before." Such an attitude may also be a case of simple ignorance: "I don't know how to build and use a team."

Why Don't We Use a Team Approach?

There are four basic reasons why supervisors resist using a team approach.

1. *Fear interdependence.* Most supervisors are given their jobs because of a combination of personal skill with the ability to work well with

others. Yet, once a person reaches a supervisory level a fear of this inter-dependence sets in. Some managers begin to feel that their continued success depends upon them taking personal action. They know that they need others, but they fear that need will show up as a personal weakness.

2. *Ignorance.* Managers either do not know—or do not want to know—the proper roles to be played by their people. They know the people, and they know their job descriptions, but they are blissfully un-aware of what their people really can do—and should do—for the depart-ment. A hospital supervisor in Alberta confided that she was shocked by a simple exercise she learned about in a seminar. She had each of her em-ployees write out a simple, informal job description. Each person was to tell her what they actually did. The results were nothing like the formal job descriptions the supervisor thought she was working with. People were doing and not doing all kinds of things without the boss' knowledge.

Ignorance can result because of overwork. It can result from too little time to really manage what people are doing. It may even result from a fear that supervision that is too close will destroy effective delegation.

3. *It takes planning.* Most supervisors are action oriented. They like to see things moving. They know the importance of planning, but they find it easier to avoid planning in favor of getting things done. Building and managing an effective team takes a lot of planning. For many of the same reasons we fail to delegate, we fail to plan. Without plans to act as guide-lines, employees will usually do their best. They do what they think ought to be done. This is *not* team work. It is individual work in a group setting. And it is not as effective as a well-managed team.

4. *The activity trap.* An action orientation can lead to an activity trap. We become so concerned about what is going on that we can easily overlook our goals. When supervisors do all the assigning themselves, when they operate with a nonteam approach, they get the satisfaction of enjoying little victories. They can see the immediate outcome of their actions. By using a team, it is not as easy to see—and enjoy—the completion of projects. It is certain that when projects and assignments successfully run to completion, there will be a sense of satisfaction. However, when using the team-oriented approach, the frequent satisfactions come to subordinates and are not as readily available to the team-oriented manager.

How to Build a Successful Team

The challenge of turning dedicated, intelligent people into a *team* can be very satisfying. Many of the steps and techniques outlined in this article are already being used by many managers. The key to successful team building is a common-sense use of these techniques.

1. *Communicate your real goals.* A common misconception is that in order to operate through "management by objectives," one needs to have a

sophisticated, highly technical system. Managing with objectives can be quite involved. It can also be as simple as an executive setting goals and communicating those goals to the staff.

Take a few minutes to review your personal and department goals. If you don't have a list of formal goals, develop one. Write out your goals. Look at them in terms of long-term goals and short-term goals. For each set of goals, set priorities. Determine which goals are more important than others. Be brutal. There is a temptation to think that all our goals are important, but it is unrealistic to think we are going to achieve all of them.

Once you have set your goals, communicate them to your people. Explain them. Ask for—and listen to—suggestions. Be flexible. Don't assume that you know what your people are thinking. Ask questions. Use body language to show your people you are interested in them and their views. Don't make goals so impressive that they intimidate. Communicate them on a personal level, so that your people can see how these goals relate to them.

2. *Be liberal with feedback.* Studies of employee satisfaction and commitment show those most willing to support a manager as part of an effective team are those who feel they have full and open communication with their bosses. This is not the overworked "open door." It does not mean that bosses must communicate everything they know to everyone on their staff.

It does mean that bosses should provide feedback. Let your people know how they are doing and *how you feel* about how they are doing.

We all like to know how we are doing, that is, how others evaluate our work and our contributions. Too often, managers assume that their people know that they are doing a good job and that they don't need to be told all the time. The problem is, as one employee confided "all I ever hear about is problems. The boss never talks to us unless we're on the hot seat."

Let people know your good thoughts, but don't overdo it. Too much praise can seem phony. Too little, though, can make even the most motivated employee unwilling to contribute to a total team effort.

3. *Persuade.* Some managers often try to control all communication. To do this, they give orders, make statements, and generally act in a manipulative manner. This usually gets action, but it rarely gets commitment.

Commitment to a team effort on the member's behalf results usually from a persuasive managerial style. A persuasive manager is one who is supportive. He or she provides plenty of reassurance and feedback and does so by listening and asking questions. The persuasive manager persuades by communicating *benefits* to her or his employees rather than by simply reciting features.

Any time that you try to motivate an employee, you emphasize certain features that are true about whatever you are trying to "sell." Trying to persuade people by telling people about features can quickly become an exercise in forcing. People resist being told why they should do anything.

However, people do like to know how *their needs* can be satisfied, and a feature that satisfies a need and is a motivator is a *benefit*. When persuading someone, search for that person's real needs. Then communicate to him or her in such a way that it helps that person see how certain features provide for his or her needs.

4. *Remain positive.* There are two ways to communicate with your people—positively or negatively.

- A negative message says such things as "don't do this," "avoid that," "and try to watch out for this problem." It alerts people to a problem, but it gives no direction.
- A positive message accomplishes much more. It sets out targets for people, it tells them what you want them to do, and it motivates.

At a university, we conducted a simple experiment. Two identical plots of lawn were bordered by a sidewalk. On one plot, we placed a sign advising "Keep Off the Grass." On the other plot, the sign was positive: "Please Walk on the Sidewalk—The Grass Is Trying to Grow." Predictably, the positive sign had a much better effect on students' behavior. They made a conscious effort to stay off the lawn.

Be creative in the way you communicate. Let people know in a positive way what you expect of them.

5. *Become a resource.* When the boss is a resource, people come to her or him for advice, help, support, information, and decisions. When the boss is a resource, employees are more likely to work out their problems among themselves. They will consult with one another, and use more of the resources at their disposal. This is the ideal team spirit.

Being a resource is not always easy. There is a temptation to jump in to try to settle things instead of relying on people to follow through. There is often a feeling that team action means executive inaction. In a team operation, the supervisor is an important part of the overall effort, but he or she cannot be the sole decision maker or expert.

Enriching the Job

A job can be enriched by allowing employees to take greater responsibility for the work that they do. For example, employees assembling clocks that have to go to an inspector may feel that management doesn't trust their work. However, if employees assemble and inspect the clocks, and sign off on their work sheets, the increased responsibility can become a form of job enrichment.

Jobs that are part of a career ladder are another example of enrichment, because they demonstrate to employees that they are not in "dead-end" jobs. If employees are successful in a job, they should be given the idea that they are in line for promotion to a better job.

If a job can be made more challenging—that is, more enriched—do it. If a job cannot be materially changed, at least try to give employees some greater sense of personal control and decision making. Despite problems, this can be done in almost any organization, for any kind of job. Consider the success of a Florida municipal supervisor of garbage collectors. Recognizing that little in the job could be realistically changed, this wise supervisor didn't try to "trick" employees into thinking otherwise. Instead, he continually pointed out to them how important their activities were to the entire community. (If you have ever lived through a week or more of a garbage strike, you have to agree on the importance of the job.) He also relieved his people of many of the unnecessary burdens usually put on such jobs. He allowed the employees to decide who drives the trucks and who throws in the cans of garbage. He allowed them to go home when their collection routes were finished, rather than force them to hang around the equipment yard until their eight hours were in. In short, he gave employees meaningful control over parts of their jobs. This is *creative motivation* at its best.

Most employees want to take pride in what they are doing. A simple, nonchallenging job gives most employees little reason to be proud. As a supervisor, you may be pleasantly surprised at the work employees can perform if they are given the opportunity.

ACTION GUIDELINES FOR MOTIVATION

1. Recognize that each person is unique. Make a list of the individual differences, strengths, and weaknesses of each of your employees.
2. Try to apply these motivation ideas to your needs.
3. Reward employees for good performance, and do not reward them for poor performance.
4. Represent your employees to management with the same effort that you represent the policies of management to the employees. Remember that loyalty is earned, and not freely given.
5. Develop and maintain an open communication system, and keep information flowing in both directions—up as well as down.
6. Be known by your employees as someone who cares about each of them as individuals. Become employee oriented. Create a reputation by your actions that you could not have earned by your title alone.
7. Develop a work team based on trust and respect. Don't forget that reaching any organizational objective must result in a reward that will satisfy individual needs. Team building can create honest and open communication. It can help solve interpersonal problems before they become major motivational crises.
8. Never forget that the physical work environment is important. Be sure that there are no safety problems and that everything possible has been done to make the working conditions as pleasant as possible.
9. Whenever possible, match the person to the job. Don't hire overquali-

fied people and then expect them to be motivated by doing a job that is beneath their skill.

10. Whenever possible enrich the jobs of your employees. Never sell your employees short in skill or ambition. Create challenging jobs which have greater opportunities for advancement, growth, recognition, and reward.

11. Finally, try to motivate your employees in the same way you would want your superiors to motivate you.

DISCUSSION QUESTIONS FOR MOTIVATION

1. Why would a supervisor who is responsible for managing many employees ever consider individual differences when attempting to motivate?

2. Explain how expectancy might influence employee behavior toward the attainment of organizational goals.

3. Discuss the relationship that might be developed between Maslow's hierarchy of needs and Herzberg's motivation-hygiene concept.

4. Must all performance be rewarded?

5. What are the values of personal loyalty to employees?

6. When you hear that someone or some group is becoming "employee oriented," what do you think it means?

7. Does motivation based on work teams violate the concept of individual motivation?

8. What are some of the problems associated with hiring overqualified applicants?

9. Can low-level jobs be enriched?

ACTION EXERCISES FOR MOTIVATION

Instructions: Consider the following questions in terms of what you have just read about motivation and what you see in real life.

1. What are the five most important factors or incentives that motivate you and why?

2. What are the five most important factors or incentives that motivate your friends or coworkers and why?

3. What are your expectations about life and your career?

4. Break into groups of three to six and compare your answers to the three questions above. After you have read each of your responses and discussed them among yourselves, summarize what you feel you have learned from this exercise about human motivation.

CASE 16. The Real World

"Recognition? You gotta be kidding. Why, my truckers are the best paid in the area. They're not here long enough to get any recognition. If they're not on the road hauling their rigs and making dough, they're in some bar getting rid of it as fast as they can spend it. Recognition and motivation is just a lot of hooey. I drove trucks in my day, and we did it for cold, hard cash. You don't baby trucking people. You pay 'em and leave 'em alone!

"My management philosophy? It's simple. It's based on the facts of life. I hire the best men in this area, and I pay 'em top dollar. I'm not about to waste my time and energy worrying about theory nonsense that some professor spouts off. Those guys just never met truckers."

1. Do you agree with this philosophy?
2. Is it a realistic viewpoint?
3. Are there viewpoints this supervisor is overlooking? Do people want only money?
4. With this viewpoint, will this supervisor ever be able to get the maximum productivity out of his employees?

CASE 17. The Train Station

In 1973, Stan Greenbaum, a graduate of the Cornell University School of Restaurant Management, opened a unique steak and seafood restaurant in his home town of Richmond, Virginia. Stan was able to purchase eighteen old passenger and freight-train cars, and after cleaning and redecorating them, he hauled them to a field on the outskirts of town. Next, he assembled the cars in a pattern which seemed random to observers but which was, in reality, scientifically designed around a kitchen in the center. Walkways were built between the cars and a roof enclosed the remaining area. When it came to staffing the restaurant, Stan hired four experienced cooks and then ran ads in the Richmond paper for waiters, waitresses, and bus boys.

The ad stressed the opportunity for young college students to earn money while attending school.

Stan had no problem in recruiting his first staff. In the first three months of operation, things went smoothly, but then the staff began to resign one by one. Stan began to ask each of the men and women when they quit why they were leaving. The responses didn't seem to indicate that the problem was money. In fact, many of those who quit had earned good money on the job. The restaurant's service began to suffer because Stan was always breaking in new help.

Stan began to ponder the problem with another restaurant manager one afternoon over coffee. "I can't understand it, I don't think it's the money." His friend suggested that the cause of the problem might be the type of employees Stan was hiring. Stan said he had always hired the "best people" available.

1. What are the options open to Stan for creating a motivating climate for his "college student employee"?
2. Is it really possible to motivate people to do routine tasks?

CASE 18. Atlanta's New Airport

Marcy Gonzales is a ticket agent with Coastal International Airlines. The airline is headquartered in Atlanta, where Marcy works. Recently, the city of Atlanta opened a new, ultramodern "infield" airport. Terminals are in the middle of the field, and the passenger check-in counters are at one end of the field, connected to the terminals by long subways under the runways. With the new arrangement, Marcy and other ticket agents are a quarter-mile from their airlines terminal, with its shops, gates, crew and maintenance areas. At Atlanta's old terminal, ticket counters were right next to the gates and other areas.

Shortly after the move to the new facilities, Marcy was talking with a passenger about her feelings. "I'm happy to be over here, but it's not really the same. We're sort of isolated. We don't get to visit with any of our old friends—ramp agents, flight crews, and the guys in maintenance. They're all together, and we're stuck out here by ourselves in the 'gilded cage.' Oh, it's nice here, and the facilities are sure better than over at the old terminal, but I'm really having a hard time adjusting to being so isolated. Several of the gang have asked for transfers to other cities where they'll feel like they're part of the 'team' again. I sure wish management had given some thought to our needs when they were building the new airport. Of course, since we're stuck with it, it's management's problem to overcome the poor morale and rapid turnover."

1. How could "proactive" management have avoided such problems before they developed?
2. How might a "team building" approach help this situation?
3. How can supervisors deal with the poor morale, lack of motivation, and rising turnover?

Communication

This chapter, which deals with communication between supervisors and their employees, superiors, and fellow supervisors, is one of the most important in the book. When you have completed your study of this chapter, you will be able to

1. Communicate with more sensitivity to the differences between yourself and your employees.

2. Identify the potential for communication problems that exist within the sender, the receiver, and the message.

3. Recognize (and make constructive efforts to overcome) the destructive effects of distortion.

4. Use repetition to improve the impact of your communications.

5. Manage the grapevine that exists within your organization and reduce some of its harmful effects.

6. Use listening and feedback to learn how your people feel.

7. Understand more about body language and thus better "read" the nonverbal messages of others.

WITHOUT QUESTION, SUPERVISORS know the importance of good communication—between themselves and their employees, superiors, fellow supervisors, and others. Yet knowing how to communicate is not enough for people in today's complex organizations. Communication in the organization involves many dimensions that are mixed together to form an imposing challenge for supervisors.

WHAT IS COMMUNICATION?

Communication is the sending of information from one person to another, and the receipt of that message in the way the sender intends. It is also the composing of a message that arouses the kind of response we want to arouse.

How Do We Communicate?

We communicate in many ways, some that are conscious, some unconscious. When we speak or write, we send a message to other people. However, the absence of a message can be just as much of a communication as a written or spoken message. When your employees

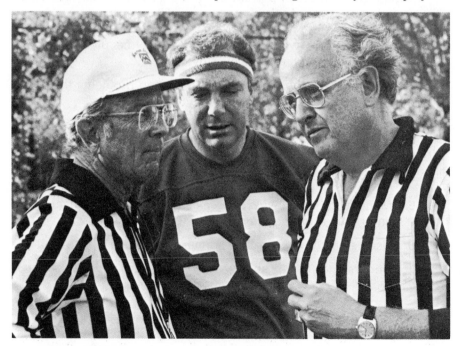

Photo courtesy of H. J. Heinz Company

ask you what happened in a meeting, and you tell them that you and the other supervisors discussed the next rotation in the job scheduling system, a message has been communicated. But, if you tell your employees that nothing took place, you have still communicated. The simple fact that you said ". . . nothing happened," tells your employees that you are unwilling to share information with them and leaves them free to speculate on just what did happen. We all have a desire to "fill in the blanks." When a message is incomplete, we will fill in the missing parts with our fears, hopes, or expectations. The resulting message may only slightly resemble the original message that was sent.

A Communication "Expert"

Some time ago, we did a communication seminar in a large Western city. At the midpoint of the seminar, when the participants were taking a break, one man in the audience came up to talk with us and proceeded to tell us that he was an expert at managerial communication. He didn't want to attend, but his boss told him to "show up or else!" He pointed to the end of the row of chairs where he was sitting, and said ". . . see that guy at the end of the row? That's my boss. I'm glad he came tonight because he does everything wrong that you fellows have been talking about. He really needs this seminar." This reaction is all too common. The problem with many of us who are exposed to communication books, articles, and speeches is that we sit in an audience, or in our lounge chairs at home, and tell ourselves that we are experts.

No one is an expert at communication. As far as communication ability goes, a supervisor is usually no better at communicating than his or her employees. Don't make the mistake of seeing the communication faults of others, while missing the places where you could improve your own communication ability.

THE PROCESS OF COMMUNICATION

The process of communication is really very simple. It involves three basic elements: a sender, a receiver, and a message (see Figure 7–1). The operation of the process is a bit more complicated than what is shown, however.

Message

Sender   Receiver

FIGURE 7–1. The Elements of Communication

The Sender

The sender is the transmitter or starter in a communication. Without a sender, communication would not occur. The sender can be an individual or a group. Senders also include mass media, businesses, government agencies, and educational or religious organizations.

As a supervisor, you are constantly sending messages. You communicate when you write a job order or complete a performance appraisal form or sign an order for merchandise or material. You are a sender when you tell someone about the progress of a job or when you give instructions to your employees. But you are also a sender when you tell someone, by the expression on your face or your tone of voice or the actions that you take, that you are not interested in their idea, or that you are upset with their report. Communication does not have to be in words, and it does not have to be conscious. You may be the most friendly person in the world, but the message you are sending to your subordinates may be that you don't care about their feelings or ideas. The sender has a great responsibility in communication, because it is the sender who starts the entire process, and it is the sender who must bear the burden of framing a message so that it will be received in the same spirit that it was sent.

Where Do Senders Fail?   Senders fail when their messages are garbled, transmitted too fast (or too slow), or filled with vague or difficult-to-understand words and phrases. Some words and phrases, even though they are apparently quite simple, can still be misunderstood. For example, if you were to suggest in a supervisor's meeting that an item on the agenda be "tabled," most of your colleagues would understand that you wanted the item held over for discussion at the next meeting. However, to some people (particularly the British), "tabling" an item means bringing it on the table for discussion. When a sender, out of carelessness, ignorance, or misunderstanding fails to make a message clear, miscommunication often results. When the boss sends a memo instructing supervisors to "tighten up this operation," does he or she mean that supervisors should cut the number of persons on the staff? Reduce overtime? Refuse to give raises? Check punctuality? Reduce quality checks? Increase quality checks? Obviously, there are many meanings possible from a simple statement. Whenever a sender leaves open the possibility of someone else putting different meanings on something said or written, he or she has failed to effectively communicate.

The Message

The message is the content of communication. It is an idea, an order, a suggestion, or a thought that the sender wants to share.

There doesn't really seem to be much argument about what a message is. The meaning is pretty clear-cut and obvious. But, as any supervisor knows, the message that is intended is not always the one that is received.

For example, a supervisor told one of his employees, "Charlie, you'd better wrap up the job." The supervisor meant that the job should be completed within the next few days. That message does not seem to have any possibility for misunderstanding. However, the employee could have understood that when the boss said ". . . wrap it up," the meaning (or real message) was that the job should be completed today, whatever the cost. Thus, a simple message can be distorted.

Some years ago, a group of Navy reservists were on a training cruise aboard an aircraft carrier in the Pacific. The reservists were doing many of the jobs normally done by regular Navy personnel. One such job was the deck officer's during the launching of aircraft. A reservist was put in charge of giving the signal to release the aircraft from the catapult on the flight deck. One reservist, when the plane was ready to take off, yelled out the order, "Fire!" The reservist operating the catapult understood the order as "fire the plane," and he activated the catapult. However, the pilot of the aircraft (a regular Navy pilot) understood the word "fire" to mean something quite different. To him, fire meant that there was a blaze on board, and that the aircraft's engines should be shut down immediately. The conflict over the meaning of the message resulted in the plane's being pushed off the flight deck without any power other than that of the catapult, and the pilot was killed. The correct word that should have been used when launching the aircraft with the catapult was "release."

The Receiver

Just as there can be many senders of messages, there can also be many receivers. When you sit down in front of the television to watch the evening news or a weekend ball game, you are but one of millions of other receivers of the broadcast message. When you write a confidential memorandum to your boss, you assume that the boss is the only one who will read it. However, if you have the memo typed, the typist will have some idea of what is going on. If that typist does not have all the facts about the situation, he or she will probably "fill in the blanks" and thus receive a message different from what was intended. Receivers, like senders, can distort or block parts of a message.

Noise

Noise is any interruption or distortion of a message. Noise can be physical, which makes it difficult for the receiver to hear or see the sender. We are usually aware of physical noise and can often take action to overcome it.

Noise can also be nonverbal. It occurs when people with different points of view attempt to communicate. They will often attach different meanings to a single message being exchanged. This noise is far more damaging to supervisory communication because usually neither sender nor receiver is aware that noise or distortion is happening. Nonverbal noise can result from our job positions. When you worked in nonsupervisory jobs, you may have been in the habit of speaking to everyone in the department and socializing with many of the other employees. When your promotion to supervisor was announced, subtle (but very real) shifts in attitudes began to occur. The fact that you were given an office, or a separated work area, and perhaps other prerequisites (such as a reserved parking space, a nameplate on the door, or frequent access to other management people and top executives) has made you different now in the eyes of your former coworkers. You are more distant from the people in your department than you were when you were just another employee. This "social distance" is a natural result of changes in relationships between people and is useful for supervisors when they must make difficult decisions, especially decisions involving their former workmates. The distance that develops because of the supervisor's status or position or responsibilities is an example of "nonverbal noise." The challenge for supervisors is to communicate in ways that minimize some of these differences in perception. This will pave the way for meaningful communication on the problems that workers and supervisors share.

THE COMMUNICATION MIX[1]

By now, you have the idea that communication is not as simple as it might at first have appeared. Your next thought should be "what is the best way to communicate?"

Unfortunately, there is no "one best way" to supervise, motivate, or communicate. Your success as a supervisor will depend on your ability to bring together a variety of techniques and ideas that best fit a particular managerial situation. Because communication occurs on many levels, some of which are beyond our normal awareness, it is very important that a supervisor develop abilities in communicating. As a supervisor, your goal should be to use communication to develop commonness. Reaching this goal means using all of the communicating dimensions possible. How you communicate will depend upon your particular talents and abilities. If you are a strong and persuasive speaker, you will obviously find it more effective to put yourself in situations where spoken communication is required (such as meetings and large group gatherings). If your "long suit" is writing, you should maneuver to put yourself into writing situations. Regardless of your abilities, however, do not overlook the impact of your personal example and your performance as a communication model. We can see everyday examples of this principle in the sports world. Good bowlers develop best when they have the opportunity to bowl regularly with bowlers better than themselves. They learn from these "superior models." Good golfers develop from competition with good golfers. The same is true in tennis, handball, and virtually every other sport. The atmosphere and attitudes you influence by your example are a vital communication link with your employees. Good examples of communication, and a willingness to "follow through" on your examples, will do much to improve the entire realm of communication within your area or department.

When your people see that you are making a conscious and continuing effort to avoid misunderstandings, they will begin to return that effort, even though they may not even be aware that they are doing so. Your job as a supervisor and manager requires that you focus all your abilities on certain problems. Your success depends upon your being able to make decisions and to control and direct the flow of work assigned to you. This, in turn, requires information. Information is sent and received by communication. Identify your personal strengths and weaknesses as a communicator, and start to develop yourself as a more effective communicator. Some of the best public speakers, the most dynamic group leaders, and the most popular and prolific writers started out in their careers with serious limitations. Their success in their work is directly related to the effort they expended in developing the skills and strengths they needed. Your success as a communicator is essential to your success as a supervisor.

COMMUNICATION IN YOUR ORGANIZATION

The best place to start looking at communications in your organization is your firm's organization chart, or job-task pyramid. The organization chart shows the relationships between people and jobs and illustrates the *official channels of communication* between people. The job-task pyramid is often called the formal organization, since it had been "formalized" or accepted by all persons in the organization.

As a supervisor and a communicator, you must learn about your formal organization. The organization chart, however, does not show all communications in your organization. Much of the actual communication in any organization occurs in channels that are not on the organization chart. These realistic channels, lumped together under the heading of "the informal organization," take many forms and directions. To understand and work in an organization, you must examine both the formal and the informal organizations.

Communication in the Formal Organization

The formal organization has three different directions of communication: upward communication, downward communication, and across or lateral communication. As a supervisor you are involved with all three kinds of communication and each direction poses its own special kind of communication problems.

Downward Communication. Downward communication is used to direct and control employees. Information must be communicated to employees before they can begin to perform their activities. Often there is a big difference between what employees need to know to do their jobs and what employees want to know about their jobs. Employees (and that includes the supervisor, too) need to have such information as what is required, when it is supposed to be ready, who is going to inspect or monitor it, and how it is to be coordinated with other activities. The what, when, who, where, why, how, and which are the nuts and bolts of any organization. Most supervisors are pretty adept at communicating this information to their employees. However, we often forget that the specifics of any job or assignment are not the only communications necessary. The things people want to know about their jobs are just as important.

What Do People Want to Know? We all want to know how a particular job or activity fits into the larger scheme of things. We all want to know that we are making some contribution, however small, to reaching a goal. We like to feel secure in doing what we are doing, and, above all, we want to know that our efforts are appreciated.

Recently the authors interviewed a supervisor who managed the work of fifty men who were doing what is one of the most thankless jobs around—collecting garbage. Our interest was sparked because the turnover in this department was far lower than the turnover in many of the more comfortable city jobs, and the employees really seemed to be motivated. Yet, when we examine the job of a garbage collector, most of us would probably find very little with which to get involved. This supervisor's secret of success was simple. He took a personal interest in each of his workers, and he communicated to them, in words and by his actions, that he was appreciative of their efforts. He also took the time to communicate to his workers the importance of their jobs in the overall operation of the city. In short, this successful supervisor told his people what they needed to know to do their jobs, but he also concentrated his downward communications on those things that his people wanted to know about themselves and the job they were doing. He also helped them remove some of the irritating parts of their jobs, so they could concentrate their efforts on the parts of the job that resulted in real success.

Downward communication is often taken for granted. Some supervisors take the attitude, "pay people enough, and chew them out when they don't produce." Unfortunately, this attitude is all too evident to the employees, and their actions will simply reinforce what the supervisor already thought was true. It is a vicious circle and one that can be broken only by developing an awareness for the "hidden factors" of downward communication.

Upward Communication. Upward communication involves the flow of information from your employees to you as the supervisor. It is information that you need in order to evaluate the results of the assignments given you by your bosses. Without upward communication, or feedback, from your employees, you would not be able to manage.

It is surprising how many supervisors deprive themselves of important information by simply blocking off the channels of communication from their employees to themselves. For example, ask yourself "How do I take bad news?" If you are the kind of supervisor who blows up whenever one of your employees brings you bad news, it won't be long before you are not getting any bad news. You have no doubt seen managers who proudly point to the fact that they never get any bad news from their employees. Be suspicious. Supervisors who give employees with bad messages the idea that the message bearer is responsible for the problem are giving a powerful message themselves. Before long, your employees will be gathering to draw sticks to decide who has to tell you bad news. The next step may be complete blockage of upward communication.

Don't let your expression, your actions, or your words convey messages you don't want to convey. Delay your reaction to things that happen. Good poker players know that the game is lost when the opponents have even the faintest hint of a reaction, and much the same is true in a work situation. Informally reinforce by your actions the positive and productive things that your employees do, and encourage upward communication by removing the roadblocks you may be unconsciously putting up.

Across Communication. Across communication involves the coordination of activities, plans, and communications with other supervisors and other departments in the organization. No department, and no supervisor, is ultimately the most important in an organization. The activities of several departments go together to make the final product.

However, it is quite common for us to assume that our particular department or activity is the most important, even though only a few people share that opinion. This condition is called tunnel vision.

Photo courtesy of Schlumberger Ltd.

ACROSS (PEER) COMMUNICATION

Tunnel Vision. Tunnel vision is something like the view through a long tube, or the view of a situation using a set of blinders. We see only a part of the entire picture. Usually, the part we see and focus on is the part in which we are involved. Earlier, we discussed the importance of communicating to the employee how he or she fits into the overall organization, and how important the job of each employee is. However, this attitude can lead to tunnel vision by each employee. At the supervisory level, it can be a major barrier to effective communication. If each supervisor takes a tunnel-vision view, no meaningful action can be taken. Problems must then be referred to higher management. This is costly, and unproductive.

The essential element in reducing barriers posed by tunnel vision is to remember that upward communication requires compromise. It is not possible for every supervisor, or every department, to get everything that their employees think they should get. Compromise is a delicate balance of the goals and requirements of each of the departments involved. Keep an open mind to the ideas and interests of other supervisors and the employees of other departments. Remember that, ultimately, you are working to achieve the goals of the larger organization, and this can be done only if all elements work together.

Communication in the Informal Organization

The informal organization consists of people who have developed personal relationships. For example, two supervisors from different departments may be in a car pool with a secretary from the vice president's office and a maintenance engineer. On the organization chart, these four persons would have no direct communications. However, the simple fact that they communicate socially, and probably talk about company problems, means that a new communication channel has formed. Thus information can "leap-frog" over the usual or formal communication lines. The same thing happens when the spouses of supervisors and employees from several departments gather together in church or social groups. Their conversations are bound to include the organization. They will be sharing information that can later have an impact on how the organization operates.

The informal organization also refers to the social arrangement of people on the job. In one department, there may be forty persons, in four groups of ten persons, each doing a different job. At coffee break or lunch, or in an after-work bowling or tennis league, the people from the four groups mix together with people from other groups and even other departments. This can lead to communication that does not follow the organization chart. It can lead to a "grapevine," and it can pose problems for you as a supervisor.

Many informal groups develop goals and attitudes which are not understood by the supervisor. When this happens the best strategy for you is to listen to your people and not just to their words, but to their actions as well. Often, employees have ideas and ways of doing things that are better than those of their supervisors. Don't see this as a threat. View it as an opportunity for increased productivity and better communication between you and your people.

The Grapevine.   The grapevine is the path that rumors take. As with most miscommunications, rumors develop and flourish not so much because someone did something but because someone didn't mention something. We all see different messages in a situation, especially where there is some uncertainty or ambiguity involved. Ask any police officer about "eye-witness testimony." Witnesses often can't agree even on the major details, much less the minor points of what happened. The same thing happens in an organization. Some incident happens, or some factual story is told and perhaps overheard. The key facts in the story are picked out by the listener and become the central part of the retelling. As each new listener becomes the teller of the story, new labels are inserted, the facts are covered with details added by what people "think" they heard, and the story changes.

Most rumors in an organization develop because there are missing details that employees want to know. These details are important, and when they are missing, substitutes are added. These additions are usually not done with any malice. Often the rumor transmitter is totally unaware that he or she is adding to a story. Yet the result is a message that can have devastating effects on the morale and productivity of a department or an entire company.

Managing the Grapevine.   There is a pattern that rumors follow. In most organizations, there seem to be a few key people who always have information hours or days before it is officially available. These people often seem to be at the center of rumors and stories that spread through the organization. This is because certain people, by virtue of the position they hold, or even the location of their office, are in the path of information (true or untrue) as it travels. Secretaries, assistants, aides, couriers, telephone operators, machine service technicians—all seem to be "where the action is." These individuals have far more control over the actual operations of the organization than many supervisors realize. What can a supervisor do about the grapevine?

The first step is to accept the fact that the grapevine is a natural part of human communication. Any time more than two people come together to work or play, there is a possibility of a grapevine forming. The attempt at eliminating the rumors in a department has been the downfall of many competent supervisors. Basically, there are two other strategies available: ignore rumors, or make them work for you.

Ignoring rumors is the dangerous alternative. Usually a rumor has at least one element of truth in it, and all rumors can be symptoms of larger problems. Ignoring rumors means that a possibly critical communication element is no longer available to the supervisor. When rumors are appearing more frequently than usual, or when the rumors begin to focus on one particular activity or situation, the wise supervisor should begin to look for the causes of the dissatisfaction and take steps to correct it. Remember, the most powerful communication is the informal, "by example" message. When your employees see you taking action, the impact and importance of the rumors will subside.

Many supervisors find that the second strategy, managing rumors, is more rewarding. Whenever possible, give employees the straight information, the facts as they are presently known. When you don't know all the facts, tell the employees that you don't. When people are honestly involved in the information flow of an organization, the desire and the opportunity for rumors to develop and grow are drastically reduced. Honesty is the best policy. It may sound trite, but it is perhaps the most effective weapon against the rumor. Managing the rumor mill also means remaining open to the information in the rumor. However, do not act solely on the basis of information from rumors. Remember that some (or most) of the material in a rumor message is probably wrong.

Managing the grapevine has its positive sides. For example, the supervisor who would like to try a new approach to the scheduling of work in the department may not want to announce the plan directly. It may be preferable to "leak" the major details of the plan to the employees, let the grapevine sift it out, and then look at how the basic idea was received by the employees. In advertising, the slogan is "Let's run it up the flagpole and see who salutes it." Politicians are masters of "managed leaks." Using the grapevine as a tool of managerial communication is a risky business. It does, however, offer you as a supervisor another dimension to your downward communications.

Feedback

Feedback is the return of the content of a message from the receiver to the sender. In simple terms, it is getting back what you sent someone else. When you give an order to one of your employees, the feedback consists of the actions that the employee performs. If those actions are consistent with the content of your communication, the feedback indicates that nothing else needs to be done. However, if the employee's actions indicate that he or she doesn't really understand you, you may want to rephrase the message, perhaps using an example, or at least using different words.

Feedback usually contains information that is valuable to the supervisor in controlling the actions within the department, and it should be encouraged. This can be done by giving praise to employees when they provide feedback. This is especially important when the feedback involves bad news. Good news is always easy to take, but the way you receive bad news is critical to your success as a manager.

Often your facial expressions, or the tone in your voice, can be a more powerful message than the actual words you use. For example, the supervisor who scowls when an employee reports that the number 3 machine just shut down is likely to find that employees are reluctant to bring more bad news the next time something goes wrong. To counter this, supervisors should develop a greater awareness of their "body communications," and try to avoid giving verbal signals that conflict with the words that they are using. Here are some other ways to encourage feedback.

Do You Have Any Questions?   This is the most common approach to feedback.[2] We've sent a message, and we ask if those who have received the message have any questions. What is the usual response?

No Questions.   Why is there no feedback? There are three very good reasons why asking for questions fails to produce feedback.

(a)   The receiver *feels* ignorant and he or she does not want to admit that a simple message has left questions, especially if no one else listening seems to have any problems with the message. To ask a question would be admitting:

"I'm not very bright"
"I wasn't paying attention"
"I'm too slow to 'get it' all at once"

The net result is no questions.

(b)   The receiver is ignorant. The receiver does not know enough about the original message to know that it was incomplete, incorrect, or subject to interpretation. In this case there are no questions, since what was heard sounds alright.

(c)   The receiver is reluctant to point out the *sender's ignorance.* The receiver has questions, but fears that asking questions would be suggesting:

"You (the sender) are so dumb. How could you leave this out?"
"You didn't do a very good job preparing what you were going to tell me."
"You are *wrong,* and I know you are wrong—and now everyone knows you're wrong."

Regardless of the reason, the outcome is the same: the predictable "no questions."

With the "no questions" response, another danger to effective communication arises. The sender may assume that no questions means that "I (we) understand." No further examples, repetition, or explanations are necessary.

Unfortunately, the result is often missed or misunderstood messages, failed instructions, wasted efforts, unproductive or even dangerous receiver behavior, and all of it arose because the sender failed to properly encourage and use feedback.

How Can We Encourage Feedback?   The active, effective listener is one who is able to draw people out. He or she is able to help others express what they are thinking and feeling, and in the process they become better communicators. Here are some methods:

MAKE THE OTHER PERSON COMFORTABLE

Use appropriate seating, lighting, and arrangements. Chairs should be comfortable, but not so comfortable that they cause the speaker to relax too much. Imagine trying to carry on a meaningful conversation while sitting in a bean-bag chair. It's hard to feel like much of a communicator when your "derriere" is lower than your knees. It's also hard to put much credence in the words of a person sitting in a very sloppy, relaxed position. Do yourself and the other person a favor and choose upright, comfortable seating.

Arrange seats so that your bodies are at an angle, rather than directly across from one another. This eliminates the feeling of confrontation from the encounter.

Don't put either of you in a position where lights are shining into your faces. A Florida executive used all the wrong advice when preparing to listen. He faced his guests into a window with sunlight streaming in, while his own chair was facing away from the window. He sat in a comfortable, cushy swivel chair, while his guest sat in a hard wood, straight-back chair—from which a quarter-inch of one leg had been cut. This made it impossible for the guest's chair to ever sit level on the floor. It was hardly an atmosphere for encouraging feedback.

ASK A DIRECT QUESTION

Because developing feedback is the sender's responsibility, ask the listener a direct question. The answer should indicate whether or not he heard you, and if he understands enough of what was said to offer a direct reply. Of course, the sender's voice tone can directly influence the reply. A barked direct question sprung on an unsuspecting listener may draw a startled or no response. This would indicate that a poor feedback-gathering technique was used rather than that a lack of understanding was present.

Properly phrased direct questions, dealing with the specific information you have been giving, will show immediately where your message is on target and where more examples or elaboration might be useful.

ASK AN INDIRECT QUESTION

An indirect question does not ask the receiver for specific information; instead, it is aimed at probing the receiver's feelings, to learn what the receiver thinks he or she heard, and how he or she feels about what was heard. There are several forms of indirect questions:

1. *Restatement.* This device is simply taking a comment or observation from a receiver, and repeating it—verbatim—as a question. For example:

RECEIVER: "That (whatever the sender has been talking about) might cause problems."

SENDER: "It might cause problems?"

RECEIVER: "I'm worried about how the employees will respond to. . ."

The sender now has some idea of the receiver's concerns. This sort of feedback permits the sender to respond to specific needs that the receiver may have for more or better information.

2. *"How do you feel?"* The use of restatement and "how do you feel about. . .?" questions are favorite indirect-questioning methods of psychiatrists and psychologists. They get the other person to express him- or herself, without the threat or pressure of "Do you have any questions?" or a direct "So, what is the capital of Bolivia?" The asking of "How do you feel about . . .?" questions permits a leisurely response in unthreatening terms. According to one psychiatrist, there is a simple reason for better feedback from this device. "When asked for questions, we feel threatened," she suggests, "but we all have feelings. If we believe the other person is really interested in those feelings, most of us are quite willing to share them openly." The result is better feedback.

3. *"If you were me. . . .?"* Ask the receiver to speculate how he or she would have presented the information you have just shared. We all like to help others. We feel good when we do, and responding to this

Photo courtesy of Pitney Bowes, Inc.

FEEDBACK: THE IMPORTANCE OF COMMUNICATION

question permits the receiver to feel helpful, while expressing his or her concerns about missing, doubtful, or misunderstood information.

4. *The "Ann Landers" technique.* This device comes from the pages of the well-read newspaper advice columns. Many of those people writing to Ann Landers, Dear Abby, and the other newspaper advisors ask for advice for ". . . my friend who has a problem with. . ." Some experts feel that 95 percent of those asking for their "friend" are really seeking help or advice for themselves. Asking for a friend is a convenient projective-type of defense mechanism, and it is especially useful when one is dealing in sensitive, embarrassing, or private matters. If you sense that the receiver is reluctant to answer direct or indirect requests for feedback, perhaps because of the delicate nature of the subject, try an "Ann Landers" approach. Instead of asking

"Bill, have you been stealing?" (direct question)

or

"Bill, how do you feel about employee theft?" (indirect question)

ask

"Bill, how do you think most employees around here feel about stealing?"

Bill can answer without seeming to implicate himself in what he might regard as a delicate question. He may say "Most people probably think it's okay as long as it's just pencils or tape or paper—nothing big like a type-writer." Judge his response for yourself. It is a good bet that you just learned Bill's attitude toward the subject of employee theft.

The Ann Landers question, or third-party question, is often used by researchers who are interested in subjects that their respondents might find embarrassing or difficult to answer. Third-party questions allow you to probe for problems without putting the receiver on the spot.

MAKE A PROVOCATIVE STATEMENT

This is a risky feedback device. If you feel that your listener isn't really listening, to test that theory, and to get some kind of reaction, you make an outrageous statement. This does not necessarily mean making a statement that is offensive to the listener, but just making one that will shake her or him up. Get the listener's attention. Make her or him respond. The risk is that the response may be stronger than expected, and perhaps even stronger than desired.

THE WRONG, STRAW MAN

This is similar to a provocative statement, and it usually results in useful feedback regardless of the other person's response. Teachers often use this device. They say, or write, something wrong, hoping that students will offer a correction. If students correct their teacher, it shows that they know the correct idea. If they fail to pick up on the wrong statement, it shows that they either don't know the correct information or that they have not been paying attention. Either way, the teacher gets useful feedback.

In a conversation, slip in an obviously wrong statement, to see how your listener reacts—or fails to react.

WRITE OUT YOUR COMMENTS

This technique works in situations where listeners may be reluctant to voice unpopular or unpleasant views in a group of peers or superiors. Simply ask listeners to write out comments or observations and pass them along to you for review and action. Of course, many people are reluctant to commit themselves on paper, especially if the subject is controversial. Still, many managers report considerable success using this approach. In the words of one who used the written response "it's better to let an individual feel that you are responsive to her or his needs and concerns. Using written questions allows me to communicate this concern."

LISTENING

Listening is a skill that supervisors often take for granted. We assume that just because we can hear, that we are listening when something is said. Yet, this confusion is responsible for many unfortunate miscommunications. Hearing is a physical process that goes on inside your head. It is the conversion of vibrations into electrical signals, which in turn form messages in the brain. Listening is an active process, which involves understanding, evaluating, and making a part of your consciousness the thoughts and expressions of others.

Many of us develop bad listening habits. We assume that we can guess what an employee is going to say; therefore, there's no need to listen carefully. We adopt a "listening posture," sitting or standing upright, eyes open, appearing to concentrate on the speaker. Having done this, we often "turn off the mind" and assume that if listening fails to occur, it is the fault of the talker. This assumption allows the listener to absolve himself or herself from blame. Ralph Nichols (an expert on listening) identified what he called the ten bad habits of listening.[3] In the exercise section of this chapter, we will use some bad habits of listening in a quiz to see if you can spot the bad listener.

Good listening is an active process, that is, one that requires concentration and conscious effort. Often, employees are reluctant to express their true feelings to their supervisor. Whether out of fear, or merely a desire to please, employees will tell the supervisor what they think the supervisor wants to hear. The job of the supervisor is to get below this level and discover what people are really thinking. To do this, supervisors would be well advised to use some of the methods of psychiatrists and psychologists. For example, don't confront an employee with a direct contradiction. If you disagree with a statement the employee has made, ask for more clarification. Ask open-ended questions such as, "You feel that the project is poorly planned?" and leave a question mark in your voice. This will signal to the employee that more explanation of his or her earlier statements would be useful. To respond directly by saying, "Well, I don't agree with you," may cause the employee to "clam up." As long as there is dialogue going on, you stand a better chance of getting to the bottom of the problem.

Be sure that there is plenty of time for a conversation to continue uninterrupted. Often, communication problems arise when a conversation is rushed or when it is concluded before the employee has said all that he or she feels ought to be said. Supervisors should find a location that is private enough to permit listening without interruption. The location should also have comfortable seats and a quiet atmosphere. The cafeteria or locker room or showroom may be fine for social conversations, but real listening, where the content of the communication is important, should be done in proper surroundings.

BODY COMMUNICATION

An important part of listening (and other parts of supervisory communications as well) is body communication. When listening to employees, give them approving gestures. By moving your body forward, maintaining direct eye contact, and keeping your hand gestures from distracting, you can make a great contribution to the success of the communication. Be sensitive to the signals that you may be giving others without being aware of them. For example, a wink combined with important warnings about safety practices may convey a message that you're not really too concerned about the importance of safety. Even though you say that you agree with something an employee is saying, your body movements (such as your arms rigidly folded across your chest, your head nodding from side to side, or a scowl on your face) may convey a different message. When messages contradict one another, we are usually more likely to accept the nonverbal message rather than the verbal one.

Watch for patterns in the body communications of your employees and your superiors. Be aware of the fact that no one gesture, posture, or facial expression means the same thing to everyone. Rather than trying to attach labels to body language, develop your sensitivity to various nonverbal signals. Examine the signals that you give others; these are more powerful than the words you say. You'll be amazed at the things you are saying.

CHARACTERISTICS OF GOOD COMMUNICATION

Good communication occurs when a sender and receiver have a common understanding of a problem, situation, instruction, or other form of message. To reduce distortion between senders and receivers, there are several practical steps that supervisors can take:

1. Reduce the number of steps that messages must pass through in order to reach their destination. If you want to get a message to Sally, then don't ask Sam to tell Dave to tell Mary to tell Sally. Each step is a source of distortion.

2. Keep messages short and simple. The human mind can absorb only a small amount of information at one time. By concentrating on the essentials, you reduce the chance of miscommunication.

3. Use examples, and repeat your main points. This gives others a chance to clear up misunderstandings even though they might have been reluctant to admit they didn't understand the first time.

4. When speaking, slow down. Talking fast is a habit that contributes to missing signals and miscommunication.

5. Use a variety of media in communicating. If you are giving instructions in writing, you might find it wise to hold a review session where you and your employees can talk about the instructions. You can also use diagrams, charts, examples, and samples to make your message clearer. The permanent nature of some forms of communication (like written instructions, memos, photographs, or diagrams) will help employees understand the material better, and it will also give them something to use for later reference.

ACTION GUIDELINES FOR COMMUNICATION

We have discussed many approaches to better supervisory communications. Remember that not all persons, whether they are employees, supervisors, or top managers, see things in the same way. We each have our own "goggles." To understand an employee, you must first consider the viewpoint of the employee.

1. Recognize the importance of informal communications or communication by being an example. The example you set and the actions you take are far more convincing than the words you write or speak. Show by your actions that you want to receive upward communication and that you in turn are willing to share with your employees all the information you have that concerns them. Openness and trust are integral parts of good communication.

2. Listen to what people are saying. Listen not just for facts, but for the feelings and attitudes of people. Identify the messages that are symptoms of areas where communication may be breaking down.

3. Whenever possible, confront communication problems head on. Hiding behind a desk or a stream of memos, or simply wishing away a problem won't work any longer. A face-to-face discussion with an employee or group having a problem will do much to remove the problem. With formal communication, the two-way exchange of information and feelings can quickly lead to understanding.

4. Become sensitive to missing information. Remember that when information that people think is important is missing, they will invent it. Deal with the grapevine as a fact of life. Use it as a tool for developing more information that can ultimately make you a more sensitive and effective supervisor.

5. Don't rely on only one method of communicating. Develop your communications skills in many areas. Improve your writing, aiming for the chance to express yourself, rather than to impress your employees with your command of the language. When you speak, be listening for both verbal and nonverbal feedback. When you listen, try to go beyond the words being spoken. When you read, ask yourself what the writer would want you to get from the writing. The critical edge for most supervisors is their ability to communicate. Begin developing your sensitivity to the broader implications of communications.

DISCUSSION QUESTIONS FOR COMMUNICATION

1. Describe how we actually communicate and what can happen between sender and receiver.

2. How do we know when we have been successful at communication?

3. Does a supervisor have full control of the communication mix? How?

4. Discuss the techniques for better upward, downward, and across communication in the organization.

5. Can the grapevine really be controlled by the supervisor?

6. Is there a real difference between what people need to know and what people want to know? Why is this difference important to supervisors?

7. How can the supervisor use the grapevine to his or her advantage?

ACTION EXERCISE FOR COMMUNICATION

Self-Quiz: Are you a good listener?

Next to each of the following questions, indicate the alternative that best represents you. When you're finished with the quiz, add up your score and compare your performance to that of an "ideal good listener" and a (hopefully) rare "bad listener."

1. I find myself falling asleep when listening to a speech, even though I'm sitting upright and paying attention.
   (a) _____ never
   (b) _____ seldom
   (c) _____ occasionally
   (d) _____ frequently
   (e) _____ often

2. When someone is talking in a dull voice, or in an unfamiliar accent, I find that I get bored quickly and lose interest in what that person is saying.
   (a) _____ never
   (b) _____ seldom
   (c) _____ occasionally
   (d) _____ frequently
   (e) _____ often

3. I listen only for facts. Facts are the only things that are important.
   (a) _____ never
   (b) _____ seldom
   (c) _____ occasionally
   (d) _____ frequently
   (e) _____ often

4. My mind wanders when I'm listening to someone speaking. I daydream when I should be listening.
   (a) _____ never
   (b) _____ seldom
   (c) _____ occasionally
   (d) _____ frequently
   (e) _____ often

5. I read things that are easy to read and avoid difficult readings. I "turn off" television programs or speakers who are "over my head."
   (a) _____ never
   (b) _____ seldom
   (c) _____ occasionally
   (d) _____ frequently
   (e) _____ often

6. When listening to someone make a presentation, I make an outline (either in my head or by taking notes).
   (a) _____ never
   (b) _____ seldom
   (c) _____ occasionally
   (d) _____ frequently
   (e) _____ often

In scoring this quiz, look closely at the items that you answered "frequently" or "often." Poor listeners often make the mistakes illustrated by these six items. Let's briefly look at each of these bad habits and see what the good listener should do.

Item 1.   The good listener, faced with a listening situation, doesn't simply assume that a "listening posture" is enough to guarantee that he or she will listen. Instead, a good listener works actively to find the meanings behind the speaker's words and finds other subjects in what the speaker is saying to pick out and review.

Item 2.   When listening to a poor speaker, the good listener doesn't simply give up. Instead, the good listener concentrates on the subject and ignores the delivery.

Item 3.   Facts are important, but so are opinions and inferences. Good listeners try to find out what is not being said. It can often be more important than the so-called facts.

Item 4.   Most adults can speak at the rate of about 210 words per minute. However, we can listen at the rate of over 400 words per minute. This difference between listening speed and talking speed leaves plenty of room for daydreaming. The good listener uses the speed difference to go back over the speaker's main points. This "review" can help to improve your ability to remember information from the listening experience.

Item 5.   Avoiding the difficult matters, whether in reading or in listening, leads to an inability to deal with concepts and ideas that are "over our heads." Good listeners challenge themselves by reading material that is difficult or listening to a speaker (or a subject) that is slightly beyond their normal abilities. In this way, they stretch their listening ability and develop positive listening habits.

Item 6.   If you try to outline everything a speaker is saying, you will end up with good mental or written notes if the speaker was speaking from an outline. If not, your notes will be a jumbled mess. Good listeners don't try to develop an outline. Instead, they divide their paper (or their mental notes) into two columns. Label one column "facts" and the other column "opinions and my feelings about the opinions." This way, you will be sure to get all the information without trying to squeeze it into some arbitrary outline.

CASES

CASE 19. Aberdeen Department Stores

Lupe Coronado supervises eighteen people in the camera and stereo equipment section of the Aberdeen Catalog Division. Her employees write, edit, and revise the catalog copy for the company's semi-annual catalog. The employees in the camera section work at desks arranged in three rows of six desks each. Three of the desks are against the windows in the room, and the others are spread throughout the room. Lupe's office is on the corner of the room, with windows on two sides.

Harvey McCormick was recently promoted to supervisor of the lingerie section in the Aberdeen Catalog Division. His desk was the one closest to Lupe's office on the window row. Lupe just hired Gloria Adams to replace Harvey, and she's decided to put Gloria in Harvey's desk next to the office. That way, Lupe can personally supervise Gloria's introduction to the catalog process (Gloria was promoted from a sales position in the Des Moines store). In making this decision, Lupe was determined to avoid the problems that developed when Helen Pierre left the department to become a buyer. When that happened, there was a general shuffling of desks, with the senior people trying to get what they felt were the better locations. While Lupe has no particular objections to "musical desks," she feels that the hurt feelings that usually result are really counterproductive. By deciding who sits where, she's sure these problems will be avoided.

Since Lupe's decision was announced last Wednesday, the section has been in what is best described as a "gloom." Something's wrong. But what? "Come to think about it," Lupe said, out loud, but to herself, "Helen's desk was taken over by Harvey, and now Gloria's moving into it. I wonder if that means anything?"

1. Is Lupe on the right track? Has she found the key to the problem?
2. What is the problem with the employees? What are their perceptions of how things are done in the Aberdeen Company?
3. What can Lupe do now to overcome this "gloom" and get the section back up to production?

CASE 20. The Bus Barn

Bob Washington was upset and was looking for Len Graham. Len is the supervisor of the maintenance yard of the Tri-County Bus Lines, and Bob is the senior mechanic on the day shift. Both men have been with the company for about twenty years, and they are social as well as on-the-job friends. However, that friendship was not much in evidence as Bob stormed into Len's office.

"Len, what's this nonsense about having to take next Friday off, and with no pay? It doesn't sound fair at all, especially with all the time I've put in on the job for this outfit. I think some consideration should be given to us hourly guys. You supervisors get your pay, no matter how many days you work, but in the trenches we only get paid when we work, and it looks like Friday we don't!"

Len was surprised at Bob's information. He'd heard nothing about any Friday layoff, although the top management did discuss the possibility of cutting back some of the hours in the maintenance area because of the general economic slowdown. But, to the best of Len's knowledge, nothing was ever decided, and surely Bob knew that Len would square with him if a decision was reached.

Len called Jerry Browne, the operations manager, and asked him about Washington's allegation. Browne assured Len that this was not the case, and that Washington must have heard an unfounded rumor.

Just as Len was planning to leave for the day, he got a call from Jerry Browne. Browne just received a note from the top management instructing him to post a notice that all hourly workers were to be given Fridays off without pay for an indefinite period. This move was necessary because of declining profits and increased competition from another bus line. The notice went on to state that supervisory and office personnel and the drivers were not affected by this move "at this time."

Jerry Browne apologized to Len for apparently misleading him this morning. "This is the first I knew about it," Jerry protested.

Len slammed down the phone and quickly dialed his friend Bob. As the phone rang, Len began to think, "Just what can I say, after my assurances this afternoon?"

1. Is this problem a common one for supervisors?
2. How would you evaluate the communication system in the company?
3. What can Len say to Bob?

CASE 21. Elmgrove Medical Center

"We're tired of being treated like children."

"They make us feel that our jobs and our feelings are meaningless."

"We demand to have a say in the decision making of this organization, and to be told what's going on."

Because of the relatively tranquil and harmonious reputation of

Elmgrove Medical Center, employee statements and attitudes like these were somewhat of a shock to Dan Thompson. As president and chief executive officer of Elmgrove, he was facing a volatile and potentially dangerous crisis. The bulk of his staff, including professional and support personnel, were in an uproar, demanding control over what had traditionally been managerial prerogatives. Communication at Elmgrove had always been open, with a "family" atmosphere prevailing throughout the organization. Patients frequently commented on the way the doctors, professional staff people, support personnel, and administrators worked together. For patients, the benefits of such an atmosphere were obvious, since the lack of interpersonal tension left each member of the Elmgrove "team" free to deal with the important medical problems they faced. It was only in the last year or so that things at the Elmgrove Medical Center began to change, and Thompson was becoming increasingly concerned that the change in attitude was related to his own arrival at Elmgrove.

Elmgrove was founded in Fillmore City over forty years ago by a dynamic young doctor, Ellis Mayer. It began as a small, rural clinic, treating patients from all over the farming regions in the lower part of the state. Dr. Mayer worked long hours, never took a vacation, and often accepted corn, preserves, or home-sewn clothing in payment for his services. Following World War II, the area around Fillmore City became a magnet for industrial plant location, the rural character of the region changed, and the population grew. By using his established reputation in medicine and his persuasive abilities, Dr. Mayer was able to build the original building of the medical complex which consisted of a 300-bed hospital, an outpatient clinic, and various support facilities.

As Elmgrove Hospital grew, Dr. Mayer kept his close personal relationship with each and every employee intact. It was not unusual to see him in an animated conversation with anyone on the hospital staff, at any hour of the day or night. He knew most of the staff (and patients) on a first-name basis and had delivered most of them into the world during his long years in medicine. Although his personal relationships with the staff were excellent and helped the staff to enjoy positive interpersonal relationships as well, there was never any doubt about who was in charge at Elmgrove. Dr. Mayer made virtually all the decisions. He promoted staff from within and searched outside for administrative talent only when local people could not be found.

Elmgrove used to be a private hospital, owned totally by Dr. Ellis Mayer. It is now a privately-held, non-profit corporation. Dan Thompson has inherited 65 percent of the corporation's stock, and he has absolute financial control, as did his father.

Dan Thompson's association with Elmgrove also goes back

many years. After he was orphaned at an early age, he was taken in by Ellis Mayer and raised as a son. From the time he was old enough, Dan worked in the hospital. During summer vacations, and after school, he was at the hospital, doing every job available, from the menial jobs to major ones, such as helping to prepare the budget. At one time, he had hoped to become a doctor, but he found that his skills were better suited to administration. At eighteen, he left Fillmore City to study public administration. It was during Dan's final year of work on his Master's Degree that Dr. Ellis Mayer died. Dan then returned to Elmgrove to take charge of the hospital.

In Dan Thompson's absence, change had continued. Shortly before his death, Dr. Mayer had begun plans to convert Elmgrove into a complete medical center. These plans were continued under Thompson's leadership, and the change occurred about nine months ago. In addition to the obvious changes involved in such a conversion, many other subtle but important changes were also taking place. For example, on his first day back at Elmgrove as the new President, Dan Thompson called all the senior supervisors and medical staff people into his office. For two hours, they met behind closed doors. When they returned to their work stations and offices, their people asked what happened in the meeting. The reply was "Nothing happened."

From then on, the Monday morning meetings continued. After each meeting, the personnel asked their supervisors what was happening, and the answer was always "Nothing."

It was during this period that the employees became restless and openly critical of the new administrative routine. They felt that they were not being told the full story behind the changes that were taking place all around them. They saw people being laid off, other new people being hired, and new research and patient care activities being started. These same kinds of changes had been happening for many years under Dr. Mayer, but now these normal changes left employees feeling fearful, confused, and "lost." Their confusion over the changes was coupled with their fears that in the Monday meeting their entire future was being decided, and they were being told nothing about it.

Jeanne Reaume was one of the senior staff supervisors at Elmgrove. She had joined Ellis Mayer in the early years of the hospital and had become one of his trusted lieutenants and close friends. On many occasions, Dr. Ellis encouraged her to assume more managerial responsibility, but she, like most of her colleagues, preferred to leave the running of the entire hospital to Dr. Ellis and deal only with her individual area of responsibility. Jeanne Reaume had great respect for the abilities of Thompson and was an early supporter of his election as the president and administrator. She was also well aware that the feelings of the employees in the hospital were changing, and she too was puzzled.

At a cocktail party, Jeanne Reaume was discussing the situation at Elmgrove with close friends: ". . . after all, Dan Thompson is like my own son. He worked in this hospital as far back as any of us senior people can remember. All the employees like him a lot, and he in turn has a genuine love for Elmgrove and for the staff that Dr. Ellis put together over all those years. Everyone in the hospital, from top to bottom, was delighted when Dan returned to pick up where Dr. Ellis left off. Dan's also very realistic. Why, his first day on the job he called all of the senior people into Dr. Ellis'—I mean his—office for a meeting. Naturally, we were somewhat nervous, but he quickly put us all at ease. He said simply. 'You people are my family. Daddy trusted and relied on you to help him make decisions. I want that to continue, and I want everyone here at Elmgrove to take a larger and more active role in decision making. No one can replace Dr. Ellis, and I certainly recognize my limitations. I want to learn from each of you, and I want you to assume more individual responsibility under my guidance and direction.' After that, the meeting became a sort of family reunion, and we talked about where Dan might build a new house in Fillmore City now that he was married. In the meetings we had each week, we never talked business. One time, we even got into a discussion about where the best bass fishing was, and we discussed golf, politics, and that new book on natural foods. Frankly, I don't understand the change in attitude on the part of the employees. If anything, they will be in an even better position, with more individual responsibility, now that Dan is in charge."

1. What happened at the Elmgrove Medical Center?
2. What should Dan Thompson have done when he first came to the medical center?
3. What would you suggest can now be done to resolve the situation before it degenerates beyond salvage?

PERSONNEL MANAGEMENT

Staffing

Objectives

After reading and studying this chapter, you will have a better understanding of the importance of staffing. You will be able to

1. Discuss some of the activities of your firm's personnel department.

2. Develop job descriptions and job specifications.

3. Discuss ways of recruiting new employees.

4. Discuss the techniques used in screening and evaluation of prospective employees.

THE SUCCESS OF any supervisor is largely determined by the people working in his or her department. Employees can make a supervisor look good, even ones who apply a minimum of effort. They can also make even the best supervisor look bad. Obviously, the staffing of a supervisor's department or work team is important, and supervisors should develop and maintain an active role in all phases of the staffing function.

Most organizations have a personnel department to assist you as a supervisor. It provides valuable services to supervisors. These services assist you in assembling and training a first-class work team, and they can relieve you of many of the burdens that fall to you as a normal part of doing a supervisor's job. Because many supervisors report that they experience varying degrees of difficulty in their relationship with company personnel staffs, let us briefly examine some of these difficulties and how they may be avoided or minimized.

LINE AND STAFF

In most organizations, supervisors are "line" managers who are responsible for achieving an organization's main goals. Usually, personnel is a staff activity that assists and advises line managers on policy and procedures, while taking some routine problems away from line people. Personnel departments often have in-house experts available to solve particularly "sticky" problems that may be beyond the range of experience of the usual supervisor. It is important to establish and maintain the authority relationship between the personnel staff and the line supervisors in any organization. Usually, this relationship is detailed in the operating policies and manuals of your organization. In practice, however, the actual relationship between line authority and staff authority may not follow the policies of top management. This happens for a number of reasons. During a certain period, there may have been real supervision in some operating departments. If, during the period, there was strong leadership in the personnel department, it is natural that the power and responsibility would go to the staff, that is, away from the line supervisors. The precise relationship between a supervisor and a firm's personnel staff is very imprecise. It is a constantly changing relationship, dependent on the skills, personalities, and goals of the individuals involved to keep it effective.

In some activities, there really cannot be any clear, single line of authority over an employee. For example, dual authority exists in training programs. Line supervisors obviously supervise the employees in participating in a training program but, if the actual training program is conducted by the staff of the personnel department, the personnel managers have nominal authority over the same people while they are in the program.

Whenever possible, it is desirable to have a clear understanding between supervisors and personnel managers on their respective authority over matters such as employee selection, training, promotion, evaluation, and dismissal. If management and supervision were an art, then surely the relationship developed between the supervisor and the staff departments would be the highest form of the art. Line–staff conflict is usually not solved by referring to the "book" or some arbitrary distinctions in company policies. A working relationship that evolves from a settlement of line–staff conflict is based primarily on individuals working together.

WHAT CAN A PERSONNEL DEPARTMENT DO FOR YOU?

In companies with a personnel department, supervisors are relieved of much of the paperwork associated with developing and maintaining employee records. These records are vital in helping the supervisor to carry out other important tasks, such as performance appraisal and recommendations for promotion or dismissal. The personnel department usually handles the major contacts with the employee representative, including the negotiations and management of a union contract. Labor relations have become very complex. It is the job of a personnel department to be able to keep up to date on the latest regulations and requirements.

Other services of a personnel department are work-force planning and developing and implementing the recruitment and training of new employees to meet the organization's objectives. A personnel department must determine the existing quantity and quality of the organization's employees, and prepare a work-force inventory which is a record of the skills, training, job descriptions, work records, education, age, previous experience, and personal objectives of all the employees. The inventory usually also includes a department-by-department breakdown on the details of the staffing. With this information, the supervisor has a reasonably accurate written record of the human resources within the department. This record, coupled with the supervisor's personal experience and observations of the work quality and work relationships within the department, is a valuable tool for planning personnel expansion (or reduction).

A personnel department helps supervisors answer questions on the type and number of employees in the departments who will need to reach the goals that they have set for themselves. Beginning with a work-force inventory and the overall long-range objectives of the organization, the personnel department can advise on the potential for promoting capable employees within the department to more responsible jobs, including transfers to other departments when appropriate. Because you and your fellow supervisors have your sights set primarily on the primary goals and objectives of your department, it is often difficult to develop and maintain a larger view, thus giving you and your employees an opportunity to move to more responsible positions within the organization.

THE "OTHER SIDE" OF PERSONNEL

There are several potential problems in the relationship between line supervisors and a personnel department staff. A staff can provide you with valuable help, advice, and service, but it can too easily become a "crutch." Supervisors who rely too heavily on the personnel department staff run the risk of losing their authority within their own departments. For example, many supervisors find it difficult to counsel with their employees about personal problems, even when such problems have a direct bearing on the employees' performances on the job. It is often easier and more convenient to have the employees counsel with personnel department staff people. This can lead to the employees identifying more directly with the staff people, thus viewing their supervisor as merely one who parcels out the work.

Many supervisory tasks are unpleasant. Because turning down pay raises, promotions, and employee requests are necessary, supervisors often find it convenient to shunt these responsibilities off on the personnel department. However, doing so may result in their authority being seriously eroded. Saying "I'd like to approve your proposal, but Personnel just won't let me" is convenient and gets the problem off your back. Saying it too often, or using the personnel department as a blind to hide behind can quickly lead employees to assume that you are merely a figurehead, with no real authority. Later, when you try to exercise your supervisory authority, that authority may no longer be recognized and respected.

The people in the personnel department are human. They have the same desires to perform and to advance within the organization. And, like you, they know that their chances for advancement and recognition will be improved if they can show performance and results. Thus, it is quite natural for the personnel department staff to be constantly looking for areas where they can exert their influence and increase their power and authority. Supervisors who leave work undone, who fail to perform adequately all the functions and responsibilities given them, or who find it more convenient to have "them do the unpleasant tasks," usually find that their prerogatives have been taken over.

The information developed by a personnel department can lead supervisors to make decisions that they might not otherwise make. However, this does not mean that personnel departments are trying to "take over." They perform valuable services for line supervisors. However, as the line supervisor, it is your responsibility to establish and maintain the proper relationship with your personnel department and its people, as well as with your own employees.

When forecasts and plans indicate that new employees are needed in a department, you begin the staffing part of your responsibilities. While working with your personnel department, you begin defining new jobs, recruiting potential employees, screening applicants (looking for the best qualified), and ultimately deciding which persons to hire.

Developing Job Descriptions and Specifications

Once the needs of the department have been established, the job descriptions and job specifications for new employees must be developed. Many supervisors think that it is possible to hire the best people in the job market and then train them to do whatever jobs need to be done. This may work for a football coach, who looks for the "best athlete" and then tailors the job to fit the individual's skills and interests. However in most management situations, the correct procedure is to define the job, and then look for people who best fit the job.

Job descriptions are written statements of duties, responsibilities, and working conditions for a job. *Job specifications* detail the knowledge, skills, personal attributes, and educational requirements that persons filling the job must have. Job descriptions and job specifications are developed after an analysis of each job is performed. This analysis is ideally done by consulting with not only the personnel department but also with the other employees in the supervisor's department. It requires that the conditions and surroundings of the job to be performed be identified. One supervisor in a medical organization has each of her employees write out their *current* job description every year. This process keeps all job descriptions in the department accurate and up to date.

An Example of a Job Description

Job title: Supervisor (Nonexempt)

Department: Production

Date: May 5, 1978

Statement of Job:

The supervisor coordinates and supervises activities in the department using job knowledge of production methods, processes, machines, and equipment. He or she reviews production schedules and determines department employee-hour and machine-hour requirements; establishes an efficient work flow based on production standards, operation sequence, completion dates, and machine-load factors; prepares reports to management outlining equipment performance, production efficiency, quality of work, and product scrappage. He or she must be familiar with long-term scheduling procedures, and may initiate personnel actions including transfer requests, employee warning conferences, discharges, and promotions. He or she may confer with employees to settle minor grievances and must report all unsettled grievances to the production manager and the personnel manager. The supervisor is responsible for ensuring accurate production counts and must resolve all count discrepancies, and she or he is responsible for explaining all company rules and regulations to the employees in the section. The production supervisor works under the direct supervision of the production manager and supervises ten to fifteen employees including production workers, leaders, and set-up persons.

Job Duties:

1. Is directly responsible for the morale and conduct of all employees in the assigned section; conducts employee warning conferences to document violations regarding substandard production output, poor product quality, misconduct, and high absenteeism or tardiness.
2. Prepares the daily efficiency reports and is responsible for maintaining a high level of production efficiency for all employees in the assigned section. Confers with the department manager as necessary to discuss individual employee performance and to determine actions necessary to increase their production output.
3. Instructs leaders, set-up persons, and production workers in the day-to-day performance of their duties. Is responsible for ensuring

Continued

that proper production methods, layouts, dies, and materials are used for each production operation. Instructs employees in the proper quality-check procedures in order to control the rate of scrap and to ensure the production of a high quality product.

4. Works in conjunction with other departments such as Personnel, Timekeeping, Scheduling, and Engineering as related to the assigned area of responsibility. Helps plan physical lay-out and set-ups for various production runs.

5. Makes routine machine inspections and issues maintenance work orders as required. Ensures that machine operators perform the necessary preventive maintenance and cleaning of machines to keep the machines at maximum efficiency.

6. Ensures that all company safety rules and regulations are obeyed and that all machinery in the section has the required safety guards installed.

7. Prepares weekly scrap report and reviews the scrappage factor with the department manager. Takes the necessary steps to correct any production operation that is causing an unacceptable level of scrappage.

Recruiting New Employees

Once job descriptions and specifications have been established, the next step is to find and recruit qualified candidates for the jobs. Usually, this is the job of a personnel department, with the supervisor acting as an advisor on specific matters. The actual placement of recruiting advertisements and announcements, processing employment applications, and checking of references is done by the personnel department. The wages to be paid to the people in the new jobs are established by using comparative wage and salary analysis. These are surveys showing the prevailing wages being paid for comparable jobs in the local area. They are used as guides for wage/salary decisions. Usually supervisors are not included in the determination of wages and salaries.

Screening New Employees

Once potential new employees have been identified, the personnel department conducts an initial screening. They drop from further consideration those individuals who do not fit the requirements of the job specifications. It is after the first screening that supervisors are usually involved in staffing. Interviews are set up with the remaining candidates for the new jobs. These interviews may be conducted in the personnel department offices or in the various supervisors' offices, and they may involve several persons in addition to the supervisor.

When planning for an interview with a potential employee, it is a good idea to have some format in mind for the interview. Many supervisors write out (or have their personnel department prepare) a list of questions that can be asked in logical sequence. This will help to get answers that can be easily recorded and reviewed. It is also useful to review before the interview the job description and specifications for the job for which the person is applying. There are few situations more embarrassing than having a potential employee ask a question about the job, the company, or its policies and practices, and having the supervisor stumped for an answer.

The setting for the interview is also important. Many people are moving away from holding interviews in cold impersonal offices, which can leave a negative feeling in the mind of the interviewee. You, too,

Photo courtesy of Jefferson Pilot Company.

TV STATIONS SPEND A LOT OF MONEY AND EFFORT FINDING THE "RIGHT" NEWSCASTERS. DO WE MAKE THE SAME EFFORTS REGARDING OUR ORGANIZATION'S STAFFING?

can be uneasy because you are away from your department, in unfamiliar surroundings. This can contribute to an unsatisfactory interview. A better place for an employment interview is a quiet private office, conference room, or area close to your department. This way, the applicant can get a "feel" for the department, and you can concentrate on evaluating the interviewee.

Remember that the interview is a two-way communication. It is designed to give you information that is useful in making your decision about which applicants to hire for a job. It is usually not possible in the first interview to learn everything necessary for making an intelligent decision, and subsequent interviews may be needed. Later interviews are usually given only for the top three or four candidates, and they involve more depth than the first interview. In this stage, it might be useful to have the remaining candidates informally interviewed by some of the senior employees in the department. Their advice can be a valuable help in making your decision.

In an interview, be honest with candidates. Don't give the impression that the job is theirs if that is not the case. Remember that the candidates may be considering other offers, and your premature encouragement may discourage them from other possibilities. Think about the applicant's point-of-view. At one time, each of us was in the same situation, which is difficult at best. Put the candidates at ease, and keep an open, informal communication going. Don't dominate the conversation with a steady stream of questions. Rather, offer opportunities for discussion and speculation. This will result in a more satisfying and profitable interview.

Example: Interview Schedule

Key information from the application blank	Questions I want to ask	Responses by applicant
Previous work experience:		
1. Ace Electronics, 1/74 to present	1. What were your specific duties and responsibilities?	
	2. What part of the job did you find most difficult?	

Continued

Key information from the application blank	Questions I want to ask	Responses by applicant
	3. What's the best feature of your present job?	
	4. Why would you consider leaving?	
	5. How much of your education and training have you been able to use on your present job?	
	6. Did you have an opportunity to gain further training with your present employer?	
	7. If yes, did you take advantage of the opportunity?	
Education		
Outside interests		
Plans for the future		
References, etc.		

SUPERVISOR'S INTERVIEW GUIDE

1. Review in detail the application blank before you meet the applicant. Make notes on any areas where you have questions that you wish to ask the applicant.

2. Make a list of the candidate's strongest and weakest points. Verify these points through questions during the interview.

3. When the applicant arrives, develop an open and friendly atmosphere. Never open the discussion with a major question. Ask the applicant a question which will help him or her relax—a question which is easy to answer and indicates a personal interest in the potential employee. Example "I see from your application you like to play tennis. How long have you been playing?"

4. Three to five minutes of small talk will generally relax the applicant, and then you should systematically begin to seek the answer to the questions you had previously developed.

5. When the applicant responds to a question with an unexpected or unusual answer, follow up the point with another question. If you don't understand the answer you received, ask for clarification. ("Did I understand you to say . . . ?" or "Did you mean to say . . . ?") Don't be embarrassed to ask for more information or to tell the applicant that you don't understand.

6. Be sure before you end the interview that you have gotten all the information possible about the applicant for every major category. Some supervisors use a check sheet to help them in collecting information. It takes longer to prepare for an interview, but most supervisors agree that the resulting thoroughness is worth the time.

7. When you are sure that you have all the information about the applicant you need, attempt to answer any questions that the applicant may have about the job. Keep in mind that the applicant is interviewing you just as much as you are interviewing him or her. Volunteer as much information as possible about the job, the company, the benefits, and working conditions. Your ability to anticipate questions that the applicant may wish to ask will often help an applicant identify other questions. Don't rush the applicant.

8. If time permits, give the applicant a walking tour of the work area and have him or her meet some of the present employees and see the actual location of the job.

9. If the applicant will be required to operate specific equipment it is often valuable to ask the applicant if he or she would like to try the equipment. (Check first with the Personnel Department to see if the applicant would be covered by the company's insurance in case of an accident.)

10. As a final part of the interview, thank the applicant for coming for the interview, and indicate when you expect to make a decision. Don't lie; if it will be two weeks before you plan to make a decision, say so. Even if you have decided that the applicant does not fit your needs and you tell him or her that employment is not possible at this time, thank the person for the interview. A little courtesy goes a long way. At least the applicant leaves with a good feeling about the company.

Evaluating Prospective Employees

When evaluating the prospective candidates before making your selection, be careful to avoid several problems that might arise. Watch for *stereotyping*. Often, we put people into categories on the basis of some rather flimsy and incomplete information. For example, when a prospective job candidate is shy and intimidated by the interview, the interviewer may incorrectly evaluate him or her as a shy individual based on the interview behavior alone. A potentially good employee may be lost by this assumption.

Another problem is to make *individual comparisons* between the people now working for you and the new applicant. Remember that there are many advantages to hiring a person from outside the organization or at least from outside your department. Often, people in a department or company have their minds made up about how things ought to work. They may have developed some negative feelings about the company or its policies. These feelings, although they are quite natural, will nonetheless contribute to lower productivity, and they will often lead to an unwillingness to learn the requirements of a new job. Persons from outside do not have these preconceived notions, and therefore they are more likely to be open to new ideas, new work methods, and new organizational arrangements.

Watch also for the "*halo effect.*" It has positive and negative overtones, both of which are damaging to your evaluations of prospective employees. When an individual in an interview expresses a viewpoint similar to that of the interviewer, or perhaps when she or he dresses or behaves in a manner that appeals to the interviewer, the natural tendency is for the interviewer to put all statements and reactions of the interviewee into a more favorable light. Similarly, if the person being interviewed expresses an idea that is directly contrary to the ideas of the interviewer (often on such nonwork subjects as politics or sports), a "negative halo" is formed. Regardless of the other statements made by the interviewee, the interviewer's mind is already made up. The evaluation has already been made.

Deciding Whether to Hire or Not to Hire

The interview of potential employees is only a prelude to the important decision whether to hire or not to hire. This decision must come only after all factors have been considered: Which individual interviewed has the skills and the temperament best suited to the job? Will the person selected be able to "fit in" with the other employees? The decision is obviously a personal choice. No one can make it but the supervisor or manager.

The staffing process does not end when the right woman or man has been selected and hired. There are few jobs in business or government today where an individual can come into the organization and operate at a normal level of efficiency. If a new employee with specific skills is hired, the "break-in" period will probably be short. For the employee coming into the organization without the necessary skills to do the job properly, a longer period of training will be required.

ORIENTATION

For all employees coming into an organization, a period is usually reserved in the early days of employment for an orientation. This orientation (which can last anywhere from an hour or two to several days) is designed to acquaint the new employee with the organization and its policies. The new employee must be processed through the various government forms and insurance and benefit applications, and he or she must be given the necessary passes, permits, and identification for working in the organization. Orientation also includes introducing the new employee to his or her coworkers. Often this first introduction determines the way the new employee will be integrated into the work group. It is the supervisor's responsibility to introduce the new employee properly and to provide some positive connection between the new employee and the work the group is now doing. For example, by saying that the new employee comes "highly recommended," or the new employee has "experience in working similar situations" during introductions will help ease the natural curiosity of the work-group members.

The introduction of the new employee to his or her new coworkers must be carefully balanced so as not to set up a barrier between the new employee and other employees. When the new employee is introduced as "the best qualified applicant we've ever had," or "the daughter of the 'big boss' over in shipping," resentment is inevitable. Obviously, the new employee was hired because he or she has certain skills or abilities needed by the department. However, if you make too much of these skills or abilities, the unstated message will be that the present work group is not performing adequately.

Orientation in some organizations can be merely formal. New employees can be given a program of speeches by top organization officials; a film or slide presentation on the organization, its products, or activities; and talks by leaders from the personnel office, the security department, the payroll department, and others. The topics in these formal sessions usually range from broad, general "welcomes" to specific information about payroll deductions, health insurance, parking regulations, sick leave and other company policies, union regulations, and legal questions. The role of the supervisor in these sessions is usually limited to no more than perhaps a brief introduction. The supervisors of new employees are usually responsible for answering questions from the new employees who are coming into the department and for providing any necessary follow-up to the formal program.

For this reason, it is wise for you to attend orientation sessions for your new employees. Company policies and requirements change, and these changes are often overlooked by supervisors who are busy with their everyday concerns. It is embarrassing for both a new employee and her or his supervisor when a simple question cannot be answered by a supervisor, or when, in fact, a supervisor is corrected by a new employee with new and up-to-date information.

If your organization has no formal orientation program for new employees, the full burden of orientation falls directly on you. Most supervisors view this task as a "necessary evil." Yet, this is perhaps the best single opportunity that supervisors have for developing a productive employee. You will be required to review with each new employee the various company policies, regulations, and requirements, and many supervisors stop right there. However, a brief discussion with the new employee about the work being done and the supervisor's personal policies and supervision philosophies, and a brief tour of the work area (or even the entire organization, if time permits) can be very helpful in developing a rapport between employee and supervisor. The relationship established during orientation can be very helpful in overcoming problems usually encountered during the employee's first few weeks on the job, where much of the initial turnover problem starts.

A SUPERVISOR'S ORIENTATION GUIDE

THE ORGANIZATION

1. What does this organization do?
2. How does our work group fit into the overall organization?
3. How important are we to the organization's success?
4. What is the chain of command?
5. What does the future look like for the organization?
6. Are there any key projects the group is or will be working on?
7. What has been the history of this organization, and what are some of its major accomplishments?

THE PERSON'S JOB

1. What exactly will I be doing?
2. What tool or equipment will I be working with?
3. What employees will I be working with regularly? What can you tell

the new employee about his or her fellow workers which will help the new employee adjust to the new job and his or her new teammates?

4. What are the work hours on the job? When are the scheduled breaks?

5. Will the employee go through a training program?

6. How long is the new employee's probationary period?

7. When and how is the employee's work evaluated? Who will do the evaluation? Will the employee be notified of the outcome of the evaluation? If the evaluation is bad, can it be appealed? If so, to whom?

THE WORKING CONDITIONS

1. How safe is this job? How is the worker protected against injury? What are the safety regulations of the job?

2. Does the job require that the employee join the union? If so, whom should the employee contact, and how long does he or she have before being required to join?

3. What is the routine of the job? When are the breaks for meals and other rest periods? How long are they? Can employees leave the facilities? Is there a place to purchase food and drink on the company premises? Are the prices reasonable? What do most of the employees in the group do for meals?

4. Is smoking permitted at the job site? Are there areas where smoking is permitted?

THE EMPLOYEE'S PAY

1. When is payday? Will the employee be paid during the first pay period of employment, or does it take one pay period for the payroll records to reflect the new employee?

2. If the new employee is hourly, must he or she use a time clock? If so, which one should be used, and where is it located? Are there any specific regulations about the time clock and its use?

3. Does the employee have the right to refuse overtime? How much does the organization pay for overtime work? Do salaried employees receive overtime payments also? If so, at what rate?

4. When traveling for the company, will the employee's expenses be paid? Will all expenses be paid, or only those up to a certain amount? What are the procedures for collecting for travel? Can the employee receive an advance for travel, and if so, how is it applied for?

5. When do reviews for salary increases take place? What is the procedure? What has been the average raise for the past few years? Are the pay raises automatic or are they based strictly on merit? If it tends to be a combination, how is it determined?

FRINGE BENEFITS

What are the fringe benefits of the job?
Fringe benefit check list:

- Company paid life insurance? If yes, what kind?
- Company paid disability insurance? If yes, what kind?
- Company paid accident insurance? If yes, what kind?

- Company paid medical and hospital insurance? If yes, what kind?
- Company paid dental insurance? If yes, what kind?
- Company paid pension or retirement plan? If yes, what kind?
- Company paid sick days? How many?
- Company paid vacation days? How many?
- Company paid military leave (National Guard or Reserves)?
- Company paid education benefits?
- Credit Union?
- Time off for religious observances?
- Personal days allowed for illness and death in the family?
- Jury duty?
- Child-care (maternity) leave?
- Physical exam: Is one required? If so, does the company pay?
- Profit-sharing plan?
- Leaves of absence?
- Educational loans for children of employees?
- Others

ACTION GUIDELINES FOR STAFFING

1. Establish a well-defined working relationship between yourself and the personnel department. Reach an agreement with personnel about when you are to be involved in the hiring process. When an opening exists, meet with personnel and use a job description to give their staff as much information as possible about the skills and experience you want to see in the applicant. Personnel can use this information to screen all applicants and can then schedule interviews for you with the best-qualified persons. The important point is that the supervisor make the employment decision. Similar relationships must be established with personnel to cover activities such as training, promotions, transfers, performance evaluation, discipline, and termination.

   Maintain a cordial working relationship with all staff departments, but retain your rights over decisions which affect your group.

2. Use the personnel staff in the way they were meant to be used—to help you make better decisions and implement better programs. Staff is supposed to help management manage. Give the staff professional the opportunity to do so. Seek out the staff's advice. Remember, they are working for you.

3. Beware of the staff "crutch." It's often easy for supervisors simply to let the staff people do the difficult or unpleasant jobs. Doing so can cause problems later, because the outcome of those jobs is the direct responsibility of the supervisor. Also, dumping the work on staff can lead to increased staff power, and when that happens no one is to blame but the supervisor.

4. Work with the personnel department in developing accurate job descriptions. Job descriptions form the basis for many other functions that will be performed by supervision. Some of these include the deter-

mination of wages and the requirements for training. Review the job descriptions every two years, or following any major organizational or work-process change. Inaccurate job descriptions may be causing employees to be inequitably paid and may well be the cause of much employee unrest.

5. Supervisors should stay informed about the current labor situation in the local area. Ask the personnel department to send you copies of local wage and salary surveys. Even if you are not currently hiring new employees, it is wise to keep up with the local scene. Supply and demand factors may influence where your present employees will be looking for work with other organizations.

6. Develop your own orientation program for new employees and coordinate it with personnel. This can help to reduce overlaps. Get a commitment from personnel as to *exactly* what items they will cover in their portion of the orientation program. Even if it is a simple, ten-minute chat on the new employee's first day on the job, an orientation can be the start of a profitable and satisfactory work relationship. In the development of an orientation program for new employees, make a list of questions you would like answered if you were new on a job. Next, list where that information can be obtained. Circulate your list to a couple of other supervisors or employees and ask them to add items you may have omitted.

DISCUSSION QUESTIONS FOR STAFFING

1. How can the personnel department help supervisors do their jobs better?

2. Does the personnel department ever step beyond its bounds and interfere with the line activities of supervisors? If so, give examples.

3. How can supervisors overcome some of these encroachments on their authority?

4. What is the proper role of supervisors in recruiting new employees?

5. What is the "halo effect"? How can it hurt the supervisor's efforts in staffing?

6. What should be included in a supervisor's orientation of new employees?

7. What is the supervisor's role in training, and what methods are best to accomplish the objectives of such training?

ACTION EXERCISES FOR STAFFING

1. Pair off and practice interviewing for a job. Decide on the specific type of job applicant desired.

(a) *Interviewer:* Make a list of the questions that you feel need answering in order to obtain the information needed to make an employment decision.

(b) *Applicant:* Develop a method of presenting to the interviewer your strongest features. Develop confidence in your presentation.

(c) *Both parties:* Honestly review the interview simulation. Score each other on areas where you feel improvement could be made.

2. Develop an orientation program for a new student at your school or new employee in your organization.
   (a) What information should be given the incoming individual in written form? Which information will be verbal? Which information is delivered both ways? Why?
   (b) When should information be given?
   (c) How large should the group be?
   (d) Who should participate in the program?

3. Develop a list of the qualities that you would personally prefer to be rated on. Does this list contain primarily personal characteristics, job-performance characteristics, knowledge and skill characteristics, or general characteristics?

4. In some previous job, you have no doubt been given an orientation program. Review that orientation program and list the various steps and activities involved in the orientation. Next, beside each activity in your orientation program, indicate your impression of that particular activity while you were actually in the orientation program. Third, what is your *present attitude* about the value of each orientation activity, now that you have the benefit of experience on your side? Finally, if you were designing an orientation program for your new employees (with complete control over what went into the program), which activities would you include in your program? Which activities would you omit? Why?

CASES

CASE 22.   Mr. Jones

Five new employees are brought in a group to the assembly line by a personnel clerk. He takes them over to the new supervisor who is sitting at his desk drinking a cup of coffee and smoking a cigarette. Clerk: "Good morning, Mr. Jones, these are your new workers starting with you today." As the personnel clerk leaves, Jones, glaring at the new people, puts his cigarette out slowly, takes one last swig of his coffee, and gets up from his desk. Jones: "O.K. Did personnel give you people a list of the safety rules, policy rules, and a time clock badge? O.K. First, I will show you, one time and one time only, how to clock in and out. This badge is your paycheck, and, if you don't clock in or out you will not get paid and I couldn't care less. You people have one week to learn this job and I'll be watching you closely. I'm the boss and we do things my way. I okay overtime, I assign duties, I recommend promotions, and I can make your life here good or bad. I have been known to overlook a long coffee or lunch break and give a day off with pay once in a while. You make my day easy for me, with no kickback from upstairs or grief from the line, and we'll get along real fine. Louse me up, and it will take an act of God to save your skin."

1. Supervisor Jones clearly has the formal authority in his department. However, did he do a proper job of communicating his authority to his new employees?
2. Are these new employees likely to be productive? Are they likely to be creative?
3. How would you communicate to new employees?

Training
and
Employee
Development

Objectives

Supervisors usually have some role in the training process in their departments. That role may be a direct or an indirect one. After studying this chapter, you will be able to

1. Choose from among the various forms of on-the-job and off-the-job training.

2. Appreciate the proper roles of the supervisors in training activities.

3. Assist in developing a training program.

4. Apply some basic principles of employee learning.

5. Begin developing a training program where you act as the primary trainer.

NEW EMPLOYEES USUALLY need some type of training before they can become productive members of your work group. Skilled employees who are familiar with the work being done require training for only a few minutes or hours; sometimes complete training may be conducted during the orientation period. Other employees, without some skills or unfamiliar with the details of your operations, will need additional training. This training may be a general review of your department's operations, the kinds of work being done, and the responsibilities of the new employee. For employees in certain types of work, a longer training period is usually necessary.

The role of the supervisor in training varies among different organizations. In some organizations, all training is handled by the personnel department. In these cases, the supervisor merely reports back to the personnel department on the progress and acceptability of the new employee once the training period is completed. In other organizations, the supervisor is directly responsible for teaching a new employee all the skills and information necessary to be a fully contributing member of the work group. In this situation, the supervisor has a number of options available for the conduct of the training, so long as the training method that is selected produces the desired results.

Increasingly, supervisors are being forced to deal with employees whose skills and abilities have declined or have become obsolete because of technological innovations. Training for these people will become a continuing responsibility, and not merely something that occurs when new people come into your department.

TWO TYPES OF TRAINING

There usually are two types of training in which supervisors become involved: *off-the-job* or *vestibule training* and *on-the-job training*. The main difference between the methods lies in where the actual training takes place.

Off-The-Job Training

Vestibule training takes place away from the place where the actual work is being done. It is often done in a classroom or in an office. The employee may be given books, films, manuals, or similar aids designed to develop a knowledge of the process and the terminology of the department. Simulators are often used to give the new employee "hands-on" experience with a machine or piece of equipment, while not disturbing or interfering with the flow of work in the department. In vestibule training the trainer usually familiarizes the employee with learning materials and then permits the employee to read and review the materials independently. Because the supervisor's main responsibility is to supervise departmental operations, vestibule training involving more direct instructor time is usually done by the personnel or training departments, using their people. Thus, most of the training activities that most supervisors partake in can be considered on-the-job training.

On-The-Job Training

On-the-job training is conducted in the department, using machinery, equipment, and personnel actually involved in the department's activities. The trainee is in the actual work area and is given increasingly more challenging assignments until he or she is judged capable of independent operation.

Supervisors approach on-the-job training in one of two ways. Some supervisors prefer to teach, that is, they directly supervise the learning activities of their new employees. In this manner, the supervisor is there to demonstrate how things ought to be done and to provide new employees with a good start toward productive on-the-job activity. Other supervisors prefer to put new employees with other employees as soon as they start work. The new employee will observe for a time before actually operating equipment or performing operations, and will then be put to work, learning by making errors and experimenting. When this is done, most supervisors ask one of the more experienced employees to act as an advisor. In this way, the new employee is able to meet fellow employees and begin developing social contacts with coworkers.

Clearly, both methods of on-the-job training have advantages and disadvantages. When a supervisor takes a direct hand in on-the-job training, it limits the time he or she has to perform other supervisory tasks. Training, especially when there are many persons being trained, can be time-consuming. It can also become dull and repetitive. It can lead to inadequate training, or to steps in the training process inadvertently being left out. Also, when an experienced employee is responsible for on-the-job training of a new employee, it is possible that the new employee will develop attitudes and feeling toward the work that are counterproductive. Also, such work group training can be disruptive, especially when new employees are being trained while departmental work is going on.

Most supervisors report that the best on-the-job training results are achieved when some reasonable mix of the two methods is used. The supervisor may begin training, and she or he may then turn over to a group leader or senior employee the responsibility for continued training. The supervisor, of course, must make periodic checks on the progress and performance of the trainee.

FACETS OF TRAINING

Continued Training for the Supervisor

Because most supervisors are responsible for some training within their departments, it is essential that you maintain a high level of skill in the operations of your department. You should also be aware of new techniques for effective supervision. Many organizations offer supervisory training classes or seminars, while other organizations leave this continuing education up to individual supervisors. Either way, continual updating and training for the supervisor can be performed properly only when the supervisor is able to make critical judgments about the work being done. Proper training for new employees and retraining for present employees helps to assure good work performances on the job. Supervisory development and continuing education encourage proper performance evaluation and supervisory judgment of employee actions.

The Supervisor's Role in Training

Today's supervisors may have the feeling that their role as trainers and developers of employees never ceases. Considering the changing demands of the job, they may be right. A modern training program includes all of the firm's efforts to improve an employee's ability to perform either a present job or a future job. Too many supervisors forget to include the employee in the planning of training programs. Instead, we assume that learning will occur if we simply teach. Experience shows that employee development requires an employee to have a desire to learn. Employee motivation is critical to the success of any training program.

For these reasons, supervisors should share work directly with the training professional in the design of the training program. They should share the reviewing of the progress of training, and they should both evaluate the results. In many cases, supervisors will actively serve as trainers in addition to their other jobs. It is therefore in your best interest as a supervisor to ensure that the best candidates for training are chosen, that the correct material is being taught, that your employees are benefiting from the training, and that proper training follow-up is done.

Reasons for Training

Employee training is expensive. Organizations spend millions of dollars annually on the training and development of their employees. Does a firm really know if it is getting its money's worth? Some training is essential and serves to ensure that each employee is capable of doing a particular job. All too often, we find that organizations throw training dollars at a problem without first attempting to discover if the training will result in achieving its objectives.

Failure to reach increased productivity goals may be caused by factors that are not directly related to training. If low productivity is caused by some factor other than employee ability, additional training may have little effect on employee output. Often supervisors who do a poor job of managing their people complain about the lack of ability that the individuals have when actually the problem is a lack of motivation.

Photo courtesy of Eastman Kodak Company.

Also, those attending a training session must have the capability to comprehend what they are expected to learn. The best training cannot be effective if the participants are incapable of learning. Industry and government learned in the 1970s that training for the "hard-core unemployed" required a substantial revision in the training methods used. Trainees were often motivated to learn but lacked the basic skills in reading and math that regular corporate training programs assumed everyone had. When remedial training was provided, the level of accomplishment increased. Without the remedial training designed to improve the basic skills of the hard-core employee in math and reading, the regular training would have been a complete failure for the firm and another failure for the individuals involved. If these individuals were allowed to fail, their self-concept and motivation would have been shattered. The results could have been disastrous for all involved.

While it is important to ensure that our firm's investment in training is appropriate to our situation, we should never lose sight of the potential payoff in increased employee productivity from a properly planned training program. Although training costs are high, their effects can be long-lasting. Some experts argue that training expenditures should not be considered as a cost but rather as an investment. The benefits from the development of an individual employee's knowledge and skills more than offset the initial development expenses that show up in the annual financial statement. Training and development comprise an essential part of the employee's growth as a person and as a valuable contributor to the organization. Employees with high personal growth needs tend to be highly motivated. A work environment that provides them with the assistance to become all they are capable of becoming helps to encourage motivation. Many of today's new employees have high expectations about what they can become. A supervisor who actively works to develop such employees to the peak of their potential will be rewarded with employees who generally deliver maximum productivity. The answer to our question of why we should invest in the training and development of employees is that the long-term payoffs in increased productivity and employee retention are substantial.

The Training Department

As a supervisor, do not let your training department make all the training decisions! Become an active partner in the training that your employees receive. In most organizations, you will need to take the first step. Have a development plan for each of your employees. You will then be in the position of asking the training experts for their help while retaining the right to accept or reject their suggestions. Most training specialists find it better to aid supervisors in tailoring a training program when there is a documented plan for employee development. Consider your relationship with the training specialist as a partnership. You know about your employees' jobs, how they are changing, and what more your employees may need and want in the way of training. Your firm's training specialists are experts on the best methods for accomplishing the training that you need. Together, you can produce effective training programs for your employees.

Development of a Training Plan

You know your people and what they will need to know better than the training department. Consequently, when you are making a request for training, take a positive approach. Recognize that different people in your group will need different types of training. You can better appreciate those needs than can anyone else.

BOX 1   What Results Should Be Obtained by the Training?

> A. Set training targets
>   A.1.   What will be learned?
>   A.2.   What new behaviors or skills will the participant be able to
>   demonstrate?
> B. When will these behaviors and skills be needed on the job?

The training plan should begin by stating the purpose of the training and what the expected results should be (keep in mind that every training plan should be *results oriented*). Make sure you have clearly defined your *training targets*. How can your jobs be improved through training? What will employees learn during the training sessions? Emphasis needs to be placed on new or improved behaviors and skills. Use each employee's present or future job description and job specifications in your description of the needed skills and behaviors. Relate the training need to each employee's present or potential job. This method will help you to define the exact nature of your training needs. Your plan should clearly show how the training will improve each employee's job performance. Spell out your training outcome. Your plan should indicate when training is needed. For example, some training, such as orientation training, is necessary soon after the arrival of a new employee or the transfer of an employee to your department. The installation of new equipment will give rise to employee training. Often such training will be conducted in advance of installation at the manufacturer's facilities or in-house on a simulator. With good planning, we can experience no significant time loss because of training, and each employee will be involved with the new equipment before it is installed.

Any training that requires time to complete and analyze must be well-planned. Presupervisory training is one such example. A presupervisory program may involve participants on a part time basis (that is, three hours a week), for four to six months. Evaluation of the results takes additional time. Some participants in presupervisory programs will recognize that they would prefer not to be considered for promotions to supervisor. Management may identify a need for additional training in areas of weakness. Planning will allow you to set priorities in the training program in terms of when results will be needed. The training plan should be built to match the needs of specific employees.

Box 2   Whom Are We Attempting to Train?

A. Recognize the individual differences between people.

B. Tailor the training program as best you can to facilitate learning for the candidates involved.

Who are the candidates for the training program? The more you know about the present level of knowledge and skills of the candidates, the better you can work with the training department to tailor a program to watch their specific needs. Both individuals and groups develop at different rates. We recognize the concept of individual difference and what role it plays in the tailoring of the training program. If, for example, we are attempting to develop a job skills training program, we would examine the manual dexterity scores of the potential candidates as well as the amount of experience each has had on related jobs. The careful grouping of candidates who are at the same learning level will facilitate the training process, will lower costs, and will reduce the frustration among those who find that they cannot keep up. It should be noted that intelligence levels, although important for many jobs, is not the sole criterion for learning a skill. Experience with similar work and tools is often more important. By grouping the candidates with the most similar job-related characteristics together, the training function will be faster and smoother. We are asking individuals to take a short step in the learning process. This concept is illustrated in Table 9–1. In group A, we have a collection of persons with no real preparation for the job. In group B, each of the candidates has moved through a progression of jobs that have gradually increased the skills and knowledge of each. Training group B will be much quicker because their previous job experience has given each a common body of knowledge and set of skills. It is likely that each person in group B is to some degree familiar with the requirements of the new job. It is a short learning stop for people in group B from where they are presently to the new job. For those in group A the training problem is very different. The men and women in group A may be very intelligent and have great potential to master the skills of the new job, yet the gap between where they are presently and where they need to be is very wide. As you can expect, the individual differences in people will be more pronounced when a broad gap needs to be closed. In addition to being more time consuming and costly, the likelihood of failure or drop-outs is significantly increased when we try to train inexperienced people.

When you have a good training plan with identified training targets based on job description and job specifications, then a careful match between training needs and current employees will result in reduced costs and more efficient results. The greater the awareness of the knowledge and skills of your employees, the more you will be able to assist your employees in attaining their optimum potential. Knowing the skills of your people pays off. Be sure you include skills that may not be directly related to the employee's present job. Employees often have skills that are not presently required in their job. Check the employee's application form in search of additional skills. Conduct your own inventory of their skills. We are often surprised to find that we already have the skills we need in our present employees.

Group A	Skill and Knowledge Required for New Job	Group "B"	Skill and Knowledge Required for New Job
		E	
		D	
		C	
No Skills or Experience		B	
		Job A	

TABLE 9–1

LEARNING

Principles of Employee Learning

Learning is more likely to occur among employees who are highly motivated to receive the training. Once you have selected employees who are capable of learning what is being taught, the next step is to develop in each employee a reason for learning. Employers must provide an atmosphere of self-motivation directed toward the outcomes desired of the training. Because you are the trainee's primary supervisor, you should spend time explaining the entire training process and the expected outcomes. Explain what will be taught, how it will be taught, where it will be taught, and when the training will take place. Try to remove or minimize any fear that employees may have about the training. By communicating what employees can expect to encounter during training, you will prepare them for what follows. Your explanation of why they have been selected for training and what the training will be, sets the groundwork for later on-the-job motivation. Be sure to help them to view training in a positive way. Being selected for training should, except for remedial training, be a sign that management has confidence in that employee's potential and has been impressed with her or his performance to date. Tie your discussion to the employee's past performance evaluations and individual career plans. The employee should know why he or she will be successful. Employers will want answers to important questions: Will the training lead to an upgrading of the job? Will it lead to a possible promotion? Will it provide a step toward a future reward?

The outcomes of a successful training program should be made as clear as possible. Don't overstate the outcomes or rewards. Level with your employees about what their successful participation may mean to them. Communicate outcomes in terms of the employee's rewards, not what the company needs and wants, and keep in mind that we are motivated by satisfaction of our needs, not by those of others.

For many employees the new knowledge and skills that they can acquire from the training can be source of personal satisfaction. With young professional employees, the amount and quality of training that they receive is a critical element in their decision to stay with a given organization. The ability to keep abreast of new and changing technologies in their professional disciplines has become an essential prerequisite to job satisfaction for some professional and technical employees. We are experiencing employees who already have a positive attitude toward training. In some cases they are demanding that their organizations provide training that they feel is necessary for their career development. The supervisor is an important link between the employee and the training specialists, because the training specialists may not have the technical expertise to understand the precise nature of the needed training. Furthermore, your employees will be judging your ability as a supervisor by whether or not you "can deliver" in an area which is very important to them.

Active Learning

Recognize the value of active learning or involvement on the part of participants. Research shows that people learn more when they are directly involved in a "hands-on" experience. When trainees have been shown how to accomplish a task, the next step is to let each person become directly involved in doing the task. Being able to apply what is being taught is a positive reinforcement to learning. Good training programs provide trainees with a continuing series of opportunities to show themselves and their supervisor or instructor what they are learning. Each such opportunity also results in immediate feedback. The participant is actively learning by doing. Each success is direct and carries immediate feedback. Positive results produce positive reinforcement and a heightened level of motivation. You must work to develop training programs based on these training principles.

Complexity of Learning

The nature of the training being conducted further influences how it will be conducted. As the complexity of a topic increases, it becomes important to spend time reviewing with the participants what the whole learning task is designed to accomplish. Too often, participants become lost in the details of the training, and they lose sight of what the overall process is about. Instructors must highlight the whole process and outcomes and then break the learning into separate parts for detailed examination. As each part is covered in the training, it must be related back to its place in the overall process or prospect.

BOX 3   Keys to Effective Learning

A. Motivate employees. Motivated employees learn more than non-motivated ones.

Continued

B. Explain to each participant what he or she can expect in the training process.
C. Explain why they were selected. Build up the employees' confidence in successfully completing the training program.
D. Explain to the employee the outcomes if the training is successfully completed. Put the benefit of the training in terms of employees' needs and wants.
E. Work to develop a training program that employs active learning.
F. Ensure that feedback of results to participants is immediate.
G. Use a positive reinforcement method of training.

Learning Is Not Continuous

Keep in mind that learning is not continuous. All individuals do not learn at the same rate. We each go through periods where our learning seems to peak and fall. This plateau is a natural part of any learning process. When each plateau is reached, the employee should receive encouragement from trainers and supervisors. Reassure each employee that these temporary plateaus are to be expected and that this is a common part of all learning. If employees are not given some warning about plateaus in the learning process, they will begin to blame themselves for failing. Participants may feel that they are "too dumb" to learn. This can be especially frustrating when the learning has come quickly up to that point. By recognizing that employees will have these plateaus and by preparing them for it, it is possible to minimize the potential danger to the attainment of training objectives when these plateaus are reached.

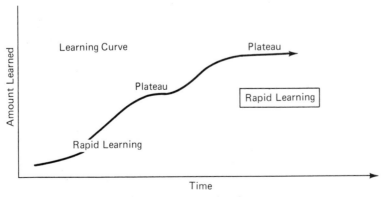

FIGURE 9–1 Learning Curve

THE SUPERVISOR AS TRAINER

There are many occasions when you will be conducting the training of your subordinates. When this opportunity occurs, prepare yourself well in advance. Review the tasks to be taught. Decide exactly what the participants must learn. Break the complex job into simple steps, and blend steps into a complete process. Develop a lesson plan for yourself to insure a smooth and logical sequence of each learning part. Conduct an inventory of the participants to determine their level of knowledge and skills before you decide what is to be taught. Adjust your presentation and techniques to the group that you will be teaching. Always keep in mind that you have done a good job only when the trainees learn. Be sure that you have a proper place to conduct your training and that all necessary equipment and supporting materials are in place and ready. Your choice of location is important. Avoid a location where the participants feel that others are watching. Except for on-the-job training, trainees should have some privacy, to reduce interruptions and keep individual mistakes from being seen by everyone. Trainees need a place where only you and they know that they have made an error. Such privacy will result in a lessening of group pressures.

The U.S. Army has chosen to use a "self-paced programmed learning" method in many of its job training programs. Each individual is placed in his or her own learning environment. The fast learners are not frustrated by a class geared to those of slower learning rates. The slower learners will not be passed over or feel frustrated by their inability to learn at the same pace as others. Instructors can recognize the exact nature of each participant's learning. Learning plateaus can be quickly identified and actions taken to assist the individual in overcoming the specific barrier.

Presentation

In your actual training presentations, be willing to vary your teaching techniques to fit the needs of the subject being taught and the skills and needs of participants. In most cases, you should use a variety of teaching techniques. Each technique should reinforce other methods used. A lecture is usually a way to start. Use illustrations and examples to clarify your lectures. Whenever possible, let your trainees become involved. Show them how a task should be done and then let them have access to the equipment to show you what they have learned. Use questions to teach if trainees seem to know the relationship between how the job is done and why it is done that way. The more questions that a trainee can answer, the more confident he or she will be about the learning process.

Beyond Training

Once the teaching portion of training is completed, the training is not complete. The next step is to have the trainee actually perform the job under normal operating conditions. While the employee is working at the job, you can take this opportunity to review what he or she has learned. Often the same questions that you asked during the presentation stage of the training have more significance now that the employee is actually on the job. Encourage trainees to ask follow-up questions. When corrections are needed, instruct in a positive manner. Seldom is *everything* wrong. Praise the positive and work with the trainee to correct errors. When corrections are needed, make it a point to recheck the employee soon to see if he or she has finished the needed corrections. If they have, praise their success. Continue the *inspection-instruction-praise cycle* until you are convinced that each employee has successfully mastered the job or skill.

Follow-Up

The last phase in the training process is the continuing follow-up you perform as the supervisor. This phase begins when you tell employees that you believe they can do the job and then assign them. Make it clear to your employees that for the next few weeks you will be spending more time checking their work than those of more experienced employees and that this is to ensure that the new employee gets off on the right foot. Encourage newly trained employees to ask questions when they arise. Be open to feedback and reassurance needs. Often it is useful to assign a new employee to team with an experienced worker who is not in a supervisory position. This "partner" can provide considerable assistance when questions arise. The follow-up may continue for weeks. At the point when you feel an employee has become proficient in the new job, you should return to your normal level of supervision and again, congratulate the employee on his or her achievements.

ACTION GUIDELINES FOR TRAINING

1. Relate training directly to the employee's present or future job. Employees should always know the objective of the training. They should know what is expected of them, why they are being asked to learn the work, and how their new learning affects their work situation.

BOX 4 The Training Process

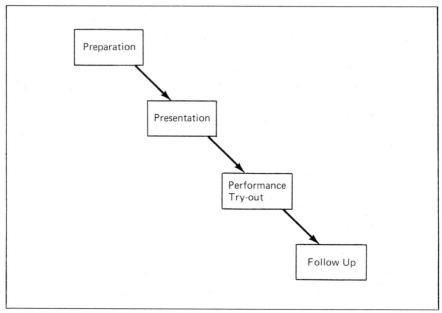

2. With new employees, explain during the orientation program what training they are going to receive and how the employees' performances during training will affect future opportunities.

3. Make training an active process. As soon as possible, involve employees physically with equipment or paperwork. The present employees should be made aware that additional training is one of the major keys to future success in the organization. You cannot force people to attend training class to improve their skills.

4. Demonstrate that higher-level skills learned by the employees are the "ticket" to promotion and pay increase. In short, relate training to future reward.

DISCUSSION QUESTIONS FOR TRAINING

1. Where would one use the various kinds of on-the-job and off-the-job training? What kinds of topics might be appropriate for each type of training?

2. In past training experiences that you have had, what has been the role of your immediate supervisor? How could she or he have helped you more during the training process?

3. List and discuss some situations in which trainee involvement would not be possible during the training activities?

4. What do you feel are some of the possible reasons for the plateaus that commonly occur during an employee's training efforts?

ACTION EXERCISE FOR TRAINING

Use a chapter in this book as the basis for this action exercise. Assume that you are a supervisor whose employees require training in that subject (such as "developing a safety consciousness"). List some assumptions and factors about your employees that you would want to consider in training them. Then develop a training plan for presenting that topic to your people. Flesh out the details. Who should attend? What is the schedule of training sessions? What training room layout and arrangement will there be? How should you break up the topic into individual lessons? What will the choice of cases for discussion be? What type media will you use? What follow-up testing and evaluation will be done?

CASE 23.   The Perpetual Learner

Helen is an inexperienced nurse who has been involved for the past two months in the hospital's nursing intern program. You have given her all sorts of extra time and help, and put some of her responsibilities on the other employees, but she seems to be a "perpetual learner." Helen's fellow nurses complain that she is getting favored treatment while they get the shaft.

1. What are some possible reasons for Helen's apparent lack of progress in training?
2. As her supervisor, what would you do now?

Performance Appraisal

Objectives

Many supervisors find that appraising their employees is their most difficult challenge. They resist performance appraisal, feeling that it involves too much control over an employee's work life and career. They feel that they are poorly prepared to handle the difficult interpersonal communication problems that arise when appraising employees, especially those employees who have not been working up to accepted standards. After studying this chapter, you will be able to

1. Understand and begin developing abilities in the role of coach and counselor to your employees; this is a vital part of the performance appraisal process.

2. Identify the vexing problems with performance appraisal.

3. Give "bad news" in a constructive and behavior-modifying way.

4. Communicate with your employees in ways that will result in better performance and productivity, and fewer negative reactions.

AN IMPORTANT PART of every supervisor's responsibility is performance evaluation and appraisal. Periodically, supervisors must report the progress and performance of employees in their departments to those higher up in the organization. This performance appraisal is used to determine wage or salary increases, promotions, job transfers, and other staffing decisions. Usually, supervisors are involved in the decision making when the time comes. However, the supervisor has a direct influence on staffing by the quality and usefulness of the evaluations performed.

Box 1   Performance Review—Hourly Employees

Employee's name ＿＿＿＿＿＿ Date ＿＿＿＿＿＿
Employee's title ＿＿＿＿＿＿ Supervisor ＿＿＿＿＿＿

Instructions: Please review the performance of the employee whose name is listed above on each of the following items. In order to guide you in your rating, the five determinants of performance have been defined.

Rating Points

5   OUTSTANDING

A truly outstanding employee whose achievements are far above what is considered to be acceptable. Has consistently performed far beyond established objectives and has made significant contributions beyond current position. Requires minimal direction and supervision. (Relatively few employees would normally be expected to achieve at this level.)

4   SUPERIOR

An above-average employee whose performance is clearly above what is considered to be acceptable. Has usually performed beyond established objectives and, at times, has made contributions beyond responsibilities of present position. Requires less than normally expected degree of direction and supervision.

3   AVERAGE

A fully acceptable employee who consistently meets all requirements of position accountabilities. Has consistently met established objectives in a satisfactory and adequate manner. Performance required normal degree of supervision and direction. (This level of performance should apply to the majority of employees.)

Continued

---

2 BELOW AVERAGE

A somewhat below-average employee whose performance, while not being unsatisfactory, cannot be considered fully acceptable. Generally met established objectives and expectations but definite areas exist where achievement was substandard. Performance required somewhat more than normal degree of direction and supervision.

1 UNACCEPTABLE

A far below average employee whose performance was barely adequate enough to consider that the requirements of the position are being met. Generally performed at a level below established objectives with the result that overall contribution was marginal. Performance required an unusually high degree of supervision. (This level is considered acceptable only for employees new to the job.)

JOB CRITERIA   POINTS

1. Amount of work. Consider here only
    the *quantity* of the employee's
    output.   _____

    Supervisor's comments: _____
    _____
    _____

2. Quality of work. Consider how well
    the employee does each job assigned.
    Include your appraisal of such items
    as accuracy, thoroughness, and
    orderliness.   _____

    Supervisor's comments: _____
    _____
    _____

3. Cooperation. How well does this em-
    ployee work and interact with you
    and coworkers for the accomplish-
    ment of organization goals?   _____

    Supervisor's comments: _____
    _____
    _____

Continued

4. Judgment. Consider this employee's ability to reach sound and logical conclusions. _____

   Supervisor's comments: _____
   _____
   _____

5. Initiative. The energy or apti-tude to originate action toward the organizational goals. _____

   Supervisor's comments: _____
   _____
   _____

6. Job knowledge. How well does the employee demonstrate an under-standing of the basic fundamen-tals, techniques, and procedures of the job? _____

   Supervisor's comments: _____
   _____
   _____

7. Interest in job. Does the employee demonstrate a real interest in the job and the organization? _____

   Supervisor's comments: _____
   _____
   _____

8. Ability to communicate. How well does this employee exchange needed information with others in the work group and with supervisors? _____

   Supervisor's comments: _____
   _____
   _____

9. Dependability. Consider the em-ployee's absences, tardiness, punc-

Continued

tuality, timeliness in completing
job assignments, and the amount of
supervision required. _____

Supervisor's comments: _____

_____

_____

10. Adaptability. Consider the degree
to which this employee demonstrates
adjustment to the varying requirements of the job. _____

Supervisor's comments: _____

_____

_____

TOTAL POINTS: _____

Supervisor's general comments: _____

_____

_____

_____

Instructions: After you have rated the employee and have made whatever comments you feel are pertinent to each criterion and the employee's overall evaluation, schedule a meeting with the employee
and review each item with him or her. If the employee wishes to
make any comment about the evaluation, please ask him or her to do
so in the following space.

Employee's comments: _____

_____

_____

_____

_____

_____

Evaluation review meeting took place on
Date _____
Supervisor present (Name) _____
Employee's signature _____
Date _____

Notice to employee: Signing the form does not imply that you either
agree or disagree with the evaluation.

Employee performance appraisal or evaluation is also a good opportunity for a supervisor to motivate employees to better performance, to report those who have been performing well, and to counsel those whose performance may not have been up to standard. For this reason, many organizations have instituted a formal performance appraisal throughout the organization. Employees at each level are evaluated by their supervisor, and the results of the evaluation are then shared with the employee and with those higher-up in the organization. Regardless of whether an organization has a performance appraisal system operating, it is useful for a supervisor to conduct periodic reviews of performance.

How Does Performance Work?

There are many variations. Most performance appraisal systems have at least a two-stage operation. The first stage consists of the supervisor's evaluating the performance of each employee in the department according to some standard. Often a questionnaire or evaluation form is used to focus the supervisors on those activities and traits being evaluated.

While considering each employee in turn, the supervisor records as objectively as possible his or her feelings about the employee on that particular item. Usually, there is space on the evaluation form for written comments, because the usual questionnaire responses do not always apply in every case.

BOX 2 Supervisor's Employee Evaluation Guide

1. Recognize that performance appraisal takes place whether you conduct it or not. People tend to compare. An employee will automatically compare his or her work with that of others. If the process of evaluation or comparison is natural, then it is necessary that the supervisor formalize the process whereby the greatest value can be obtained for both the individual and the organization.

2. Recognize that not all employees want a good evaluation system. Employees who know that their performance is below standard *do not* want the supervisor to do accurate evaluations. These employees will resist the use of an accurate evaluation system.

3. Beware of any bias you may have. Prejudice which is personal in nature does not belong in supervision or evaluation. Every employee has a right to a fair evaluation of performance.

———— Continued

4. Review the employee's performance for the whole period. Don't just look at or remember the last few months. Consider improvement made by the employee.

5. Be as complete as possible. Have all the facts. Be prepared for the evaluation interview. Have all your notes and records.

6. Supervisors have found the following procedure to be effective in good performance evaluation meetings.

% of time of the meeting	Nature of the Discussion
5	Get the employee to relax and describe to the employee how the evaluation works.
20	Review with the employee the negative features of the evaluation and specific areas where improvement is needed.
20	Review with the employee the positive features of the evaluation and specific areas where his/her performance was outstanding.
50	Mutual discussion of what the employee should do for the next evaluation period. Specific targets of performance are agreed upon by both supervisor and employee. Agreement is reached as to how the supervisor can help the employee reach that goal.
5	Set a next meeting where the employee can report as to his/her progress in reaching the goals.

As you can see, 50 percent of the time is spent on planning for the future. You cannot change the past, so put your efforts into improving performance in the future.

TABLE 10–1 Guide to Employee Performance Appraisal Performance Degrees

PERFORMANCE FACTORS	Far Exceeds Job Requirements	Exceeds Job Requirements	Meets Job Requirements	Needs Some Improvement	Does Not Meet Minimum Requirements
Ability	Leaps tall buildings with a single bound	Must take running start to leap over tall buildings	Can only leap over a short building or a medium one with no spires	Crashes into buildings when attempting to jump over them	Cannot recognize buildings at all, much less jump
Timeliness	Is faster than a speeding bullet	Is as fast as a speeding bullet	Not quite as fast as a speeding bullet	Would you believe a slow bullet?	Wounds self with bullets when attempting to shoot gun
Initiative	Is stronger than a locomotive	Is stronger than a bull elephant	Is stronger than a bull	Shoots the bull	Smells like a bull
Adaptability	Walks on water consistently	Walks on water in emergencies	Washes with water	Drinks water	Passes water in emergencies
Communication	Talks with God	Talks with the angels	Talks to himself	Argues with himself	Loses those arguments

215

When the evaluation form for each employee is completed, the counseling phase of the performance appraisal system begins. Supervisors meet privately with each of their employees. The supervisor and employee discuss the employee's ratings and reasons for these ratings. At this time, the supervisor can indicate where performance or behavior has been good or where it might need some improvement. These discussions give the employee valuable feedback on performance. The discussion should include an opportunity for the employee to respond to ratings that he or she considers unfair, and steps can be initiated to correct the alleged unfairness. Once the meeting with the employee is concluded, the supervisor sends to higher management the evaluation form and a report of the meeting with the employee.

Coach and Counselor

Performance appraisals serve two purposes: Planning for, monitoring of, and training of the subordinate and the administration of salaries and rewards.[1] Both are extremely important and both put the manager into a classic role conflict. Can a supervisor be a friend, confidant, counselor, and trainer while still being the coach and the keeper of the purse strings? It's a difficult position because a supervisor can't be sure which role should get more attention and commitment. This situation poses alternatives from which each manager must make a choice. From a communication standpoint, the critical issue is which of the roles do employees perceive the manager to be emphasizing? The conflict between being a coach and being a counselor adds to the discomfort and conflict during the performance appraisal process.

Problems with Performance Appraisal

Performance appraisal is an effective supervisory tool, both as a control of staff activities and as a motivational device to reward or stimulate behavior. However, there are some problems reported by supervisors doing evaluation.

Objectivity

One major problem faced by most supervisors is that of objectivity. In order for the performance appraisal to work correctly, it must be objective. Each employee must be judged according to standards, not according to the personal feelings of the supervisor. Unjustified high ratings are just as damaging to an employee and to the organization as are unjustified low ratings. Supervisors are human and often fall into the trap of considering "average" to be a negative evaluation. Such feelings frequently result in high ratings for everyone in a department. Clearly, this is both statistically and practically impossible. Objectivity is difficult to achieve, and few organizations expect absolute objectivity in the ratings that their supervisors give to employees. However, a record of consistent evaluations based on a standard that is known and understood by employees can make the evaluation process a valuable supervisory tool.

Use of Forms

Supervisors also report difficulty in reading and interpreting the performance evaluation forms that they are asked to use. While it is usually beyond the power of an individual supervisor to immediately make changes in the performance evaluation form, many supervisors simply ignore the form and give ratings that are largely meaningless. A supervisor's responsibility legitimately extends to the design of the questionnaire or evaluation form used by the organization. If the form does not meet the need for an adequate evaluation, the supervisor should make his or her feelings known to the personnel department or to the person in the organization who is responsible for designing the form. Only by establishing the usefulness of forms can the supervisor have an instrument that provides useful information.

Contamination

Another difficulty that supervisors encounter when they perform evaluations of their employees is what might be called a "contamination" of the evaluation. Often, it is necessary for a supervisor to rate an employee as "poor" on one specific characteristic or area. What happens is that the poor rating in one area affects the ratings that the supervisor gives to that employee in other areas, where performance might well have been good or excellent. To avoid this problem, many supervisors attempt to rate each employee in the department on a single item or characteristic, before moving to the next item on the form. For example, you would rate each employee in the department on his or her record of absenteeism. Once done, you would next rate each employee on his or her contribution to the morale in the department, and so on. This procedure helps to prevent contamination of the evaluation and contributes to the objectivity that is so essential to performance appraisal.

Supervisor-Subordinate Interaction

The interaction between supervisor and subordinate can be extremely difficult. It is easy to compliment a subordinate on an outstanding performance or to offer an employee a raise. Unfortunately, the process of doing the following is not always pleasant: criticizing an employee; informing the person that he or she will not be promoted; or persuading someone to come to work on time—or else!

Giving Bad News

Superiors dislike giving "bad news" almost as much as subordinates dislike getting it. For that reason, employee appraisals are often avoided completely. The problem of vanishing appraisals is important to managers because the absence of feedback undermines the effectiveness of any motivation program.

One way managers avoid giving negative criticism is to tell all employees that they are performing well. If a manager rates 80 percent of his or her employees as good or outstanding, but only gives raises to 20 percent, there appears to be an enormous communication breakdown, at least from the subordinate's viewpoint. The subordinate has every reason to believe that he will be rewarded, since he was told that he was performing well. When the reward doesn't come, distrust and bad feelings are sure to emerge. Even if animosity doesn't occur, the employee has no way of knowing how to improve, because the manager evaded his responsibility for giving accurate feedback. By attempting to minimize the discomfort of both subordinate and superior, the supervisor may have created an even bigger problem of employee dissatisfaction.

Dehiring

Another way supervisors avoid the unpleasantness of negative performance appraisals is "dehiring." If a supervisor doesn't want to tell the employee that performance is not up to standard, "dehiring" helps to avoid the problem. "Dehiring" the employee doesn't solve the problem, but it may make the problem go away. Using this strategy, the supervisor attempts to make life on the job as miserable as possible for the employee who, on reading the signals, will leave voluntarily. If dehiring is effective, the supervisor never has to give the "bad news." Despite the fact that managerial unwillingness to exercise responsibility can hurt both the employee and the company, "dehiring" is very widely used in all kinds of organizations.

COMMUNICATION STRATEGIES
FOR PERFORMANCE APPRAISAL

Identify the Behaviors

In order to achieve a desired performance, the employee must know exactly what is expected of him or her. The manager's responsibility is to provide the employee with a complete, precise, and clear understanding of the behaviors that are desired. This provides the employee with a greater appreciation of what is to be done, and it forces you, as a supervisor, to be more specific in your expectations and, therefore, more objective in your evaluations of the employees. When it is properly done, the identification of desired behaviors can create a less defensive atmosphere between supervisor and subordinate.

If you tell a subordinate to "take care of that problem," there is a good chance that he or she may not completely understand how to proceed. On the other hand, if you tell an employee to perform three specific tasks, the employee has less uncertainty about what is to be done. Defining expected behaviors provides the direction and focus needed by many employees, even though there is a risk of restricting employee creativity and initiative.

Once you have identified specific behaviors, employees can be evaluated in terms of how well the goals were attained. Because the standards are established ahead of time, the manager can be more objective in evaluation.

Finally, and of most importance, a focus on behaviors can minimize defensiveness in an evaluation interaction. Consider the difference between the following statements:

1. "Jim, you really didn't do a very good job on the report."
2. "Jim, the data collection, and writing style in the report were fine but the punctuation was inappropriate in the spots that I have indicated."

In our first example, the manager evaluated Jim's performance, but this kind of feedback did not give Jim any idea as to how to correct his failures. In the second example, Jim was told what behaviors were acceptable and the sources of difficulty were identified. Description, rather than evaluation, creates a more supportive communication climate. It is important to make the distinction between person and behavior. When you have to give negative feedback, resentment is minimized when you can say "I like you, but I don't like these specific behaviors."

Photo courtesy of Sears, Roebuck & Company.

THE MOST EFFECTIVE PERFORMANCE APPRAISAL IS CONTINUOUS APPRAISAL

Identify the Criteria

A supervisor can make the evaluation of employee behavior much easier and much less subjective if he or she defines clear and precise criteria for "comparing" employee performance. The criteria should include all relevant job activities, and they should be weighted as to their relative importance. They give the manager a "yardstick" with which an employee may be evaluated more objectively. Complete objectivity, although it is desirable, is an unattainable goal because the manager is always perceiving employee behavior with his or her own biases, prejudices, blind spots, and unique frames of reference. Such perceptual influences can never be eliminated totally, but their impact can be reduced as additional criteria are used in performance appraisal.

If the criteria for employee behavior are not clearly established, the manager takes the risk of falling into the trap of giving some employees the benefit of the doubt to the point where favoritism emerges. The "halo effect" is a real danger and can create dissension among other employees. If all employees know the criteria and feel that the manager is using those criteria, they will know what to expect. Because their doubt and uncertainty have been removed, the employees then know what must be done to earn rewards. If the criteria are well established, employees can feel that changing their behaviors and "shaping up" will produce personal benefits. The potential for increased motivation won't appear until the relationship between behaviors and rewards is clearly spelled out and the employees see what it is that the manager is going to reward.

Don't Just Focus on the Negative

It is often very difficult to get employees both to hear what their bosses are saying and to appreciate the implications of those messages. All too often, employees may hear but not really listen to the intended message. To achieve the desired results, a message must be presented in a way that is at least minimally acceptable to the employee.

When an employee is in a threatening situation, that person's natural response is to seek protection. If someone throws something at another person, it's only natural for the latter to duck and try to avoid the object. The same is true of an employee being criticized. As soon as the inevitable ". . . or else" is heard, the defensiveness begins.

Sandwich

Supervisors should develop communication strategies to minimize defensiveness in performance appraisal. One strategy is to use an indirect approach which *sandwiches* the negatives between positive evaluation and praise. While some studies have suggested that praise doesn't affect this process one way or another, the research failed to take into account the positioning of bad news in relation to praise. When being criticized, a subordinate's first reaction may well be ". . . and I suppose I never do anything right." When the manager recognizes and praises positive behaviors of the subordinate at the beginning of the interview, this counterargument cannot be used. The criticism can be put into perspective and may then be perceived as being more fair.

"Sandwiching" negatives is really just the use of empathy. Putting yourself in the employee's place may lead to better prediction about how a subordinate may react. In advance, the manager may decide to avoid a particular approach. Empathy leads to looking at the employee's particular set of circumstances rather than operating from some neutral stance or from an arbitrary set of rules. Empathy may reduce defensiveness, and thus it may help employees hear and understand what is being said.

Minimize the Differences

Another way to reduce defensiveness is to minimize the differences in role status when giving feedback. Instead of telling a subordinate that he or she has a problem, emphasize a joint concern that must be overcome. This mutual interest allows the employee to feel less alone or stuck with the problem. Defensiveness can also be reduced if the evaluated person is not made to feel inferior or second-rate. When a supervisor assumes an arrogant attitude, flaunts his superiority, or shakes her head in disbelief, an employee will invariably become defensive. This is not to suggest that supervisors must renounce their superior role or be on a first name or "buddy" relationship with employees in order to prevent defensive attitudes from forming. However, supervisors must treat subordinates with genuine respect even though some employee behavior may be unacceptable. A manager must first demonstrate, at least, a minimal concern for the employee if work behavior is to be improved materially.

Again, it is obvious that the multiple roles of the supervisor may create conflict. The manager suggests that while the failure to attain organizational goals is a mutual problem, the employee will get no raise because of his or her poor performance. The manager is also to be a counselor, so the problem is compounded. But, the manager must *also* be an administrator of wages, which, by definition, is a superior role. One way to reduce this conflict is to conduct employee improvement interviews separately from those in which salary matters are discussed. This won't eliminate role conflict, but it may help to minimize the negative consequences of such conflicts, and it may make possible greater behavioral changes.

Don't Gunnysack

By giving negative feedback, you may want to "correct" one or two things in the employee's behavior. Yet, the overall objectives often get lost once the discussion begins. When a performance confrontation starts to get really rough, the participants start digging out all of the ammunition they can muster. All of those little things that have been "under one's skin" finally have a chance to burst out. Everyone has been guilty of that kind of defensive argument, but what are the results of that approach?

Assume that you come into the performance appraisal session with one or two behavioral items which you want to correct. When the employee puts up a fight or gets defensive about some of these things, you may feel backed against a wall and strike out with whatever is at hand. You'll use all those little gripes that have accumulated in the supervisory gunnysack for presenting at the right time. "Gunnysacking" detracts from efforts to correct real problems. The employee can now justify his or her behavior because "obviously the boss is just nit-picking." The message to the employee is diluted if too many additional issues are injected during the discussion. A better strategy is to resolve these minor issues as they arise. If the issues aren't important enough to be brought up as they occur, then they should be forgotten. Gripes must not be allowed to accumulate. When they do, they create an obstacle when something really important arises.

The effectiveness of feedback often depends on when that feedback is given. When feedback is given immediately following a behavior, the feedback is more likely to be effective. It doesn't make sense to reprimand a child several hours after he has misbehaved. Similarly, it doesn't make sense to withhold evaluative information from an employee until the next six-month evaluation. Feedback, both positive and negative, should be given continuously. Regular feedback allows the subordinates to modify their behavior when necessary, while it reinforces existing desirable behaviors.

Recognize the Difference
Between Can't and Won't

Too often, managers fail to identify the cause of poor performance. Performance has at least two major elements: motivation and ability. If performance is poor, a common managerial response is to assume that the employee won't perform; this is a motivation problem. While that may be the case, there are many times when lack of performance is due to the employee's low ability or lack of training. The two factors in poor performance demand very different corrective strategies. If an employee won't perform, you must evaluate the motivation strategies being used. However, if the employee can't perform, your responsibility is to train the employee if possible or find an alternative solution such as a transfer or termination. The important distinction between "won't" and "can't" must be made. One way to do so is to directly involve the employee in the performance appraisal process. A joint evaluation procedure not only helps managers to more accurately perceive problems, but it also provides employees with a better understanding of evaluation. It leads to a greater employee satisfaction with the entire evaluation process.

Split the Conflicting Roles

Many supervisors have little or no real control over the details of their firm's performance appraisal system. The timing of the supervisor-subordinate joint review session is given, as is the general format of the meeting and the suggested method for presenting bad or negative information. For these supervisors, the strategy to split conflicting roles will not be possible.

However, for those with a flexible performance review system, a productive approach is to hold two face-to-face sessions with each employee: One should deal with the administration of salaries and rewards or punishments and a second should deal only with the counseling/planning/training function. While such an arrangement clearly takes more time—in effect, it can double the actual amount of supervisor-subordinate contact time on each review cycle—the benefits of a split strategy are many. Above all, it permits the supervisor to wear one hat at a time; thus, she or he concentrate on a single task without the necessity of shifting from one role to another.

If the first of the two meetings is devoted to the salary/reward phase, the employee has an interim period of time to digest the feedback. If the initial feedback was negative, both the news itself and the employee's offhand reaction can be isolated. The counseling phase, or meeting number 2, can then be held in a more open or productive setting, that is, one relatively uncharged by an emotional response. Also, the employee has the benefit of reflection on the first evaluation. With this reflection, the counseling in the second meeting can usually be directed toward more clearly defined and agreed-upon goals. The employee's mind is reasonably clear of evaluative information and is better able to focus clearly on the planning/training session objectives.

Supervisors using a split-session strategy must exercise caution in the second session. Some employees, usually those given low ratings or negative feedback in the first session, will try to resurrect the subject of their rating in the counseling session. It is here that you must exert discreet but firm control if the benefits of the split-appraisal approach are to be realized.

Watch for Supervisor Defensiveness

A new and interesting, if not potentially damaging, phenomenon in performance appraisal is the problem of the supervisors perceiving negative employee ratings as reflections of their own supervisory abilities. Recently, several supervisors in management seminars conducted by the authors have pointed out this new barrier to communication in performance appraisal. In such a situation, the supervisor feels that an employee's poor performance directly reflects his or her performance as a manager. With that perception, the manager is reluctant to criticize and becomes highly defensive whenever a low-rated employee's defensiveness seems to backfire on the supervisory performance. In some instances, the supervisor's attitude results in the employee's gaining practical control over the performance appraisal process. The minimum cost of such an occurrence is a higher-than-deserved rating. At worst, the entire appraisal process for all employees can be seriously compromised.

There is no simple remedy for such a communication problem. However, should such defensiveness occur, it may well indicate a performance appraisal failure of another sort at the next higher organizational level. The defensive supervisor's immediate superior has perhaps failed to communicate properly or to conduct meaningful counseling activities with that supervisor. Thus, the defensiveness of the rater may well be a symptom of problems higher up in the chain of command.

SUMMARY

All managerial strategies ultimately depend on the efficiency of the employee evaluation process. Efficiency requires readily understood appraisal procedures and effective managerial communication skills. Despite the incentives used and the objectivity of appraisal mechanisms, evaluation efficiency ultimately depends on the way that you communicate with your people. It is your responsibility to be aware of both the pitfalls of the evaluation process and the available communication strategies. Managers facing forthcoming employee performance reviews are advised to consider carefully the ideas and suggestions presented in this chapter. Watch for signs of resentment, gunnysacking, defensiveness, and "fuzzy" criteria. Develop with each employee an acceptable, understandable relationship between the suggestions and standards applicable to the employee and his or her personal interests. The recognition and minimization of the differences between the employee's interests and the standards being set is a positive first step toward effective performance appraisal.

ACTION GUIDELINES
FOR PERFORMANCE APPRAISAL

1. Learn as much as possible about your firm's performance appraisal system and other organizations' process of performance appraisal.
2. Analyze yourself as a coach and counselor. Are you able to make objective judgments about employees while still being able to provide human concern for them and their problems?

3. Avoid even the appearance of "dehiring." It can give all employees—and not just those being dehired—a feeling of being under siege. That is not a very productive atmosphere in which to supervise.

4. Be specific in identifying the behaviors that are wrong, the behaviors that you will want to see, and the criteria by which you plan to judge the counseled employee during the next appraisal period.

5. Remain positive. Too much focus on the negatives and the problem behaviors of the employee may cause him or her to feel threatened or put-upon. Such defensiveness interferes with the employee's commitment to changing her or his problem behavior.

6. Sandwich bad news between layers of good news. Let the employee know that, on balance, there are some (even many) positive aspects to his or her behavior.

7. Minimize the differences between where an employee's performance *is* now and where you want it to be. The setting of goals too high for the employee often results in goals not being met.

8. Watch for the temptation to gunnysack. When there is a problem with a person's behavior, tell him immediately. Don't wait until the next regular performance appraisal session. By then, it may be too late.

9. Watch and avoid your own defensiveness. It can be a real source of compromise for any performance appraisal system.

ACTION EXERCISE FOR PERFORMANCE APPRAISAL

Use the sample form at the beginning of this chapter to appraise your own performance either as a student or as a supervisor. Then, with a classmate or coworker who has done the same thing, swap forms, and review each other's evaluations. This will result in two benefits: First, you will have an appreciation for the performance appraisal process, and second, you will be given a revealing look at yourself as the appraised individual. Both benefits can be very useful as you approach your first or next performance appraisal where you are doing the rating.

CASE 24. The Workaholic

Juan is a compulsive overworker. He arrives hours before the shift starts, stays after everyone leaves, and never stops in between. His work is first-rate, but you are concerned about the long-run impact of such behavior.

1. Is Juan a problem employee?
2. If he is, what can you do about it?

CASE 25. The "De Facto" Boss

Mary Jo, a middle-aged person, had been with the department for seventeen years. She had been an administrative assistant for the past decade. During that time, she had had several bosses. Her manager for nine years had gradually abdicated many of his internal duties so that Mary Jo gradually assumed more and more of the managerial responsibilities. Mary Jo's office and that of the department manager were on the third floor, but other staff desks and offices were on the second floor. To say that Mary Jo's manner was gruff was to understate the case. Her approach with others was usually straight on, and she often spoke in a loud voice. Needless to say, others in the office knew she was "the boss" and assumed a deferential stance toward her.

There was recent evidence to indicate that the other staff members were prone to taking longer-than-normal lunch hours. Also, one of the staff had been absent from work on frequent occasions lately. A new department manager, who had been on the job for approximately one month, heard of this situation. She instituted a "sign-in/sign-out" sheet in the main office to control matters because the between-floor separation made continual monitoring impractical. Two younger staff members who reported to Mary Jo had a very strong negative reaction to this new control policy, and they requested a meeting with the manager. The manager readily agreed to meet with the complaining staff members on the same day that it was requested. As it happened, Mary Jo was out sick that day.

The meeting was quite useful. Tensions and concerns were aired on matters that went beyond the control technique itself. In the meeting, they discussed such matters as Mary Jo's approach and attitude toward employees although this was of minor importance under the current circumstances. Mary Jo happened to call the office later on during the day of the meeting. The fact of the "gripe" session was more or less off-handedly mentioned to her and she exploded! How could a meeting be held without her? She prided herself in her ability to manage the office and was particularly piqued that she had been a topic of discussion when she was not there to defend herself. The tone of her voice, and her emotional state grew more intense the longer she spoke. At one point, she slammed the telephone receiver down abruptly. Shortly thereafter, she called back and continued her tirade.

---

*This case was written by Dr. William D. Litzinger, Division Director of Management and Marketing, The University of Texas at San Antonio.

1. What has given rise to this violent outburst? What immediate and latent problems exist?
2. Could anything have been done to alleviate the situation in an organizational sense? In a physical one? Emotional one? Managerial one?
3. What actions should the new manager have taken immediately? What should she do the next day when Mary Jo returns to work?

CASE 26. Underqualified?

A long-term employee for many years has worked in the same job and has been moved from one supervisor to another as programs and requirements changed. Over the course of the years, he had been promoted to a senior position at a premium rate of pay. The appraisal of this man's performance had passed through many supervisors with apparent approval. Now with a new departmental reorganization, he was assigned to a new group but still was performing the same type job. At first his performance seemed acceptable. But as time went on it became apparent that he was lacking in many areas and was failing to meet the performance level set by his immediate supervisor. These problems were discussed with him, and areas requiring improvement were outlined by his supervisor. This action did not bring about an improvement in his performance. On recognizing that he was having no effect on the employee, the supervisor discussed the problem with his boss and a decision was made to give the employee a written warning advising him he was in an overpaid position and if his performance did not improve, he could be dismissed. In the end, the department head had to transfer this employee to a lesser responsibility in a different group.

1. Was this the right decision?
2. How will this decision affect the company?
3. What actions could the supervisor have taken to avoid this confrontation?
4. Is this problem a common one for supervisors, especially with older employees? Why?

Managing for Safety

Objectives

This chapter deals with the safety and health of you and your employees while in the work area. After reading and studying this chapter, you will be

1. More conscious about the importance of safety.

2. Able to begin developing a program of safety consciousness for your employees.

3. More aware of the role of the supervisor, the organization, and the government in the mission of maintaining safety.

4. Better able to deal with the unthinking attitude many of us develop when it comes to accidents, that is, the attitude that "it can't happen to me."

SAFETY DOES NOT add additional costs to a company or any additional responsibilities to a supervisor. On the contrary, an effective safety program can result in lower accident rates and a greater confidence in the employees. The supervisor's role is critical to the success of any safety program.

One of the basic factors affecting employee attitudes about management is the quality and safety of the physical working conditions, that is, the environment on the job. As one supervisor noted, "You can't stress quality, productivity, or cost savings when employees are afraid to work in what they feel may be unsafe surroundings." Today, managers are dedicated to maintaining a work environment that is as accident-free as technology and people can make it. Equipment is continuously redesigned with the safety of the operator in mind. Working conditions on the job have been improved by work methods engineering. There is no question that working conditions in most organizations today, while perhaps not as safe as standing in an open field, are the safest ever. (In fact, standing in an open field can even be hazardous, especially when there's a thunderstorm brewing.)

DEVELOPING AN EFFECTIVE SAFETY PROGRAM

The first step in developing an effective safety program is to gain the cooperation of all management levels. Management is interested in safety programs because of the savings in cost and improvement in morale. By assuming the initial responsibility for a safety program, management should set specific policies about safety and health for the entire organization. Supervisors should be involved as much as possible to ensure that the policies established by upper management truly relate to situations being faced by the organization's employees. Top managers can then establish the responsibilities of each member of management for carrying out the policies. Through such an arrangement, upper management demonstrates the importance of the safety program and accepts the responsibility for its accomplishment.

A second step in developing an effective safety program is to search for the causes of past accidents and investigate where similar conditions still exist in the work place. Every supervisor, with the assistance of every employee, is encouraged to approach safety as an effort to protect each employee personally rather than simply as a cost savings technique. Every source of a potential accident that is corrected may save a life. As a supervisor, you must constantly remind your employees to be aware of potentially unsafe situations and to report them to you promptly.

The supervisor must also pass along the results of his or her safety work to the company or plant safety committee or official. A committee is usually headed by a staff person from the safety or personnel department, whose function it is to coordinate the efforts of the organization's supervisors on all matters related to health and safety. Often new supervisors assume that if an organization has a safety person on the staff, the supervisor's responsibility for job safety is eliminated. This is not the case. Staff safety personnel can be a great help to you in becoming aware of potentially dangerous conditions. However, it is always the supervisor who has the greatest opportunity to spot unsafe situations first. Thus, supervisors are a firm's "first line of defense."

The final step in making the safety program effective is to share information with other supervisors. If you or your group find that a particular technique is successful in developing or improving a safe working environment, pass it along at a safety committee or supervisor's meeting. The same is true for any new safety problems that you find. Your warnings may prevent accidents and save lives in other work areas. Good safety communication keeps everyone aware of potential problems, aids in planning new safety programs, and helps other supervisors effectively deal with potential problems in their work areas.

FACTORS INVOLVED IN SAFETY

Risk

Without question, certain jobs involve risk. No amount of engineering and no safety program can remove those risks. Risk involves calculating the probability of danger and taking measures to minimize that risk. For example, movie stunt people take risks in performing their stunts, just as athletes and circus performers take risks. However, they also observe strict safety measures to keep the risk that they are encountering to an acceptable minimum. Safety engineering and effective safety practices perform the same function in organizations. They reduce the risk of working in that environment to an acceptable level, while making the work situation economical for productive effort. Clearly, it is impossible to engineer all danger out of any environment, just as it is impossible to manufacture a completely safe automobile. However, the problem is the same—the safety measures would make the automobile (or the work situation) totally uneconomical. Thus, in most human activities, we accept risk. We maintain vigilance, reward employees and supervisors for safety innovations, and pay a premium to those persons who must assume greater risks in their work activities.

Photo courtesy of Pullman, Inc.

SAFETY IS ESSENTIAL IN A REFINERY—OR IN ANY ORGANIZATION. IS IT IN YOURS?

As a supervisor, your safety goal should be the elimination of safety hazards wherever possible. It should also be the development of a safety consciousness among all your employees.

Stupidity

An organizational safety program is usually aimed at reducing the potential for accidents and injuries caused by unsafe acts. These unsafe acts can be divided into two categories: (1) those acts that injure people or damage property when employees are properly performing their assigned tasks and using proper safety measures, and (2) those violations of safety that result from the conscious or willful negligence of employees (or supervisors). Organizations usually have a greater success controlling accidents caused by mechanical failures. However, the latter kind of accident usually results in the supervisors asking themselves "why are people so stupid?"

For a variety of reasons, people believe that they can "beat the safety odds." Supervisors are often ignored when they talk with their employees about safety practices. This is usually because people don't believe it can happen to them. The danger in this kind of thinking is that it can lead to lapses in normally cautious behavior. When the United States lowered the maximum speed limit to 55 m.p.h., the purpose was to reduce gasoline consumption. However, another benefit of this action was to reduce the accident rate on the nation's highways. Safety statistics from the National Safety Council have shown a much lower rate of accidents and fatalities after the speed limit dropped. However, these statistics fail to impress many drivers, and the evidence can be seen daily on the highways, as many drivers violate the posted speed limits. Again, the logic appears to be, "It can't happen to me, so why worry?"

Accidents happen in organizations mostly because people, although aware of safety and risk, commit unsafe acts with the misplaced confidence that they will not be injured. Usually, such confidence is developed gradually. One unsafe act is performed with no ill effects. The worker assumes that the safety rules really don't apply, or that the rules are silly, because the danger is minimal. Next time, the same employee is likely to further exceed safety limits. A process of violation and success stimulates the employee to further excesses. Ultimately, this unfortunate cycle may come to an end, and the result is often tragic. Breaking this "poor safety cycle" is a major (and continuing) challenge for all supervisors.

A note of caution. Supervisors are often prey to the same assumptions that befall the men and women working for them. Clearly, safety consciousness is important in those situations where equipment or machinery poses a real safety hazard. However, many supervisors in less dangerous situations (such as offices and stores) assume that safety planning and safety consciousness are for the factory and machine shops. This assumption is faulty and potentially dangerous. Safety is a concern for all supervisors and all people in organizations.

SAFETY FACTS

The Bureau of Labor Statistics reports that approximately 6 million work-related injuries or illnesses occur in the United States each year, and similar statistics are reported from other industrialized nations around the world. An estimated 28 million workdays are lost each year due to job-related injuries or illnesses. Ninety-seven percent of the 6 million persons hurt are injured in accidents, and the Bureau estimates that an injury occurs on the job to one in every ten workers. These facts make it imperative that supervisors recognize the responsibility they have to the health and well-being of the people assigned to their departments. The employing organizations are forced to struggle with the staggering cost of injuries, which are estimated at an annual rate of $2 billion lost production and $1.5 billion lost wages. This is approximately ten times the amount lost by organizations in all forms of labor actions, including strikes.

These facts speak for themselves. They depict a serious problem. How can supervisors help improve the safety record of their workgroups?

WHO IS RESPONSIBLE FOR SAFETY?

The Organization's Responsibility for a Safe Working Environment

Organizations are responsible for developing and maintaining safety consciousness. This is done in the initial orientation and training that are given to new employees and it is carried throughout the contacts the organization has with its employees. Posters, safety campaigns, awards, and suggestion systems all contribute to the safety program within the organization.

Organizations are, of course, responsible for maintaining work environments that conform to the various regulations of the various state, provincial, and federal governments.

Beyond these actions, what can the organization and upper managers do to help reduce accidents and improve working conditions? To begin with, supervisors can continually make every effort to report potential safety problems upward in the organization until the potential problem is remedied. This reporting function helps the organization to keep its attention focused on this issue.

Some organizations have successfully developed a safety-by-objectives program in which the entire organization attempts to set standards for the improvement of safety conditions. One firm, through such a program, was able to cut the accident rate throughout the organization by 70 percent in eighteen months. The program resulted in the reduction of time lost by employees due to accidents and in increased employee morale. Through the safety-by-objectives program, every potential safety problem was acted upon and the employees began to recognize that management was indeed serious about improving the working conditions. All suggestions for improvements were reviewed by a panel composed of representatives from labor and management, and their recommendations were promptly acted upon.

It is always difficult to define reasonable standards of safety. Here again management and labor can work together to set standards that protect the employees while not going overboard costwise. At this point, the role of supervisor becomes extremely important. The supervisor's daily contact with the problems put him or her in a critical role in the maintenance of a safe work environment.

The Supervisor's Role in Safety

In addition to his or her role as an example of safe work practices, the supervisor is responsible for maintaining a high level of safety consciousness among employees. This task is often difficult, because the goal of a safety program is a reduction (or total elimination) of unsafe conditions and personal injury. To achieve this end, many supervisors and many organizations keep and post the actual job time lost through accidents and injuries on the job. This is a commendable action, because it can help maintain safety consciousness. However, by publicizing the fact that there have been few or no accidents over the past few months or years can also be strangely counterproductive. As more and more time passes since the last accident or injury, memories fade. Employees and supervisors alike forget to maintain their vigilance for unsafe conditions and practices. They are lulled into thinking that accidents are a thing of the past and are no longer of any real concern. Clearly, one cannot stage an accident occasionally just to impress workers with the seriousness of safety on the job. Such informal communication, while it is powerful, is simply not practical. However, many supervisors report great success in achieving safety on the job by holding informal discussions with their employees whenever an accident occurs in their organization or in an organization doing similar work. These groups discuss the details of the accident, and they even bring in experts or persons with a first-hand knowledge of the accident to give a better account of what actually happened. These discussions are followed by "action exercises," in which the group members analyze their own work area to see if conditions similar to those from the accident scene are present. In this way, supervisors and employees alike are "tuned in" to thinking about safety and to taking positive steps to improve safety consciousness and safe conditions.

Supervisors are the conscience of the employees when it comes to safety. The employees are often too involved in the actual operations to think directly and continuously about safety. The supervisor, however, should help by setting examples and by taking action to keep safety in the forefront.

Supervisors can train each new employee in the "safe way" of doing a job. During this training session, you can use your experience to warn new employees about so-called short cuts and explain why these short cuts are potentially dangerous. Time spent in such training can prevent time lost due to accidents later.

During normal operations, be on the lookout for employees who seem to have a bad attitude about safety. Employees who do not care about safety not only endanger themselves, but they endanger others around them. It is important to emphasize that such persons are not "brave" because they can flirt with danger, but they are instead a danger to everyone. In cases of repeated offenses, disciplinary action should be taken promptly. Safety rules apply to all employees. If one person violates these rules and is not corrected, others will soon believe that no real danger exists and they will begin to follow suit.

When an accident does happen, and medical treatment is required, begin a step-by-step analysis of why the accident took place. Avoid the initial "it wasn't my fault" answer. At this time the accident has taken place and you are less interested in fixing blame than in attempting to find out what really happened so that steps can be taken to avoid a recurrence. When the cause of the accident is determined, action should be taken immediately to correct the problem and to inform others of it.

Dr. Larry Klatt has compiled a list of some of the more common environmental and mechanical hazards found in industry. These are shown in Tables 11–1 and 11–2. These lists can be a useful starting point for a safety analysis of your work area.

Most supervisors are by now familiar with the Occupational Safety and Health Act. This act set up standards for safety in a wide variety of organizations and established the Occupational Safety and Health Administration (OSHA) to administer the law and deal with violators. The declared purpose of Congress in enacting this legislation was to "assure as far as possible [that] every working man and woman in the nation [have] safe and healthful working conditions and to preserve our human resources." The intent is certainly honorable and worthy of support.

Yet, for many managers and supervisors, enforcement of this and subsequent laws is a different matter. Some of the statements in the law are vague and subject to various interpretations. For example, the law states that an employer ". . . shall furnish to each of his employees employment and a place of employment which are free from recognized hazards that are causing or are likely to cause death or serious physical harm to his employees." Any employee who feels that the working con-

TABLE 11-1 Environmental Hazard Check List

Congested work area.
Congested aisles.
Ventilation problem: mist, smoke, dust, odor, heat, cold, draft.
Faulty lighting: glare, too dim, too great contrast, flicker.
Littered floors.
Slippery floors: waxed, wet, subject to spill.
Uneven or damaged floor (check also safe load limits).
Bad stairway: uneven risers, sub-standard handrail.
Ladders: not available, wrong kind, defective.
Catwalks and elevated platforms: sound? railing and toeboard?
Crawl space above false ceiling (support a man's weight?)
Foundation crawl space: nails, broken glass, seepage.
Pipe tunnel and pipe shaft condition.
Doors and doorways: Open directly on step or stair?
                       Swing wrong way for emergency exit?
                       Need window to prevent collision?
                       Remote control device needed? In good condition?
Furniture: chairs, stools, desks, benches, racks, etc.
Tripping hazards.
Pressure vessels: safety devices, periodic inspection.
Control of foot traffic (especially at rush hour).

Some of these you can correct. Others may simply need to be clearly marked with a warning signal. Add below the special environmental hazards in your plant.

Source: Supervisory Safety Seminar Handouts. Dr. Larry Klatt, Florida Atlantic University.

TABLE 11-2 Mechanical Hazard Check List

General: Pressure vessels, elevators, piping, electrical circuitry and panels.
Circuitry and panels, switches, grounding.
These are usually maintained in safe condition by the maintenance department. Some are inspected by outside agencies. If in doubt, or if any incident occurs, check with the responsible person.

Machine Hazards:
Accessibility of controls, emergency stop. Is operator off-balance?
Operated only by trained person.
Provision for lock-out and written procedure.
Accessibility lubrication points.
Check source of unusual noise. Arrange for noise control, if shouting is necessary to give instruction or to get help.
Proper clothing (no loose sleeves, jewelry, hair protection, etc.).
Personal protection, eyes, face, toes, etc.
Is the whole drive mechanism safely enclosed or protected?
Are points of operation guarded as well as possible?
If push stick, soft nosed forceps, suction cup, etc., is used, is feed device adequate and used properly?

Source: Supervisory Safety Seminar Handouts., Dr. Larry Klatt, Florida Atlantic University.

ditions are not in compliance with the law (and are thus unsafe) has a right to ask for an inspection of the facilities. Penalty provisions of the law apply only to employers, making the role of the supervisor even more important as a watchdog for unsafe conditions.

OSHA further requires that employers comply with all occupational safety and health standards and rules developed by the National Institute for Occupational Safety and Health. In order to assure compliance with the regulations, inspectors from the Department of Labor physically examine organizations across the country. These inspectors have the power to issue citations and levy fines on organizations whenever violations are found. As a supervisor, you cannot refuse to admit an OSHA inspector (although recent court decisions have somewhat limited the powers of these inspectors). The best way for a supervisor to deal with the OSHA is to cooperate and have all records up to date and available for inspection. If a safety violation is found, it should be corrected at once, not only to avoid penalties, but to prevent a mishap from occurring. Learn all you can about the OSHA regulations and your employer's policies concerning safety and the OSHA. Your compliance and your careful concern for safety will pay off for you, your employees, and your organization.

It is beyond the scope of this text to include a detailed explanation of the entire OSHA act. Regulations are constantly being updated as the federal government attempts to legislate safety in the work environment. The organizational safety office should provide each supervisor with updates to the law as they become available. Read these updates and then pass the information along to the employees. Safety really is everybody's job.

ACTION GUIDELINES FOR MAINTAINING SAFETY CONSCIOUSNESS

1. Become familiar with the safety regulations that affect your work environment. Determine the "whys" of safe behavior. If you can't tell an employee why performing the job is safer your way, you won't convince that employee to change and perform safely.

2. Coordinate your efforts with those of your safety director or the personnel department. The most successful safety programs have the support of top management and employees alike. Coordination is essential for maximum impact.

3. Ask the safety director or personnel department for current information on the injury and illness rates in your work area. Such specific information can help make the safety program a personal concern for each employee. Don't generalize; be specific.

4. Demonstrate safe practices, but don't "lecture" to employees. Use your imagination to create a safety-conscious environment.

5. Make safety a part of the job by updating the job descriptions to include responsibility for safety planning and maintenance. Follow up with safety checks with each employee and with some program of regular safety discussions. New employees should be given a "safety orientation" in addition to the regular orientation on responsibilities, benefits, and so on.

6. Get professional help to perform periodic safety checks on all equipment and work areas. Coordinate these checks with the safety director or personnel department.

7. When an accident or injury occurs, conduct a complete and open investigation of the entire incident, even if other authorities are conducting similar investigations. The information you gain from your investigation and those of the organization will be useful in helping you to brief your employees about what happened and to take steps to prevent a recurrence of the event.

8. Have adequate medical treatment materials and facilities on hand and periodically conduct "safety drills." Know the best routes to move help through the work area if an injury should occur that prevents the injured worker from being moved. Know precisely the procedure that the organization wishes to have followed when an injury occurs. Such a policy should be developed using the best information available; improvisation can result in a waste of valuable time when an injury does occur.

DISCUSSION QUESTIONS FOR MAINTAINING SAFETY
CONSCIOUSNESS

1. What are the major provisions of the OSHA that apply to your work area? What are the recent regulations or court decisions that also affect your safety program?

2. What, exactly, should you do when an injury occurs on the job? If this information is not readily available, begin at once to assemble the information.

3. Should the state and federal governments take a greater or smaller role in the administration and monitoring of safety practices?

4. How can employees be encouraged to develop safety ideas on their own?

5. As a supervisor, what is your responsibility with regard to safety?

ACTION EXERCISE FOR MAINTAINING SAFETY CONSCIOUSNESS

Perform an inventory of your work area. Identify safety precautions and those areas where potential safety violations may be present.

Next, list the various ways that the safety violations you identified can be corrected. In particular, identify those things that you as a supervisor can do and those things that the organization must do to overcome the unsafe or potentially dangerous conditions. If you are using this text as a part of a course in a college or university, perform the same sort of examination of the school environment. This practice can be most helpful in developing your own safety consciousness.

CASE 27. Perez Petrochemicals, Inc.

As with most companies manufacturing and dealing with noxious and combustible materials, Perez Petrochemicals has stringent safety rules. Many of these rules (and the practices which follow from them) are dictated by OSHA and other federal and state agencies. The chemical industry has long maintained its own standards for safety that go beyond the minimum levels set by law, for rather obvious reasons. In a typical chemical plant, there is an ever-present danger of an accident or a lapse of caution that could lead directly to a major explosion or to the escape of dangerous substances. This could result in injury and death to personnel and could result in major capital losses as well.

Anton Petrovski realizes the importance of safety regulations. As the supervisor on the swing shift at Perez, he has seen enough accidents and injuries to convince him of the value of proper safety training. Yet, as with most supervisors, he has constantly faced the problem of convincing his employees (especially the younger workers) of the importance of caution and safety around dangerous chemicals and equipment. Perhaps, he thinks, these young men and women simply haven't seen any accidents to impress the message on them. None of them has ever had to go to a young wife with three children and tell her that her husband was just killed in a "minor explosion" at the plant. Anton has had to do it on three different occasions, and each time was more painful to him than the last. Since coming to Perez as a supervisor ten years ago, Anton has had no fatal accidents in his department, and he has experienced only a few minor incidents that required hospitalization for some employees. The department's record (the best in the plant) is currently 1,623 days without a work hour lost due to accident or injury on the job. Anton is proud of this record, yet he is concerned because his employees don't seem very impressed by its meaning. Perhaps they will find out when something happens, but by then it may be too late.

Billy Thorburn has been Anton's major problem employee for some time. Billy is considered something of a "rebel" by the other employees, mainly because he delights in taking chances and violating minor safety rules whenever he thinks he can get away with it. He has been written up for violations four different times, but no one violation has been serious enough to require anything but a reprimand from the company safety director.

Walking past the cleaning equipment storage room, Anton has noticed Billy and another employee (also a troublemaker) smoking within five feet of an open vat of cleaning chemicals. This is, of course, a direct violation of company rules. Anton knows that if an explosion should occur with this particular chemical, the blast will be loud, fiery, and impressive, but it won't likely do any real damage to personnel or facilities. This, Anton thinks, might be the perfect opportunity to teach these two guys (and the rest of the department) a lesson they won't soon forget. Why not let them go ahead and smoke? If an accident should occur (and conditions are right for an accident), the scare might impress Billy enough to make him mend his ways. Anton could then use the accident to "bring home" the safety message he has been preaching. If he simply reports the smoking to personnel, Anton is sure the response will be just another warning.

1. If you were Anton, would you let the "accident" happen?
2. How should a supervisor deal with safety violations when warnings don't work?
3. Regardless of how you answered question 1, what are some of the consequences of letting the "accident" happen?

CASE 28.   Public Gas and Electric

"Safety's fine for the guys reading the meters and the people over at the pumping station, but my people never leave the office!"

Mary Ruth Munro's comment seems all too common to Ellen Bowers. Ellen is responsible for supervising five departments at Public Gas and Electric, including the billing section, where Mary Ruth is a supervisor. Her employees work at individual desks with a keyboard and display screen to review individual customer bills before the statements are printed and mailed out. Mary Ruth had worked in the department for six years before being promoted to a supervisor, and she is well-regarded by her subordinates and superiors as well. The men and women in her department receive the company's safety bulletin, but the general feeling in the department is that safety is someone else's problem.

Mary Ruth feels that this attitude (and her attitude as well) is a direct result of the emphasis of stories in the safety bulletin. Because the company operates three natural gas pumping stations and four coal-fired electric power generators (and is building a nuclear generating station), the stories and items in the bulletin usually deal with these situations. When a consumer-oriented environmental group began protesting the safety practices at the nuclear power stations in other parts of the country, PG & E began an intensive media campaign to inform the public about the company's current safety practices and the policies proposed for the new nuclear plant. The emphasis in the bulletin continues to be on industrial activities, and seldom is any mention made of the safety problems in the so-called "clean" environments, such as in offices and computer facilities.

Ellen Bowers has just returned from a company-sponsored safety conference put on by the University Continuing Education Division. She is interested in developing a greater safety consciousness among her employees and has expressed this desire to her five subordinates. These subordinates (including Mary Ruth), are to develop a very specific list of potential safety hazards or problem areas within their department for discussion and distribution at the next supervisor's meeting. It is after receiving this assignment that Mary Ruth has made her comment about safety being someone else's problem. Still, the assignment must be completed, and Mary Ruth is stumped. "Just what is the purpose of safety training in an office?"

1. Developing a "safety orientation" is vitally important. Despite the fact that your supervisory interests may not be in office management, one excellent way to develop your safety consciousness is to think about potential safety problems in areas outside of your own. With this in mind, develop a list of potential hazards or safety problems that could exist in Mary Ruth's office or in any office situation.
2. Is the Public Gas & Electric Company's apparent preoccupation with "industrial" safety a common situation? Does such a preoccupation have any particular disadvantages?
3. If you were in Ellen Bowers' position, how would you design a program to encourage your supervisors and their employees to become more safety conscious?

Keeping Order and Discipline

12

Objectives

This chapter is important for all supervisors. After studying this chapter, you will be able to

1. Better identify problems before they become serious.

2. Develop a system for handling complaints.

3. Understand how a grievance procedure works under a labor-management contract.

4. Discuss the supervisor's role as a counselor.

5. Differentiate between directive and nondirective counseling and understand the elements of each.

6. Discuss the supervisor's role in discipline.

7. List the advantages of positive discipline.

IF THERE IS one part of supervision that supervisors (new and experienced alike) agree is a major problem, it is in keeping order and maintaining discipline. This is a negative side of supervision that is only occasionally discussed in supervisory training. It is usually assumed that anyone can keep order, but in fact, this may be the most difficult part of your job. One experienced supervisor described how a first encounter with a discipline problem can change your attitude about employees and be reflected in how they handle future problems: "No supervisor is immune to discipline problems and to employees whose attitudes are not in agreement with those of the organization. It's how they handle those first problems which will influence their career as a supervisor."

DISCIPLINE—WHAT IT MEANS TO THE
SUPERVISOR AND TO THE SUBORDINATE

Discipline is defined in a number of ways, all of which seem to focus on behavior in compliance with rules and work rules. Most supervisors agree that discipline must be both preventive and punitive—characteristics that some experts call positive and negative discipline. *Preventive discipline* is designed to help employees become aware of the need to follow rules and to avoid possible injury to others. The purpose of preventive discipline is to develop in subordinates an attitude of "self-discipline." Self-discipline exists whenever employees are willing to follow the rules without being forced. *Punitive discipline* involves specific punishment for offenses. Supervisors must be willing to use both methods if they wish to maintain order and discipline in their work area.

Identifying the Problems
Before They Become Serious

There is an old football saying that "the best defense is a good offense." This idea certainly applies to supervision. Any supervisor would like to have a situation where nothing ever goes wrong and where employees are always pleased with their supervisor and their work environment. Unfortunately, this doesn't happen in the real world. In every organization, problems arise at the supervisory level which must be identified and solved. Failure to recognize problems at this level can result in more serious problems, such as work slowdown, strikes, or even sabotage. Generally, poor morale will be reflected in grievances against the firm or the immediate supervisor. Employees who feel that they have a legitimate complaint and that no one pays any attention to them, will "find a way to be heard." In most organizations, there is a formal grievance procedure which describes how grievances are to be handled. We'll discuss this topic later in more detail.

What is most important for supervisors is to have the ability to recognize complaints that have real substance. All of us have certain dissatisfactions about our jobs at one time or another. You may have thought to yourself, "I wish this machine worked more smoothly," or "I wish we had next Friday off." These are common with all individuals. However, when a dissatisfaction is allowed to continue, it becomes a complaint, no matter whether it is spoken or put in writing and brought to the attention of the supervisor. This is a big point. Acting upon complaints at this time can often result in the elimination of grievances. A complaint becomes a grievance when formal written action takes place. In a union work situation, specific procedures govern the grievance system. In a nonunion work situation, some established format for filing grievances is usually used. If a complaint is important to the employee, management should know about it and try to deal with it satisfactorily.

Complaints and grievances from employees are ways of telling the system that employees perceive some inequity or injustice. All too often, new supervisors don't take a positive attitude toward complaints, and they are often unwilling to invest their time in identifying what the real problems might be. A supervisor should never disregard a complaint because it does not appear to be grounded in facts. Employees are just as upset about what they *feel* is true as they would be if a situation actually were true. If it seems true to the employees, it means the supervisor may have a problem.

In cases in which employees feel that they cannot complain about certain issues, a second issue is substituted, one that is "appropriate" to complain about. For example, a supervisor in a Midwestern insurance company tells this story about an employee whom the supervisor determined had been mistakenly left off a list of employees who were to be publicly recognized for their efforts on behalf of the company's community charity drive. Although the employee was very hurt, she felt it would be wrong to make a fuss over being omitted from the program. Instead, every day for the next two weeks, the employee complained to her supervisor about the temperature in the room, a draft at her desk, and a variety of other nonexisting problems. The employee was reacting against the company in a manner that she thought was acceptable. What she would rather have complained about was that she had not been given the credit for the work she had performed.

Why Have a System for Handling Complaints?

As we see in the above example, what you observe is not always what is really happening. The idea of having a system that reports complaints up the chain of command stems from the need of middle- and upper-level management to know all of what is happening at the other levels. Upper and middle management have plenty of reports to tell them how productivity and costs are behaving. One more report on the organization health of the employees won't overwork them. Such a report helps make managers who are removed from the work place more aware of their employees' problems and frustrations. Such a communication system usually includes a summary of the number of complaints on a specific issue, their source, the supervisor's evaluation of the problem, and the supervisor's recommendations. Figure 12-1 is an example of one such complaint form. Use it as a starting point in preparing a form to fit your organization or department. The important thing about any form is the extent to which it enables the supervisor to communicate to the managers about the problems that employees perceive.

Employees who complain may actually be better employees than those who don't. Employees who feel that they can go to their supervisors with a problem or complaint are more likely to be able to get their problems out in the open. This permits the supervisor to begin work on getting the problem solved. That old adage that "your problems are my problems" is absolutely true. If an employee feels that something is wrong, the employee has a problem. That problem is bound to begin to affect the employee's work and the work of fellow workers. An unattended problem seldom cures itself. Sometimes the problem will simply go away, but in most cases it will not. As the supervisor, you may now be experiencing a situation of decreasing productivity and increasing costs and have no idea of the cause. Many inexperienced supervisors react by trying to cure the symptoms (declining productivity and increasing costs), and they may use methods that eventually aggravate the real problem. The result is that the problem still remains, but everyone is now upset over new problems.

When employees feel that they can come to their supervisor with a problem or complaint and the supervisor will take some action on the problem, they may be doing you a real favor. Employees who complain are giving you the opportunity to work on a problem *before* it gets out of hand. Experienced supervisors feel that some of the greatest problems they face come from their failure to deal with what they thought were frivolous or groundless complaints. Other employees reacted to the supervisor's attitude instead of to the complaint itself. The results are often unfortunate.

Employees expect their organizations to have a system of justice,

FIGURE 12–1 Complaint Report

To: Department

From: Supervisor's name
        Department or Division Name

Specific complaint (in the words of the employee as much as possible) _____
_____
_____
_____
_____

Similar complaints in the past year (be as specific as possible) _____
_____
_____
_____
_____

Your evaluation of the seriousness of the problem(s) outlined in the complaint _____
_____
_____
_____
_____
_____

What actions have you taken in dealing with the problem(s) outlined in the complaint? _____
_____
_____
_____
_____

What additional actions would you recommend be taken to solve the problem? By whom, and for what purpose?

Recommended actions	By
1.	1.

For the purpose of
1.

that is, a way of handling their problems. Employees expect that their supervisor will not be a dictator. They expect to exercise their right to be heard when they feel an injustice has occurred. They also feel that they are entitled to an appeal when their supervisor has taken actions against them which they feel are perhaps unfair. These rights and assumptions are merely a part of the society we find ourselves in during the last quarter of the twentieth century.

THE SUPERVISOR AS COUNSELOR

One of the most significant functions that supervisors perform is dealing with employees who themselves may be a source of problems. This involves disciplinary counseling. Supervisors must get closer to the employees and their problems if they want to avoid a glut of discipline problems.

There are generally two types of counseling used by supervisors: directive and nondirective. Whether or not a supervisor wants to be a counselor, psychologists tell us that he or she is looked to for advice. The position as formal head of a group creates for some employees the feeling that the supervisor really does know what's best. This is a very important responsibility and should not be taken lightly. Counseling is a tool that the supervisor should use to improve the working relationships on the job and to prevent problems before they arise.

Directive counseling is very simple and something every supervisor does every day. In fact, we might conclude that directive counseling is much like the basic concept of supervision itself. In directive counseling, the supervisor listens to the employee's problem, decides what the employee should do, and instructs the employee on how to proceed. All training involves directive counseling. This type of counseling is extremely useful when the supervisor is the source of knowledge or expertise for the group being supervised. For example, if the supervisor alone knows how to operate a machine or do a procedure, the supervisor will find employees seeking advice and counsel on problems related to that expertise. Directive counseling is generally limited to those situations where employees respect the opinion and knowledge of the "expert" and where they are willing to seek advice. Supervisors enjoy the recognition given them by employees who voluntarily seek their advice. Yet, this doesn't usually help with problem employees. The problem employee is not likely to respect the judgment of the supervisor. Telling the problem employee the answer, even when you are right and the employee is wrong, does not result in a change in behavior.

Nondirective counseling is more difficult to learn and more time consuming to do, but it can be very useful in dealing with problem employees. Nondirective counseling methods do not involve the supervisor directly helping employees by giving advice. Rather, employees are encouraged to express their true feelings about a situation or problem. Through this expression, employees gain a better understanding of themselves. This method requires that employees develop solutions to their own problems. Supervisors must recognize that there are some employee problems that they (the supervisors) cannot solve. Experience suggests that supervisors should help employees find professional help when problems such as alcoholism, drugs, or serious family difficulties interfere with work activities and threaten the stability of the work group. These "big three" problems are better handled by men and women who have years of professional experience developing the best techniques for dealing with these problems. However, the supervisor may be the person in the best position to bring about change in employees' behavior when their problems are work related.

With a nondirective style, the supervisor must learn the basic rules of counseling: The employee must be in control of the counseling session. It is the employee's problem, and the employee alone can solve it. Never use your position as supervisor to "put down" an employee. Approach the employee as an equal during the counseling session. Emphasize to the employee that he or she will be making the ultimate decision and that he or she will be able to make better decisions in the future if they learn now to act independently. As a supervisor, it is your responsibility to help by asking probing questions and by listening openly. If you're unsure what the employee means, ask for clarification. Focus on the feelings behind statements. Ask the employee to restate ideas and be sure that you both understand what is being said. Learn to use phrases like ". . . are you saying?" or ". . . did you say . . . ?" or ". . . does that statement imply that . . . ?" When the supervisor uses these techniques, the employee will begin to better understand his or her own feelings.

It is not useful to have the supervisor act as if he or she is judging the feelings of the employee. Neither is it useful to praise or blame. In fact, the supervisor should try not to show emotion when an employee is discussing personal feelings. Very often, the employee will be testing your attitude. If you overreact, and lecture the employee on how his or her attitude is out of line, the employee will simply write you off. What you must do is *listen*. Listen for what the employee is saying, how he or she is saying it, and what the employee is *not* saying. After a while, you will develop the ability to "read between the lines." You'll find yourself able to ask probing questions which will help the employee to see the problem clearly. Ask questions which emphasize the deeper feelings of the individual about the *real* problems and not just the symptoms. Never push so hard as to antagonize the employee. Nothing is ever gained through argument.

Counseling is preventive supervision, because its effects may never be directly measured or observed. Indirectly, however, counseling may help in creating a positive work atmosphere. Counseling can help the employee to develop self-confidence. It is a very personal form of communication, because it allows the employee to reduce anxieties by talking about problems with a supervisor who is sympathetic and supportive. After talking, the employee may be able to view the problem in such a way that a solution becomes obvious. A counselor should do little but listen, while the employee finds his or her own solution. By asking for clarification and interpretation of the meaning behind statements, the supervisor can help the employee see what he or she is really saying. When you listen, search for the assumptions that the person speaking is making. The key to many feelings lies in assumptions that are deeply rooted in an individual's mind and feelings but are not really based on facts. For example, while interviewing an employee in an organization with low employee morale, we asked him why he had a negative feeling about the plant's management. When asked to clarify his statements by giving examples, he couldn't recall any. When asked why he had no trust in supervisors, he recalled that when he was a young man, his father told him that management was no friend of the ordinary worker. Although years had passed, the father's words were still accepted: "Management cannot be trusted." Facts do not always overcome feelings. Any supervisor who is armed only with facts and is unwilling to deal with employees' feelings is doomed to disappointment. Counseling can help supervisors reach all employees, and not just on a surface level. Being able to prevent problems is much more productive than being forced to react to problems that are out of control.

HOW TO DELIVER THE BAD NEWS

What do you say when you must deliver bad news during a discipline interview? Delivering bad news makes most managers feel very uncomfortable.[1] As a result, they mishandle interviews in which bad news must be delivered.

Much can be learned about giving bad news from the way bad news letters are written.

In a bad news letter, the bad news is likely to put the receiver in a poor frame of mind. The letter writer must convey the bad news message without further antagonizing the receiver. This means sending the bad news while maintaining whatever good will can be salvaged.

In a bad news interview it is best to take an indirect approach. Using a slower pace and emphasizing the positive at the beginning and end of the interview can help overcome some of the negative effects of the bad news. This is the "sandwich effect"—the bad news is delivered between the good news.

For example, suppose a person's request for a transfer must be turned down. Assuming that you want the employee to remain motivated and productive, you should give the message in a way that minimizes negative effects.

As you begin the interview, briefly outline some of the employee's strengths. Point out some of the features of his or her work profile that makes this person a sound prospect for future promotion or transfer consideration. The bad news can then be given using the "you" viewpoint. This will help the employee understand the reasons for the turndown from his or her point of view. The interview can then be closed on a more constructive note.

There are problems with using a sandwich approach for presenting bad news. Many people want to receive their bad news directly. Because you may feel capable of handling personal bad news without the sandwich, you may also want to treat everyone in a similar way. However, psychological studies show that when bad news must be delivered, the sandwich approach is the most effective way.

It is important when delivering bad news that you separate the person from the behavior. The interviewee should be shown the "bigger picture" and helped to identify certain behaviors which are counterproductive. It is also important to reduce as much uncertainty as possible. People should be told what to expect and how to behave if they want to be more favorably considered.

When giving bad news messages to people in an interview situation, it is wise to avoid references to the bad news that will be coming. This is a strategy very similar to writing a bad news letter. You should try as much as possible to avoid statements such as, "You are not going to like what I am going to say in a few minutes." Statements such as this needlessly raise anxiety and do very little good.

Often, we use such statements to prepare ourselves to deliver a bad news message. This sort of message does not really help the receiver understand or accept the bad news. It is better to hide negative messages by first building your case and explaining reasons with a "you" viewpoint. When the time comes for the bad news, make it as specific as possible.

At the close of a bad news interview, try to make it upbeat. Don't recall the problem or continue to back-slap in an attempt to overcome the negative effect of the bad news. It is far better to leave the interviewee feeling that he or she has had a full hearing than it is to have you suggest that you really wish you could have helped the person.

If you have successfully reduced some of the personal threat while delivering the bad news message, such a closing may undo all the good work that you have already done. Don't make the other person appear stupid or unworthy. Make it clear throughout the interview that the other person's interests are also your main concern.

Interviews that contain bad news are unpleasant for both the interviewer and the interviewee. However, it is part of your job as a manager to learn the techniques of successfully conveying bad news. It probably will never become easy for you to conduct a bad news interview, but by learning the techniques you will at least be able to make the bad news easier for the interviewee to handle.

DISCIPLINE

Every supervisor wishes that his or her work group will conduct itself in an orderly fashion and will follow the prescribed rules of the organization. When this happens, good discipline exists. However, when order does exist, this does not necessarily mean that employees are following the rules of the organization willingly. Three discipline conditions can exist in an organization. First, rules and regulations are being followed by the employees because they feel the rules are reasonable and that it is to their personal advantage to do what is right. This situation is

Photo courtesy of Exxon Corporation.

CONSTRUCTIVE DISCIPLINE

called *self-discipline*. Every supervisor should work to create a situation where employees can develop self-discipline. The second condition exists when employees are following the rules and regulations of the organization because they fear the results if they disobey. Too many supervisors believe that this is a reasonable, stable situation and the way things ought to be. In reality *discipline by fear* may be the most dangerous situation of all, because the supervisor never really knows when the fear of punishment will cease to restrain employees. Everything looks calm, but the supervisor cannot measure the latent hostility toward the organization, nor can the supervisor know when trouble might begin. The third condition is where an employee violates the rules and regulations of the organization. This can happen either because of a chronic troublemaker, or because of a random occurrence of misbehavior.

Once we discover and admit that a lack of discipline exists, the next step for the supervisor is to determine the "why's" of such behavior.

Reasons for Discipline Problems

Some of the major reasons that employees fail to conform to the established rules and regulations of any organization are

1. The rules and regulations are viewed by employees as meaningless. "Why do we have that stupid rule?" indicates a failure on the part of managers to effectively communicate the reasons behind the rules. It is important to recognize that there is a great deal of difference between an employee's being told about a rule and his or her learning the why behind the rules. A "no smoking" rule or sign has no meaning if the employees do not know the reasoning behind the rule (that is, if the rule is violated, an explosion may occur).

2. Violation of the rules occurs when employees no longer fear punishment for violations. Depending on an employee to fear punishment is not sufficient to ensure that all rules will be followed. In one example, an employee seemingly had had enough "static" from the overbearing supervisor. Heated words were exchanged between the two men and the supervisor warned the employee to control himself or suffer the consequences (in this case, being fired). A fight broke out, and the employee "decked" the supervisor with a well-placed right hand. Staring down at the semiconscious supervisor, the employee said, "That's OK, I planned to quit anyway." Such situations are (hopefully) rare, but they do emphasize the futility of depending on fear of punishment to force employees to follow the rules.

3. There are employees who will violate rules because they feel underpaid or perhaps because they feel that management discriminates against them. Much of the employee theft in organizations is directly related to employees who feel it is all right to take tools, supplies, or merchandise for their personal use. "They owe it to me. If I were working for (the competition), I could be making more money." This

rationale reflects management's failure to make clear exactly what the organization's discipline policy is, why it exists, and what the consequences are when it is violated.

4. By being a discipline problem or creating undetected discipline problems, some employees see this as an excellent way to retaliate against their supervisors. The boss reprimands an employee for being late again this week. To retaliate, the employee misdirects some important correspondence or misuses some equipment, which causes expense and delay. There are as many ways to retaliate as there are people doing jobs. Yet, it is important to understand that discipline is related to the human-relations efforts of supervisors.

5. Some violations of the rules are truly unintentional and reflect a lapse in memory or caution. We find most of the discipline problems as well as the bulk of the safety problems in organizations in this category. Forgetting to comply with safety regulations is generally unintentional. It is, however, an indication that the supervisor needs to re-emphasize the reasons for the safety regulations. A brief presentation or discussion once each month on the "why" behind specific rules will do much to reduce the time lost to accidents.

Steps in Disciplining Employees

Every organization has its own rules and regulations, including a written schedule of punishments for various offenses. The steps in the disciplinary process vary according to the offense and the individual committing the offense. Some very serious offenses involve immediate dismissal, while others involve a whole series of actions (counseling, oral warnings, written warnings, disciplinary lay-offs, even final dismissal or discharge). The following chart summarizes the offenses and punishments typical of most organizations.

A complete set of rules for an organization includes every possible offense. It is essential that every *employee* and every *supervisor* know the results of violating the work rules. Supervisors must follow these steps in punishing employees for work violations. Consistency and fairness in the application of punishment are basic to maintaining morale among other employees.

So far, we have focused on discipline problems and the nature of an effective discipline program. It is hoped that most discipline problems can be reduced by identifying potential problems early and then effectively handling employee complaints and grievances.

Positive Discipline

Positive discipline is based on the belief that employees who know the rules and the reasons behind the rules will conform more willingly to those rules. If employees find that they are rewarded in some way for

TABLE 12-1

OFFENSE	1st Offense	2nd Offense	3rd Offense	4th Offense
Theft	Suspension	Dismissal		
Gambling	Written warning	Suspension	Dismissal	
Drinking on the job or drunk on the job	Written warning and counseling	Suspension	Dismissal	
Fighting	Suspension	Dismissal		
Insubordination	Suspension	Dismissal		
Sabotage	Dismissal			
Chronic Absenteeism	Oral warning	Written warning	Suspension	Dismissal
Chronic Tardiness	Oral warning	Written warning	Suspension	Dismissal

following the rules, they will be further motivated to comply. The Army gives "good conduct medals" which serve to demonstrate to the others in the work groups that behavior in compliance with the regulations of the organization is not only required but also rewarded.

If an employee wants to work in a peaceful, disciplined environment, positive discipline must be practiced by the supervisor, and rewards for conforming to the regulations must be evident and available. Employees who are serious about their jobs do not want to work in conflict. They also know that the individual who steals tools from the toolcrib today may tomorrow steal from purses or lockers. Thus, there are many group forces that a supervisor can use to help develop an atmosphere of positive discipline.

Ten Keys to Effective Discipline

The following rules and ideas can be applied by all supervisors. Because your relationship with your employees is severely put to the test when discipline problems disrupt the work environment, the application of some of these ideas to your situation can prove profitable.

1. *Don't be a discipline ostrich.* Never be indulgent and fall into the pattern of overlooking violations. When you recognize a violation, immediately take action to reprimand or overcome the difficulty. If you fail, you are simply inviting continued violation and possible confrontation

later. Other employees not directly involved in the discipline situation will begin to question your ability and fairness as a supervisor if discipline is put off or ignored. The employees will begin to assume that all the organization's regulations are worthless. Borderline employees will be drawn into rule violations by the examples of uncontrolled violation around them. The situation can quickly get out of hand.

2. *Become "Caesar's wife."* Your behavior as a supervisor must be above reproach. There can be no question in the minds of the employees about your personal adherence to the rules and regulations. You cannot expect employees to practice self-discipline when their supervisor does not have an equal commitment. Seeing the supervisor "bend" the rules promotes lax behavior throughout the work group.

3. *Practice the "hot stove" rule.* Douglas McGregor developed a very useful analogy for supervisors facing discipline problems. Basically, he said that when you touch a hot stove, *the reaction is immediate.* There is a clear cause-and-effect relationship. Also, everyone knows that when you touch a hot stove, you will be burned. The result of the action is well known in advance by everyone. *Discipline should be based on known rules.* Each and every time you place your hand on the hot stove you will be burned. *Discipline should be consistent.* No matter who touches the stove, that person will be burned. You will be burned because of what you do, not because of who you are. *Discipline must be impersonal.* McGregor's concept of the hot stove is easy to remember, yet it is not always followed by supervisors. The failure to act immediately or inconsistent or partial action will retard rather than improve discipline progress.

4. *Never lose control.* The only acceptable time to touch an employee is when you are required to stop a fight or give aid to an injured or sick employee. Except when your supervisory authority has been publicly challenged, employees should be disciplined in private. The public reprimand of an employee can cause the employee to resist your efforts at discipline, because he or she may feel that this public display has caused a personal loss of dignity before fellow employees. The resentment may cause the employee to overreact to protest the loss of pride, and this in turn can cause more discipline problems later.

If other employees viewing a public reprimand feel that your actions are too severe for the violation, the disciplined employee will quickly become a martyr, and the reason for the discipline will be effectively lost. If the public discipline is seen by employees as your attempt to humiliate their fellow workers, your future efforts at team building will be wasted. Group morale will suffer, and effective control will be lost for some time.

In situations where your supervisory authority has been directly and publicly challenged, it is essential that you regain and maintain your personal self-control and act in a calm, mature manner. Your failure to act will result in a loss of respect for you, and your authority will be further eroded. It is hoped that this situation will not often arise. When it does, remember to beware of taking steps backwards. Hold your ground physically and managerially. Your behavior in this situation will affect how others view your authority in the future.

5. *Be instructive.* When you are required to take disciplinary action, the employee being disciplined should be told exactly why the action is taking place. The supervisor should tell the employee that other alternatives are available for redress of a grievance if that individual does not agree with your assessment of the discipline. Don't hide anything from employees, especially when their discipline is at stake. Be open, and discuss the situation in a mature and reasonable way.

6. *Be firm.* If you expect the employee to feel that discipline is important, you must maintain an open, honest attitude about the reasons for the discipline. Never joke about discipline. If you act as if the matter is serious, the employee will respect your actions and your authority. But remember that being firm does not mean being harsh.

7. *Stay out of the employee's private life.* An employee's private life is just that—private. It does not have any bearing on your assessment of that employee's performance on the job. As a supervisor, you are responsible for the work being done under your direction. It is essential that you avoid making judgments about employees based on nonrelevant information. Personal value judgments about employees can often lead to discrimination against employees, with an eventual loss of respect for you as a supervisor.

8. *State the rules and regulations in a positive manner.* It is important to avoid the extreme negative feelings that many employees have about rules and regulations. State these rules in terms of positive actions and expectations. Statements such as "Employees are expected to abide by all safety regulations and be safety-minded at all times," or "Employees are expected to respect the property rights of the organization and the rights of fellow employees" are much better than the standard "NO . . ." rules that we often use. If they are put in a positive and mature manner, rules and regulations can be effective guides to positive actions.

9. *Don't be a discipline magician.* Avoid becoming the supervisor who "pulls rules out of his hat." One of the keys to success in maintaining discipline is to be sure that all employees are aware of all the rules and their meaning. Keep everything out in the open, and don't spring new rules or variations on employees *after* a violation has been committed. Give employees every opportunity to be in compliance with the organization's rules and regulations.

10. *Be precise.* Whatever your organization's procedures for discipline may involve, be sure you are precise in your interpretation and application of those procedures. Begin with an accurate statement of the problem. State clearly what has occurred, which rules were violated, and how they were violated. Determine the relevant circumstances and who was actually involved. If more than one person was involved, determine

the role that each played in the violation. Never jump to conclusions. Search for all viewpoints before making a judgment about guilt, fault, or blame. Your employees will respect your efforts when they see your concern for truth, and not a desire for easy disposition of a difficult situation.

ACTION GUIDELINES FOR KEEPING ORDER AND DISCIPLINE

1. Recognize that keeping order in the work area is a basic requirement of the supervisor's job. Disciplining employees is never pleasant, but it is often necessary.

2. Be sure that all employees in the work group are familiar with the rules and regulations and that they know the "whys" behind the rules.

3. Remember that you cannot depend on the fear of discipline to keep the employees in line. Once employees no longer fear the penalties, the "penalty-prone" supervisor will find it difficult to continue maintaining order.

4. Watch for employees who feel that the organization "owes them something." At some point, they often decide to help themselves to it.

5. Don't avoid taking actions when an employee violates a rule. Overlooking violations will do nothing except lower the esteem in which you are held by your employees.

6. Never violate the rules yourself. You can't establish two sets of rules. To be an effective supervisor, don't put yourself above your employees, especially when it comes to the rules and policies of the organization.

7. When you must discipline an employee, never lose control. Handle the situation privately, and treat the offending individual with dignity. Your behavior in these unpleasant situations establishes your character in the minds of the members of the work group.

8. Recognize that complaints are often warnings about potential serious problems. Learn to spot legitimate complaints, and take prompt action before the trouble gets out of hand.

9. Try to settle problems at your level, rather than forcing the matter up to higher levels. Naturally, not all problems can be solved at the supervisory level, especially when complex and legal issues are involved. However, your success as a supervisor (and your potential for future promotions) is directly related to your ability to keep such difficulties from requiring the involvement of higher authorities.

10. Develop your ability to counsel comfortably. Practice and learn everything you can about how you can better serve the needs of your employees by helping them deal with their problems.

DISCUSSION QUESTIONS FOR KEEPING ORDER AND DISCIPLINE

1. What is the best strategy for dealing with troublemakers?

2. Why should supervisors make middle management aware of employee complaints?

3. What role does the shop steward play in a union grievance procedure?

4. What are some of the techniques that work for you in nondirective counseling with your employees? Why are those techniques successful?

5. What are some of the major employee reasons for discipline problems?

6. Which are some of the most effective keys for discipline?

ACTION EXERCISE FOR KEEPING ORDER AND DISCIPLINE

1. Break into discussion groups of three to six and assume that you have just been selected as a committee to write a new set of rules and regulations for the school or organization. Using the simple chart below, write as complete a set of rules and regulations as possible. Where differences of opinion exist, make note as to what issues are involved and the nature of the differences.

2. List the differences of opinion that exist and the degree of difference.

3. Using the same group, write an introduction to the rules and regulations you just wrote, stressing what you believe to be guides to a new supervisor or school administrator on how to apply these rules and regulations.

Rule or Regulation	PUNISHMENT OR ACTION			
	1st Offense	2nd Offense	3rd Offense	4th Offense
1. _____				
2. _____				
3. _____				
4. _____				
5. _____				
6. _____				
7. _____				

Continued

Rule or Regulation	PUNISHMENT OR ACTION			
	1st Offense	2nd Offense	3rd Offense	4th Offense
8. _____				
9. _____				
10. _____				
11. _____				
12. _____				
13. _____				
14. _____				
15. _____				

 CASES

CASE 29. Mammoth Manufacturing

Mammoth Manufacturing recently won a contract to produce a complete line of integrated circuits. The people who were hired for these jobs were mostly inexperienced in a work environment and young (about 75 percent were under 25). Most were recent high school graduates with no previous work experience. Ida Wilson, the manager for a group of twenty of the employees (mostly women), came in one afternoon to her supervisor, Ralph Herrera, with her problem. "Ralph, how would you handle a problem like this?" Ralph could see Ida was frustrated. "Five women in my unit have slipped into some bad work habits, Ralph. They come into work on time or a few minutes late, but they have their hair in curlers. Then, they go to the ladies room and don't return for work for ten to fifteen minutes. Then, there's the coffee. They all sit and drink a cup of coffee before they start work. Sometimes it is 8:20 before the whole group is working." Ida seemed relieved to be discussing the problem. "The older, experienced workers resent this carefree attitude and behavior. In fact, on Friday one of them asked me to do something about it. I told them that they might catch on to the proper behavior if one of the older and more experienced women had a talk with them about proper work behavior."

1. What would you say to Ida if you were her supervisor?
2. What are her alternatives?
3. Should Ralph take direct action, or should he simply advise Ida?

CASE 30. Mammoth Manufacturing, Part II

Time passed. The younger women did not "fall into line." Instead, the older employees also began to come in later and start work slower. In fact, the group's productivity was beginning to reflect their behavior. Ida was summoned by Ralph to report on why her group was 8 percent behind last month's production quota. "It's your responsibility, Ida. Let's get this play-time cleared up and get back on track!"

1. What does Ida do now?
2. How does she reestablish her supervisory authority?

CASE 31. The Practical Joke

The employees sat back and took a good look at their new supervisor, Jack Newland. Chuckling to themselves, they commented that they had more years experience working on oil rigs than that kid had had on earth. Their fears and suppositions were confirmed when Jack was introduced. He was a college graduate, with only two summers' experience in supervisory positions, neither of which was in oilfield technology. In school, he majored in manufacturing, and his experience was in a local machine shop.

According to top management, Jack's strength was in planning and scheduling, and the front office thought he would be a big help in implementing new administrative procedures.

Jack's new employees were nothing like himself. In fact, they were totally different. The youngest man in the work group was forty-five years old, and the oldest sixty-eight. Few of them had even finished grade school, but they had one thing Jack didn't. All of them had twenty-five years or more experience in the oilfields. There was little about drilling and drilling equipment these men didn't know. As a group, they were proud of the work they had done and the experience they had. They were rough men, used to living in bad conditions and making their rules as they went.

Some of the group members decided to give Jack the "new supervisor's test" to see what kind of man he really was. Elmer Borman called Jack over to the rigging shed Friday afternoon. Jack had just finished his first full week on the job and was looking forward to his first day off. Elmer began, "Mr. Newland, how should we rig the hydrostatic armature to the boom hitch?" Naturally, neither of these parts existed, except in Elmer's mind. The group wanted to see Jack's reaction, and it didn't take long in coming.

Jack stammered, looking uncomfortable. He knew the words sounded familiar, but he hadn't the foggiest idea what Elmer was talking about. Still, his pride wouldn't let him admit that he didn't know. "After all," Jack said later, "supervisors should know what's happening on the job."

Just as Jack was ready to go back to his bunk to pull out an old textbook, Joe Sweeny and Elmer began to laugh. Soon the entire room was roaring with laughter, and Elmer was falling to the floor. Jack's face turned about four shades of red, from embarrassed to mad.

Jack lost his composure. "You think I'm a big joke, huh? Just wait until Monday, and we'll see who's laughing then!"

1. Should a new supervisor in this kind of situation expect to be "initiated" into the job?

CHALLENGES
OF
SUPERVISION

Successful Conflict Management

Objectives

This chapter deals with the thorny problem of handling—and hopefully managing—conflicts. After reading this chapter and studying the strategies and examples, you will be able to

1. View conflict as a "process" rather than as an isolated incident or problem to be tackled by itself.

2. Understand better why many managerial conflicts develop.

3. Deal with the fact that not all conflicts can be solved or resolved through better communication, and that in some cases, better communication can actually make the conflict worse.

4. Analyze five major strategies for handling conflict, and be able to evaluate each of these strategies in terms of their potential benefit and cost to you.

5. Take a "problem solving" or "optimizing" approach to the conflicts that you face.

MANAGEMENT AND CONFLICT go hand in hand.[1] Because we associate "conflict" with concepts of aggression, hostility, or warfare, the word suggests negative and unproductive behavior which must be avoided. However, in today's business world, conflict can also have some very positive outcomes—if it is managed correctly.

For example, creative conflict over differences in business policies or operations can result in better planning, working, and greater profits. Within an organization, properly managed conflict between a manager and staff can help produce more interest in the organization's affairs. Conflict can also keep the employees "on their toes" and aware of their responsibilities.

Dealing with conflict may sound like risky business, but it is often better than dealing with a lethargic, "who cares" attitude that can infect employees. A frequent comment from managers in our conflict management seminars is: "If we didn't have some occasional conflict in my department, I'd have to create some just to keep my blood moving."

WHAT IS CONFLICT?

Conflict is any situation in which the goals, methods, aims, or objectives of two or more parties are in opposition. It is also a situation in which potential solutions appear to be mutually exclusive.

HOW DO CONFLICTS DEVELOP?

Many conflicts arise over the allocation of scarce resources. If the personnel department wants a major educational program this year, and the supervisors believe that this year is the time for major reorganization, conflict is likely to occur over how to spend the firm's limited time and money. The choice of spending for a major education program may mean little or no funding for reorganization, and vice versa.

Conflicts may develop over standards, location of a meeting, the management handling of the budget, the roles of various supervisors and paid officers, or even the color of the carpet in divisional headquarters. While some of these conflicts have a major impact on an organization and others seem trivial, none can be completely ignored for very long.

COMMUNICATION AND CONFLICT

Many conflicts are caused by one person's ignorance of another person's position. For instance, a supervisor reads a statement issued by the training director and interprets the statement in a negative way. Yet, on further examination, both people want the same things. Their conflict stems from a problem with semantics and can be resolved by better communication. Therefore, communication is often cited as a major strategy for resolving conflict.

It is well advised to improve communication if the source of a conflict is ignorance of another's similar position. However, suppose that two parties in a conflict who feel that if they more clearly explain their positions, will find some common ground, begin to communicate, and discover that they are in fact miles apart. Furthermore, suppose that they also discover just how strongly the other person feels about his or her position. When they become armed with this new and more accurate information, the battle lines are hardened and the conflict intensifies.

Worse still is the situation where two parties are in apparent agreement on every detail except one. To resolve the remaining barriers to total agreement, they begin to communicate more about their respective positions. In doing so, they may discover that what they thought was agreement was really ignorance of each other's conflicting position. Now the battle really begins.

In general, good, open communication is better than poor or nonexistent communication. But don't be misled into believing that better communication automatically leads to reduced conflict.

THE LINGERING NATURE OF CONFLICT

Our usual goal is to resolve a conflict, and get on with productive activity. We think that when conflict is settled, it goes away and is no longer a concern. Yet, few conflicts are really resolved with no trace or aftermath.

Often, one person wins and another person loses. In a democratic system, the losing side gets behind the winner and the conflict is resolved. But do losers always forget their differences and join hands in a spirit of solidarity? More often there is some residual of resentment to any conflict "resolution." The loser is likely to feel that "they beat me this time, but I'm not through yet. I'll go along for appearances, and wait for another time to make my move." This loser attitude of "don't get mad, get even" is the reason why few win-lose conflicts can be resolved permanently.

Throughout history the "resolution" to one conflict became the basis for future conflicts. The Treaty of Versailles "ended" World War I. Yet many historians feel that the treaty's conditions and stipulations created the springboard for the rise of Hitler and World War II. In the same way, the "solution" to the conflict over the carpet color at the office may leave a loser unwilling to rest until he or she has "showed 'em they can't treat me that way!"

CONFLICT MANAGEMENT

The challenge to the supervisor in handling conflict is to behave in a way that will minimize the damaging effects of the present conflict and minimize the possibility of future ones. There are several commonly used strategies for managing conflict, and each of these strategies has long-range and short-range implications that the supervisor should know about.

Compromise

The role of compromise in conflict resolution or management is interesting. Often we use compromise to resolve a conflict. Both parties agree they can't get everything they want, and they settle for something instead of nothing. A well-designed compromise that benefits both parties and reduces hostility is an effective way to manage conflict. However, a compromise does not guarantee that future conflicts will not develop.

Suppose there is a conflict over who will head a fact-finding committee. A compromise is reached, where a person from one department gets the appointment, while a person from another department agrees to wait until another time. The bargain is struck, the committee is formed, and everyone is happy. This is the end of a conflict, right?

What happens if those in the second department feel that their manager sold out? Will the compromise hold if the manager on the committee feels that the top candidate is reneging on certain commitments?

When bargaining is used as a strategy for managing conflict, there is always a danger that the bargain will come unstuck and that the conflict will flare again. If each party to a bargain trusts the other, the compromise may hold. If there is a strong third party involved, such as an arbitrator or respected statesman, he or she may be able to keep the parties faithful to their bargain. However, the very nature of a bargain is that each party wins some and loses some. Thus, the perception of loss can be the most important ingredient in determining the potential for future conflicts.

"Do It My Way, Or Else"

This is a win-lose strategy. The winner has more power and can force the loser to accept whatever solution he or she imposes. But a forced solution can lead to sabotage or resistance on the part of the loser. At best, a forced solution gets the loser's cooperation at "gunpoint," with little or no enthusiasm for or commitment to the principles of the winning side. And a succession of losses can stifle creativity, leading to an unresponsive, static organization.

One Big Happy Family

In some conflicts, we respond by pointing to the futility of an open battle, and instead suppress the conflict in hopes that it will go away. Smoothing over a conflict may involve getting the warring parties to lower their public voices, shake hands, issue joint statements pledging mutual love for each other or for the industry. This strategy is based on the assumption that emphasizing the positive will defuse a conflict and make it go away.

In the short run, smoothing may actually work, in the same way that a ceasefire stops the battlefield shooting. However, smoothing does little to get at or handle the causes of a conflict, and it rarely leads to a long-term solution. It is a strategy for stalling, perhaps in hopes that things will change and that the need for a conflict will cease. Taken at its extreme, smoothing becomes appeasement, and both world history and management history show the dismal record of appeasement in resolving conflict.

I Don't Want to Talk About It

While the aforementioned bargaining, forcing, and smoothing all do something about a conflict, withdrawal is doing nothing about a conflict. An ostrich with its head in the sand makes an enemy disappear to the same extent that ignoring a conflict makes it go away. Yet there are situations where even withdrawal can be useful in managing a conflict episode. Suppose that at a meeting one participant is very upset, shouting and raving that the manager and his "cronies" are "conspiring" to make the "progressives" look bad. Tempers are heated, facts become opinions, and logic turns to gut-level reactions. Continuing to argue the merits of various positions would be futile, and it could even lead to remarks in the heat of battle that could damage the group's ability to govern. In this situation, the forcing of a vote or smoothing over of the differences in the group might lead to further trouble. When forced to go in an unacceptable direction, the "losers" might attempt to sabotage the decision. They could withhold information or support, or they could actively subvert the majority's efforts. Smoothing might leave both sides feeling that they have been "had" or have been given the "treatment," which can build into smoldering resentment. Withdrawal or avoidance is useful here because you remove the opportunity to continue fighting. Simply adjourn the meeting. Walk out. Change the subject abruptly or diplomatically, or refuse to comment in any way until tempers have cooled.

Withdrawing or avoiding a battle is an effective short-run ploy if it is used to gain an advantage by allowing for a better time, place, or situation for a confrontation. It can also be useful when you are facing several simultaneous crises. If you try to handle them all, you can drain your energy and reduce your effectiveness and that of the others involved. Instead of fighting four fires at once, you might select the two most critical and consciously ignore the other two. You would minimize the total damage from the four conflicts, although you would still have two "back-burner" issues to be confronted eventually.

OPTIMIZING CONFLICT

All the strategies that we usually associate with conflict have advantages and disadvantages. The common factor in all of them is the potential for future conflict, the so-called latent conflict. In the short run, these strategies may help you to resolve conflict, although it may cost you in the long-run.

Photo courtesy of A. B. Dick Company.

The best overall resolution for long-run conflict management is optimizing or confrontation. It involves changing the focus of a conflict away from blame, starting points, causes, and specific solutions toward an overall remedy for the problem. It is often called a problem-solving strategy because it requires the participants to seek common points of agreement, not as a compromise solution, but as a basis for a comprehensive problem solution. Optimizing produces no losers, and thus it minimizes the aftermath of a present conflict. This means that all parties to a conflict commit themselves to an optimal solution instead of grudgingly agreeing to a "half-a-loaf" compromise while waiting for a chance to "get it all."

ACTION GUIDELINES TO OPTIMIZING CONFLICT

Here are eight guides to managing conflict through optimizing or problem-solving:

1. *Direct confrontation between opposing parties is essential.* This is the key element in an optimizing strategy. The opposing sides must be willing to face each other (and each other's ideas) head-on. There is no opportunity for ducking side issues, smiling to make things appear friendly, or lining up to bargain chips for swapping later.

Confrontation in a supervisor's meeting may result in the following dialogue:

AL: "Harry, we've both been letting off a lot of steam here and frankly I'm worried about the effect upon the company. I feel your comments on the proposal are actually potshots at me personally and that you're trying to make a grab for power. I don't mind telling you that it scares me, not because you'll win or I'll lose, but because of what the battle may do to our firm's position. Tell me, Harry, how do you feel about me personally?"

HARRY: "Hey, I don't mean anything personally, Al. Look, I'm just as interested in this company as you are—maybe more. After all, I've been here fifteen years. I love this business, and I'm committed to this company."

AL: "Harry, everyone here appreciates you and your efforts. But you're ducking the issue. How do you feel about me as a person?"

HARRY: "Why, is it important?"

AL: "If we can't confront each other honestly and openly about our feelings toward each other, those hidden feelings will just get in our way as we try to work out our problems. Listen, let me tell you, no holds barred, what I feel about you—the goods and the bads. Fair enough?"

Obviously, this approach is dangerous. Harry may welcome the chance to really let you have an earful about your shortcomings and alleged weaknesses. However, Harry may also respond with an honest assessment of his feelings toward you and your performance as an executive. Direct confrontation on a person-to-person basis (rather than on a position-to-position one) is the way to begin managing a conflict.

2. *Get personality feelings up front first.* In your first contact with your opponent, try to talk about how you feel about each other. Often conflicts are heightened and solutions made more difficult because there is a "hidden agenda" in the conflict. People are conflicting over their relationship as well as the issue at hand; the relationship conflict is the road back to agreement. It is also a major contributor to a conflict aftermath.

When two political factions argue over a bond issue for public works, they are rarely talking about public good and the merits of the bond issue. What they are disputing is the question of who will be in charge at city hall. Handling the power relationship is the key to managing the conflict—the actual issue is secondary. When a manager challenges a boss' decision on the site for an upcoming meeting, is the manager really arguing that he or she prefers Podunk for the meeting? Or is he or she trying to assert some sort of power over the boss?

The personality issues rarely go away when an issue is settled. Regardless of whether the bond issue passes or fails, regardless of the outcome of the "anywhere but Podunk controversy," the relationship issues will remain. They form the basis for the next conflict. Conflict management reduces the probability that future conflicts will arise, and it reduces the hostility and damaging aftereffect of those conflicts that do arise.

Thus, it is important to get the relationship conflicts out in the open first before tackling the issues. You won't necessarily change your opponents' feelings about you, but at least you will be able to separate their feelings about you from their feelings about your position on an issue. Of course, you will be doing the same for your opponents.

3. *Minimize status differences.* When confronting a conflict head-on, it's best to keep the opposing parties on a reasonably equal footing. In working out staff conflicts, the status differences are important. Imagine your boss, sitting in his or her office behind an executive desk, Gucci-clad feet propped up on the desk, while you sprawl uncomfortably on a too-low sofa separated from the boss' desk by an expensive Persian carpet. Can you communicate as equals and ignore the differences in your relative status? Hardly!

A better approach is to find a neutral site for the confrontation if your objective is to work out an optimal solution to the conflict. Remember that if your objective is to enforce your position, the status advantages weighted on your side are useful. However, this is forcing a conflict solution, not optimizing one.

4. *Don't try to identify blame.* In most conflicts, the participants spend a lot of time trying to shift the blame for the problem from one side to the other. If one side can successfully fix blame on the opponents, it's possible for them to "win" the conflict. In an optimizing strategy, fixing blame serves no useful purpose.

5. *Delay commitments to specific solutions.* When we try to solve a conflict, we often contribute to the difficulties by holding out for a specific solution. A better approach is to delay as long as possible before committing yourself to a certain course of action. Of course, too much of a delay can give you the appearance of a poor leader, but a "tolerable" delay may help all participants in a conflict to hold open their options and remain flexible about an ultimate optimal solution.

6. *Identify areas of mutual agreement.* An optimizing solution to a conflict is one that minimizes the aftereffects that lead to future conflicts. It is also an approach that focuses on an overall solution to a problem, rather than on a winner and a loser. To achieve this outcome, try to identify early in the confrontation the areas where all parties can agree. This is often called "commitment to superordinate goals." Simply put, it means focusing the attention of the fighting parties on some larger goals that they all have in common. For example, in a conflict between factions in a group, members can always focus on the "good of the firm." Both sides will readily agree that "the company comes first" and that their position is best for the company. Rather than have everyone involved in the conflict agree that the firm comes first, and then resume their fighting, keep the attention on the mutual goal as long as possible. When one side or the other starts to slip into a discussion of their favored "solution," bring the discussion back to the larger mutual goals of both sides. When the parties in a conflict can evaluate their common goals and how to achieve them instead of defending their predetermined positions, an optimal outcome of the conflict is possible.

7. *Emphasize mutual benefits.* When a natural disaster hits a community, the usual bases for conflict within the community disappear. The politics, skin colors, economic positions, and historical differences of the people in the community become unimportant. The goal of restoring order and resuming life is the overall goal of everyone, and such a mutual benefit is possible only if past feelings and differences are put aside.

A large U.S. airline found itself facing a similarly dangerous threat. Without some drastic cost cutting, the company faced almost certain bankruptcy. Labor and management agreed that they could achieve mutual benefits through cooperation instead of through the usual hostility. Labor agreed to set aside some of its salary and benefit increases stipulated in the contract, and management agreed to a salary cut and a "nolayoff" policy. By working together, the difficulties were overcome.

Yet each side had a "right" to enforce its position with legal action. The emphasis on mutual benefit made it possible to set aside the traditional management-labor conflict. The focusing on mutual benefits thus shows itself to be an integral part of the problem-solving aspect of an optimizing strategy.

8. *Examine your own biases and feelings first.* Before confronting a conflict, take a close look at your own feelings and attitudes about your opponent and the conflict that confronts you. Knowing your attitudes may help you get them "up front" and thus keep them from interfering with a problem-oriented solution to the conflict.

ADAPT AND BE REALISTIC

When facing a conflict situation, assess the participants, the stakes, and the setting. Determine how important the conflict is to you and to your department or business. Keep in mind that no one strategy—smoothing, forcing, running away, or confronting—works best in all situations. Remember, too, that an optimum strategy of confronting a conflict head-on may still result in a bargain between the parties. The idea is to minimize the aftereffects and thereby keep conflicts within the association manageable.

Don't be a Pollyanna. You must be realistic and realize that some conflicts cause permanent damage despite the best efforts of all concerned to minimize the aftermath. Think of conflict management as forest-fire management. The forest service doesn't put out every fire and save every tree. If it is successful, it minimizes the damage from forest fires and keeps enough of the forest green to ensure that there will be a need for a forest service.

Remember too that after a bad burn, new trees spring to life and the forest goes on. If you've done your best with conflicts, you'll still be in business and in control of those seeds of growth in your organization.

DISCUSSION QUESTIONS FOR CONFLICT MANAGEMENT

1. What are some of the major sources of conflict in your daily activities on and off the job?

2. What are some examples of historic conflicts that illustrate the notion that conflict is a process, consisting of a string of unresolved conflicts, each one helping cause the next one?

3. What are some of the disadvantages of using a "do it my way" or "I win–you lose" approach to handling conflicts?

4. What are some of the risks you see in using an optimizing approach to managing conflict?

ACTION EXERCISES FOR CONFLICT MANAGEMENT

1. In a group, role play a conflict situation in which you have recently been involved. Have several group members take the parts of persons who were actually in the conflict, and brief them on what happened. Then improvise, using all of the strategies that we have discussed in the chapter.

2. Draw up a list of the sources of conflict in your life. Then, beside each kind of conflict, list how you have typically handled that sort of conflict. What will emerge is a sort of profile of your conflict management style. Analyze the profile carefully, looking for situations in which your approach to a conflict either led to a positive solution or to a continuation of the conflict in another, later episode.

CASE 32. South Side Security Company

The South Side Security Company employs two salespeople. Al has seniority and has achieved a modest, but unimpressive sales record. The company recently decided to expand by adding another salesman, Ben. He is aggressive and wants to achieve a high sales record.

Both salesmen are paid on commission so their salary rests entirely on their ability. The company offers a wide variety of security services. Because these services are interrelated, it would be very inefficient to give any salesman jurisdiction over a particular service (guard patrol, armored truck, and so on).

When Al learned that a new man was to be hired, he quickly made the statement to management that the new man could not handle guard accounts, because he did not feel there was room for two salesmen in this area. However, Al received no commitment regarding this position, and Ben received no such directives.

When Ben came to work, he and Al became very good friends. From the very first week, however, Ben began selling at an impressive rate, which is unusual for security salesmen. Ben found that when he was able to sell one type of service, he could usually sell others—in particular, guard accounts.

Relations between the two men became very strained. This distressed Ben. At first, he avoided the problem, but he finally decided a confrontation would clear the air. In the discussion, Al said that by Ben's selling guard accounts, Ben was taking money from him personally. Al further stated that he had made every effort to be cordial to Ben as a gesture of friendship and was now being stabbed in the back.

Ben was very disturbed by these allegations. Although he had enjoyed Al's friendship, he felt selling was an open field and competition was the name of the game.

Relations continued to worsen. Ben decided to talk to the office manager.

1. What is the basic problem in this situation?
2. What might be some of the "hidden agendas" or hidden feelings between Al and Ben that are contributing to the conflict?
3. If you were the supervisor of these individuals, what would you do to resolve the immediate problem and the deeper conflict between Ben and Al?

CASE 33. "Over the Hill"

Bill is over his head on a project to redesign the hospital's computer billing system. He is 56 years old and experienced, but not as up-to-date on the technology as he should be. His young assistant (with an MBA; two years out of graduate school; 25 years old) is making Bill look bad by comparison. The assistant has asked you, as the supervisor, for the chance to "show what I can do!"

1. What are some of the possible causes of this all-too-common conflict?
2. What would you recommend Bill do?
3. How would you, as the supervisor, handle this conflict situation?

Supervising in a Union Shop

14

Objectives

This chapter deals with concerns of supervisors in a shop or department where their employees are represented by a labor union, and with those matters of interest to supervisors who face unionization of their people. After studying this chapter, you will be able to

1. Immediately set up an "action file" of materials that relate to supervisor-union interactions.

2. Better appreciate why employees join unions. This will help reduce your defensiveness if you find yourself faced with a union organizing campaign, or if you are suddenly thrust into a potentially dangerous confrontation with the union representing your employees.

3. Understand the major labor legislation that controls and influences management-labor relations.

4. Relate the role of the shop steward to your role as a supervisor.

5. Understand the union contract–mandated grievance procedure.

6. Handle conflicts in a union environment.

MANY SUPERVISORS TODAY work with employees who are represented by one or more labor unions. Although many of a supervisor's attitudes and responsibilities are the same with or without a union, there *are* some differences and special considerations when working in a unionized environment.

In this chapter, we will examine several aspects of supervising in a union shop: the reason why employees join unions; the major pieces of union legislation in the United States; the source of labor-management conflicts at the supervisory level; and some thoughts on a supervisor's reaction to a union's successful organizing effort. All of these ideas, and all of this information, is useful—but it is deliberately general. Labor-management relations are highly complex technical matters. Few top executives understand all the subtle and legal "ins and outs" involved. For these reasons, most unionized firms have labor relations specialists who handle the thorny problems of labor-management relations. Every supervisor is therefore urged to do the following:

1. Get a copy of your organization's "master contract" with the union representing the people in your department.
2. Read it carefully and often. Memorize important provisions and details.
3. Study your organization's manuals and handbooks on labor-management relations. They are written to guide and assist you through a potential management "minefield."
4. Consult with your firm's Labor Relations Department, not when there is an immediate problem facing you, but when you have time to get to know these experts and establish a rapport with them.
5. When a labor problem does develop, do not be reluctant to seek the help and guidance of your experts. Any supervisor who feels that he or she can handle all union-management problems without help is a fool. No one—no matter how well-informed—can be adept at handling the subtle aspects of a union contract while handling the other important parts of a supervisory job.
6. Don't take union-management difficulties personally, but don't assume that you have no responsibility either for the causes or solutions to problems. There are many complex reasons why union problems crop up at the supervisory levels. Some can be "blamed" on supervision; others are far beyond any supervisor's power to prevent or control. Remain sensitive to potential union-related problems. But don't let fear of union troubles keep you from carrying out your supervisory responsibilities.

Working in a union-organized environment can be a rewarding challenge. Many supervisors feel that they prefer a union shop to a nonunion shop. Others, of course, prefer to deal directly with employees, and they resent what they see as "interference" with their role as supervisor. Either way, unions are a "fact of life" in many business, government, health care, and educational organizations. Working in such an environment is part of the challenge of supervisory management.

WHY EMPLOYEES JOIN UNIONS

There are no simple answers to the question "Why do people want union representation?" There are some common reasons for union membership, although it seems that most people are influenced by a variety of reasons.

Self Interests. A major reason for union membership is *to protect and promote an employee's self-interest.* When employees feel that management does not have the worker's interests in mind in their daily dealings, employees begin to feel a need for union recognition. When power is unevenly distributed between management and the workers, the imbalance can create anxiety about managerial decisions. When this happens, workers often seek to shape a force of power equal to that of management to protect their interest. Poor supervision, lack of communication, inadequate recognition, and thoughtless decisions all create and build the atmosphere that encourages the creation and solidarity of a union. Worker fears of any arbitrary managerial action create the feeling that management does not care about the effects of their decisions on employees. All are powerful incentives to organize or join a union.

Strength in Numbers. Another reason people join unions is that they feel there is strength in numbers. Employees feel more secure when they are together discussing a problem or presenting a grievance. Workers often feel management has *all* the power. Management represents the shareholders. It is seen as a sort of David and Goliath situation. From the early days of the factory system and the industrial revolution, workers have found greater strength in staying together for mutual benefit. The actions of one worker may have no impact on the organization, but the actions of all workers will have an impact on management.

Job Security. Employees organize to protect their jobs and try to ensure fair and equitable treatment from management. Job security is a cornerstone of the organized labor movement. Labor feels that workers have a right to their jobs just as investors have a right to use of their capital. Workers often feel that without representation by the union and a contract with management, they could be fired without notice or reason. When one's job ensures one's livelihood and that of one's family, the concerns over job security run deep. When there is a lack of trust be-tween management and workers, it is reasonable to expect workers to take actions to ensure the protection of their livelihood.

Fair and Equitable Treatment. The desire for fair and equitable treatment is another reason for unionization. Everyone wants to be treated fairly. Any failure of management (whether it is real or im-agined) to treat workers in an inequitable manner will result in a cli-mate that is ripe for unionization. Because of the concern for fairness, every supervisor's actions must be above reproach. When workers feel that management is being unfair, the appeal of a union is increased.

Pay and Benefits. Improved pay, fringe benefits, and working condi-tions have always been major employee concerns. Employees often be-lieve that by joining and supporting a union, they can significantly improve their pay, working conditions, and other fringe benefits. Throughout history, this is one area where unions have been very successful serving their members. Most people wish to "get ahead" in life, to be better off materially as they get older. With a union, workers feel that management can be pressured to maintain an environment where pay, fringe benefits, and working conditions are consistent with worker desires.

Social Reasons. Many people enjoy belonging to groups where the members have things in common. Unions give their members opportuni-ties to associate with people who share their values and interests. This solidarity and the opportunities for leadership are important reasons for belonging to a union. In a union, it is possible for employees to achieve leadership roles that may be denied to them within the management of their employer's organization. Union members can become shop stew-ards, or other leaders who get respect. Supervisors must now listen to *them*. This leadership gives union members a way of achieving self-respect and equality with management. Men and women who are frus-trated in attempts to achieve leadership positions in the work environ-ment may be attracted to the opportunity to satisfy their need through the union. Some may even use the position to "get even" with supervi-sors who they feel were the roadblocks to them becoming supervisors in the organization. Of course, this isn't the only reason for a person to seek a union leadership role, but for some it can be important.

A Source of Employment. Although the closed shop, where every employee must be a union member, was outlawed by the Taft-Hartley Act of 1947, there are many segments of American industry where a union shop does exist in practice. Firms in these industries hire new employees *only* through the union. Union membership is the only way one can be hired by these organizations. In many of the situations where a union shop exists, the union has negotiated attractive wage and fringe benefit packages. New workers are strongly attracted to jobs that pay top wages and provide training and opportunities for even higher wages and more job security.

THE MAJOR LABOR LEGISLATION
IN THE UNITED STATES

Today's supervisor *must* be aware of the legislation that governs the relationship between management and labor. Since the early part of the twentieth century, the U.S. Congress has enacted laws defining the rights and obligations of both management and labor. States also enact labor-related legislation to address concerns and problems of working people in specific regions of the country.

Although employees have attempted to organize labor unions in the United States since the earliest settlers arrived, there was no national policy in support of organized labor until the 1930s. Prior to that time, management had no obligation to deal with workers who chose to unionize. In fact, it was a common business practice to declare such worker associations a "conspiracy in restraint of trade." Unions were, in this view, outside the law. With the great depression of 1930 came a political climate more sympathetic to the organized labor union movement, and many unions began their growth leading to powerful and important roles that they hold in society today. Legislation since the 1930s played a significant part in that development.

In 1932 Congress passed the *Norris-LaGuardia Act.* It prohibited the courts from enforcing contracts that employees were forced to sign as a condition of employment in which they promised not to join a union. Organized labor had always considered such contracts a denial of employee rights. Labor called such contracts "yellow-dog" contracts. Only a yellow dog would agree to work under such an employment agreement. The Norris-LaGuardia Act also limited the use of injunctions against unions when they were in the legal pursuit of their business.

The most significant piece of legislation of this period was the *National Labor Relations Act (Wagner Act)* passed in 1935. The Wagner Act placed the government firmly in support of organized labor. The critical element of the Wagner Act granted labor five fundamental rights. The law specified a series of actions which were to be considered unfair labor practices of management:

"To interfere with, restrain, or coerce employees in the exercise of their rights to self-determination."

"To dominate or interfere in the formation or administration of any labor organization or contribute financial or other support to it."

"To discriminate against any employee in regard to hire or tenure of employment or any term or condition of employment to encourage or discourage membership in any labor organization."

"To discriminate against any employee because he has filed charges or given testimony before the N.L.R.B. concerning any alleged employer violation of the Act."

"To refuse to bargain in good faith concerning wages, hours, and other conditions of employment with any union duly chosen as a representative of its employees."[1]

The Wagner Act put the teeth into these principles through the creation of the National Labor Relations Board (NLRB), enforcing and administering the new law.

The next major piece of labor legislation was the *Labor-Management Relations Act of 1947 (Taft-Hartley Act)*. This legislation was intended to pull the pendulum of government support into a more neutral position. Congress believed that labor was acting in an irresponsible manner and that restraints were necessary. The Taft-Hartley law spelled out illegal labor practices. Unions could not force employees to honor a strike, nor could they force an employer to discriminate against an employee who chose not to join the union. The closed shop was declared illegal. With a few exceptions, the Taft-Hartley Act left the union shop legal. Under a union shop, employees must join the union within a specified period of time after being employed. Such a provision, if neglected, prevents what the union terms "free riders." In the union's view, if an employee receives the benefits derived by collective bargaining, they should pay the dues.

The Wagner Act further defined what the union could not do to enforce a strike. Some types of secondary boycotts, as well as secondary strikes and picketing, were made illegal. Unions were also required to bargain in good faith with employers, in a manner similar to the provisions of the Wagner Act requiring management to do the same. It was hoped that this provision would encourage a better balance in the collective bargaining process.

Unions were no longer allowed to restrict membership by charging excessive or discriminatory initiation fees. Some unions, it was charged by proponents of the Taft-Hartley Act, held the supply of skilled labor to a minimum by restricting new membership. When labor supply is held artificially low and demand for the skilled labor is high, it is easier to raise the wages of members through the negotiation process.

The Taft-Hartley Act also outlawed the practice of "featherbedding." Featherbedding involves forcing an employer to pay for services that are not performed or which are not necessary. Unions had been accused of padding jobs with employees who were not needed and threatening a strike if these people were dismissed.

In 1959, the Congress passed the *Labor-Management Reporting and Disclosure Act.* Known as the Landrum-Griffin Act, its purpose was to provide union members with a "bill of rights". The law dealt with the regulation of the internal affairs of unions to ensure that union members actually did control, through a democratic process, their unions. Most of the new regulations imposed on union leadership were the results of testimony before a Senate committee on labor racketeering and corruption.

There is a constant flow of legislation affecting labor-management relations. Most of it deals with narrowly applied specifics and does not have the impact of major legislation. Also, much of today's labor law is actually coming from rulings of courts and administrative agencies. A wise supervisor will do well to stay abreast of changes in labor law. Arbitrary actions of an uninformed supervisor could establish a precedent which can adversely affect future incidents or negotiations. If the supervisor is within his or her rights to take certain actions, they should be taken. If there is any doubt regarding the letter or the spirit of the contract, the question should be taken to the personnel department or the supervisor's immediate superior.

Photo courtesy of Eastman Kodak Company.

WORKING UNDER THE CONTRACT

After the union agreement has been ratified, all supervisors are given copies of the contract and additional information as well. Because the supervisor must operate a department under the provisions of this document for an extended period of time, there is an obligation not only to read the contract but also to understand it. Supervisors shouldn't hesitate to question their superiors or the personnel department about any ambiguous clauses in the contract. Much time and thought go into the preparation of a final union contract, and it will stand for a stipulated period of time. The supervisor, to do his or her job properly, must live with the conditions of the agreement for the duration, for better or worse. It is not in the best interests of the organization or the union for a supervisor to attempt to ignore or circumvent the conditions provided in the agreement. No matter how noble the intentions, no one will thank a supervisor when erroneous actions cause a costly work stoppage. This is not to imply that the union agreement in any way relieves supervisors of managerial responsibility or authority. They are still responsible for running an efficient operation. However, this must be done within the confines of the agreement.

THE SHOP STEWARD

The supervisor's primary link with the union in a situation where employees are represented is the *shop steward* who is elected by his or her coworkers to be their on-the-job union representative. Shop stewards are usually well informed about the content and provisions of the union agreement.

The shop steward, in most cases, will be a regular, full-time employee, expected to do a full day's work, although there may be some specified amount of organization-paid time allotted for union business. This will be stated in the union contract. The shop steward is often in a difficult position, with divided loyalties. On one hand, he or she is a company employee and has certain responsibilities to the organization. But, he or she is also an elected union representative with an obligation to do a good job representing his or her fellow workers. A good shop steward will be able to strike a happy medium in this difficult situation. Working well with supervision provides a better relationship between labor and the organization. The steward has direct access to the "grapevine" and can alert management to potential problems before they get out of hand and cause a major crisis. It is to the supervisor's advantage to establish and maintain a good working relationship with the shop steward. In doing so, the supervisor can open lines of communication which are needed if the grievance procedure is to work effectively and with a minimum of disruption. Often, these good relationships can help to prevent grievances. The supervisor and the shop steward can work together to get to the root of a problem before it results in the filing of a formal grievance.

GRIEVANCE PROCEDURES
AND THE UNION CONTRACT

In a union shop situation, a grievance is a written complaint submitted by an employee through his or her union representative, usually the union shop steward. The grievance is raised over an issue in which the employee feels that supervision has been unfair, or in which the union-management contract seems to have been violated.

The union-management contract is usually established by delicate negotiations and a series of compromises between labor and management. Although the first-line supervisors are not present at these negotiations, their contributions (through the labor relations department) are quite important. Many of the issues under consideration are related to situations supervisors deal with in their own departments. Problems such as working conditions, work assignments, transfers, productivity, and promotion of employees become an integral part of the ultimate agreement between the organization and its employees. The supervisor must live with the contract for the next year (or longer). In order to be able to assist top level management with union negotiations, the supervisor must be aware of what is happening in his or her own department. Accurate records concerning incidents, disciplinary action, and work assignments are essential to back up the supervisor's opinions and recommendations. These records will be used by the management negotiator at the bargaining table.

The Grievance Procedure

Most union contracts outline specific, detailed procedures for processing and resolving grievances, and both the shop steward and the supervisor are obligated to follow these guidelines once a formal written grievance has been filed.

First, the written grievance is submitted to the supervisor by the shop steward. The majority of grievances can and should be resolved at this level. When the supervisor receives a grievance, he or she should attempt to get all the facts and be sure that he or she understands fully the nature of the grievance. After this investigation, the supervisor should ask the shop steward and the employee or employees involved to discuss the problem in an effort to resolve it. During these discussions, it is important that the supervisor maintain self-control. Nothing will be accomplished if those involved give way to angry and irrational arguments. The supervisor should, at the beginning, define the problem as he or she sees it, and ask if the problem is clear to all involved. When all involved are satisfied that all relevant facts have been brought out, the supervisor should attempt to determine if settlement is possible. In doing this, the supervisor must consider all the ramifications of a settlement. It may be setting a precedent which could affect other grievances and could have an impact on future union negotiations. In cases where substantial issues are raised, it is advisable to ask for help from the industrial relations or personnel departments. These staff specialists can help all parties by providing information on previous agreements or regulations which may be affected by the decisions of the group.

In settling a complaint, the supervisor must be sure that the shop steward and the parties lodging the complaint clearly understand the terms of the settlement. Ambiguous settlement agreements devised just to get the problem settled will surely leave room for more grievances in the future and may cause a serious breakdown in union-management relations.

Negotiations at the primary level are easier because they can be handled rather informally. If the grievance is not settled at this point, the problem is turned over to a grievance or shop committee, and here procedures are more formal and legalistic.

In our experience, 85 to 90 percent of the grievances can and should be settled at the first, informal level. It is unfortunate that this level of success is seldom achieved. Too often, personal feelings about who wins and who loses result in no settlement being reached. The grievance is simply sent on to the next highest level in the grievance process. The cost of handling grievances becomes much greater as each level fails to reach agreement. What is even more important is that when the first group (the supervisor, shop steward, and the employee) fails to reach a decision about the problem, the problem in the department remains. Operations of the department may continue in a way which is not conducive to cooperation. The relationship between the employees and their supervisor has failed. When the problem is not resolved here, the parties involved must admit failure. Good supervision is not based on failure. Rather, it depends on trying to solve day-to-day problems as smoothly and efficiently as possible.

When a grievance cannot be resolved at the first level, it is forwarded to what is generally called a "shop committee." This committee's membership can vary, but it generally includes union officials and the appropriate department heads from the organization. If this group is not successful in reaching an agreement on the grievance, it is sent forward to an appeal committee. The appeal committee is composed of the top industrial relations specialists of the organization, and the employee making the grievance complaint is represented by a top-ranking union official. If this appeal committee is unsuccessful in resolving the grievance, an outside arbitrator is selected to act as a judge. The decision of the arbitrator is binding on both parties. Arbitration is the "last resort," not only legally as a part of the grievance procedure, but as an admission on the part of both management and labor that they cannot resolve their own problems. Supervisors should be careful to avoid making an unwise settlement out of fright or concern for the cost and discomfort of arbitration.

Conflict in a Union Shop

As a supervisor in a union shop, you will be on the line when conflicts arise. If you are aware of some of the sources of these conflicts, you can prepare for them by developing cooperation. If you can identify an issue or situation which, from your experience, is likely to become a point of conflict, it is better to try to resolve the problem before you are forced to face it head on. Your firm's union-management contract cannot cover all problem situations that might arise. While some experts might suggest that it is best to "let the sleeping dogs lie," our experience is that the ignoring of a potential conflict will surely cost greater time and energy later when the conflict must be confronted. Making the contract work is in part the responsibility of the first-line manager. By facing the potential conflicts head on and working with the union's shop steward, you can build a relationship of trust between you which can reap valuable rewards later.

Supervisors can expect conflicts to arise when employees feel that they are in a situation where they could lose some rights or privileges. When a win-lose circumstance is in the work place, conflict will result. Avoid actions that look as though they may lead to a win-lose outcome. As a supervisor in a union situation, you will seldom win. However, if you do win a battle over an issue, you may endanger the long-term cooperation between yourself and your employees. "Shoot-outs" between management and labor can be prevented by effective communication and good faith discussions. Some labor-management issues revolve around principles that cannot be compromised. We are not suggesting that such issues ever should be compromised. The key to avoiding a conflict situation of this magnitude is to actively pursue a program of open discussion with employee representatives and employees on the issues. More problems develop from misunderstandings of the issues than from the issues themselves. Clarification of the positions of opposing parties can help manage potential conflicts.

A major source of union-management conflict is self-interest. Persons or groups often place great emphasis on what is "good" for them. When there are scarce resources, conflict will almost always exist. Often you can do nothing about the problem of inadequate resources. You can only work to reduce the negative effects of the conflict through a full disclosure of the situation. Conflict is worse when employees perceive that resource allocations are disproportionate or unfair. Employees may feel that when they are asked to take less, others will be asked to make the same sacrifice. In recent years, with a troubled economy, there are a number of examples of organized labor willing to hold the line on wage increases and, in some instances, cutting wages to help companies stay competitive. In these cases, both labor and management have focused on common goals. Both sides felt the same pinch of inflation, but both parties also recognized that the actions were needed. The workers felt that it was in their long-run self-interest to cooperate in order to stay competitive and possibly to maintain their jobs.

Conflict is inevitable when employees feel that they are being treated unfairly. No one accepts unfair treatment easily. When "the system" creates a situation in which employees feel that they have been unfairly treated, the supervisor can expect to feel the reaction. To the employee, the supervisor is the company. Employee reactions are normally directed toward you. Don't be offended when you receive the expression of their anger. Where else would they direct their anger? If you are aware that employees are likely to be unfairly treated by a management decision or policy it is your responsibility to make upper management aware of the potential conflict that will result. Your choices are few. If you want to maintain your credibility with your employees, you need to take steps to protect them from unfair treatment. If there is any area where actions speak louder than words, it is in the matter of perceived fairness. You cannot work effectively in an environment where employees feel that their supervisor is insensitive to unfair treatment. For a more detailed treatment of conflict management, in both union and nonunion situations, please read chapter 13.

DEALING WITH EMPLOYEES
WHO HAVE RECENTLY UNIONIZED

Supervisors who undergo the trauma of a union election among their employees often feel a deep and very real resentment. Some will feel that the employees' desire for union recognition is a personal affront to them and to their leadership. During a period of high anxiety between employees and management, it is important for supervisors to react in a positive and nonthreatening manner. Personal bias or prejudice toward the union, its leaders, or those in your work group who favor the union must be suppressed. Periods of anxiety may produce emotionally charged statements. A supervisor's first encounter with a union-organizing campaign can be a terrible and threatening personal experience. Men and women with whom you have worked or supervised for years now want to impose a union between you and them. You are hurt, you feel betrayed, and you are angry.

Despite your personal feelings, you must be able to withhold harsh or "knee jerk" reaction.

After your employees have unionized, be sure to avoid the creation of a "gap" between yourself and your employees. Don't behave as if the employees are suddenly members of some alien forces. They are simply men and women who have chosen to exercise one of their precious rights. The employees are also likely to be uneasy about how this new situation will affect their relationship with you. Your behavior will be closely watched by all your employees. If you create a positive climate, it is likely that the employees' fears about retaliation will be reduced.

Learn as much as you can about the details of the contract that will affect your work relationship with your employees. Focus specifically on supervisor behaviors and decisions that are no longer unilateral.

When must you coordinate with the shop steward before making a decision or taking actions? What new written procedures must be followed? Be sure that you understand the paperwork that accompanies your actions. Know the contract so that you can live up to management's end of the bargain.

Don't try to become an "instant expert" on labor relations, even though you have taken time to learn what is expected—or demanded—of you under the union contract. If you are insecure about what to do, call a labor relations specialist. Do not be concerned with looking stupid or uninformed. The smart supervisor, when faced with a situation that is unclear, calls for help from the personnel/labor relations specialist. Your interpretation of the situation may be different from those with other views. The company may wish to respond to each situation with a specific precedent.

If your firm did not have a grievance procedure previously, it will have one under a union contract. A grievance procedure system provides each employee with an opportunity to ensure that he or she is fairly treated. There will always be employees who attempt to beat the system, and some will be successful. However, if an employee has been accused falsely of violating a company rule or if there are extenuating circumstances, a grievance system will serve to protect the employee. If you show your support of the grievance system, you are likely to have few grievances filed against you.

As history has proven, supervisors who treat their employees unfairly have much to fear from a union representing their employees. A grievance system is an important part of a total labor-management relations system. Your response to employee grievances will establish the tone for the entire employee-supervisor relationship in your firm.

Respect for each employee's rights is an essential requirement for effective supervision. The imposition of a union may alter the steps and procedures that the supervisor takes, but the fundamental practices of supervision will not be altered.

DISCUSSION QUESTIONS
FOR UNION SHOP MANAGEMENT

1. Discuss in more detail, or with examples, the reasons why people join unions.

2. What could be possible reasons why people would want to remove their union membership?

3. What are some reasons why employees would file grievances against their organizations or supervisors?

4. Discuss how you would handle a conflict between a union-represented employee and you as a supervisor to prevent the employee's complaint from becoming a formal grievance.

5. What are some of the reasons why management would want to have its employees represented by a union?

6. What are some reasons why management does not want its workers unionized?

ACTION EXERCISE FOR UNION SHOP MANAGEMENT

Write to a major union headquarters, or the Public Relations office of the AFL–CIO, and ask for a copy of a typical contract that its members work under. Study the contract, and develop a list of potential problems that such a contract might pose for a supervisor. Also, look at the details of the grievance procedure in the contract. What is the role of the supervisor? What are his or her rights and allowable actions under the contract?

If you are presently employed by an organization whose employees enjoy union representation, acquire a copy of your firm's union agreement, and do the same analysis.

CASE 34. The Shop Steward

Jerri Jarrard is a person who wants the authority of a supervisor without having the responsibility. She was recently elected shop steward. She now feels that her job is to contradict her supervisor and virtually all company decisions. When an employee is dissatisfied with something, Jerri immediately blows it all out of proportion. She never tries to calm down the employee or convince her or him that there are other ways of looking at the situation. If an employee does not react *unfavorably* to a supervisor's decision, Jerri will ask such questions as "Are you going to accept that?", "You do want to fight it, don't you?" and "Do you want to file a grievance?" In private discussions, she admits that she sometimes feels that the employees may be wrong, but her job as shop steward is to be on the "people's side against supervision."

1. Is Jerri's attitude right? Should she actively seek out grievances and employee problems?
2. What do you think a supervisor's response to Jerri's actions should be?
3. What can management do to alleviate this sort of problem during the negotiation of the next labor-management contract? How would you advise *your* firm's management if you were faced with a Jerri Jarrard in your shop?

CASE 35. The Complainer

Jan is a welder assembler. His job is to assemble and weld copper tubing to use on the assembly line. His work is scheduled daily by the company scheduler. A schedule is issued to him six to eight hours ahead of the assembly line where the tubing is used. There are three other areas using the same schedule but doing different assemblies, and everyone is working well except for Jan. Jan is a very good and very fast welder, but he loves to visit other work stations. This causes him and others to fall behind in their work. When this happens, Vic (the department supervisor) steps in to find out why the work is falling behind. When he approaches Jan, Jan goes all to pieces. "What is it to you? I'm working, can't you see? Get off my tail, man! Who made *you* a supervisor? Everything was going well until you took over this department! Go back where you came from!"

Vic has known Jan for over twenty years, and at one time he worked as an assembler with Jan in a different department. Vic was transferred into management to take over supervising a department in a different plant. After several years, Vic was asked to take over Jan's department. From that day, Jan was never the same. There was name calling (such as "company lover" and "traitor"). Vic tried to talk to Jan but Jan wouldn't listen. He would say, "If you have anything to say, get the shop steward. Don't talk to me." The department has nineteen people and Jan is the only employee of the nineteen who won't communicate with his supervisor without the shop steward or a union official at his side, and he still refuses to follow instructions. Jan has been reprimanded a number of times for his actions and was twice suspended for hitting Vic. Each time the union was able to bring him back to the job. This has been going on for over a year. Vic is getting the work out of Jan's area by using the scheduler. He keeps close watch throughout the day to make sure that Jan doesn't skip all over the schedule, because he still wanders away from his work area. At times, Vic makes himself visible to keep Jan working. This ties up Vic, but it also helps to prevent an even bigger problem.

1. Comment on Vic's approach to managing this problem employee. Would you handle Jan the same way? What would you do differently?
2. What are the potential problems that Vic may be facing with the union because of Jan's behavior and his (Vic's) response to it?
3. When Jan threatens to "get the shop steward," what should Vic do?

How to Plan and Budget Your Time

Objectives

This chapter is about the management of your time. Time management involves the successful planning of one's time and then working with the plan to improve performance and reduce wasted time. After reading this chapter, you will be able to

1. Identify those activities that are time wasters and those that are accomplishment producers.

2. Recognize the difference between spending and investing time.

3. Overcome the common confusion between actions and accomplishments, and focus your activities on reaching your "time management" goals.

4. Help your employees and fellow supervisors better manage their time by discussing their time problems and applying some of the "time-saving tips" in this chapter.

As a supervisor, you have many demands placed on your time. You are responsible for many activities, and the success not only of your own department but those of others depends on you meeting your commitments. You must also deal with unexpected crises and unavoidable delays in schedules. Supervisors have only so many hours in the day to do what is expected of them, and often there doesn't seem to be enough time to do all that is required.[1]

Of all the things we value, time seems to be the most ignored. Yet, in a very real sense, time is the key to the traditional and behavioral functions we have been discussing. Without adequate time, we would not be able to plan, control, direct, communicate, motivate, or lead.

Time management has today become one of the most talked about of the supervisory skills. Each of us can use more time. We treat time as a commodity. We buy it, sell it, waste it, give it away, and save it. We frequently say that "time is money." This is true, and the sooner we start to think about time as money, the sooner we will be able to get control over our time.

HOW DO YOU SPEND YOUR TIME?

Too often, our time is spent on things that really don't have much value. It's the same with our money. We spend money on trifles, rather than on investing it to achieve significant results. One trick used by some people to accumulate money is to take all the small change from their pockets each evening after work and throw it into a jar. At the end of a year, the amount of money in the jar is often surprising, yet saving it didn't really hurt at all. If you spent the small amounts of change, it is very doubtful you could buy anything of significant value. Yet, the "budgeting" of the small change can result in a useful "lump" of money. It is the same way with time. Thoughtful planning and careful use of time yield small amounts that, added together, can give you the opportunity to accomplish something worthwhile.

Who Controls How You Spend Your Time?

In some recent studies of supervisors, we found that a significant amount of their time is spent not on productive activity, but on activities imposed on them by the system, be it the company or the realities of the industry. Even more surprising, large amounts of time are controlled by the requirements of the boss.

However, many of the time uses are self-imposed by the supervisors. They are, in effect, giving themselves things to do without any real requirements from either the system or the boss.

In a recent *time management seminar* participants were asked to list some of the things they do because they are required to do so, either by their job description, their boss, or their own sense of what needs to be done. Can you add some of the things *you* do to each of these categories?

The job requires me to

- Write letters
- Answer the phone
- Write directions, schedules
- Read and keep up in my professional field
- Follow up on projects
- Attend meetings

My boss requires me to

- Address invitations for his parties
- Wrap gifts
- Put out fires (administrative fires, we assume)
- Comfort other employees when they have problems (commonly called "hand holding")
- Answer the phone when no one else is in the office
- Conduct employee reviews

On the job, I do the following things because I *want* to, or because I feel they *should* be done:

- Make my job more meaningful
- Grade and evaluate my employees' completed projects
- Maintain a friendly office or shop atmosphere
- Visit with fellow employees, so that problems can be headed off early
- Rewrite the boss' material

Setting Priorities

The process of managing and planning your time begins with the setting of personal priorities. You must think about and ask yourself to identify the most important things in your life, on the job and off. What are you trying to accomplish? What is the most important activity on your job? What is it that your job hinges on? The answers to the question of personal and job priorities are followed by an even more difficult question. Does your time go toward the activities that are of highest priority? For most of us, the answer is no. This is a major symptom of the problem of time management.

Actions versus Accomplishments

Most supervisors are busy. In fact, we have been taught that the busy manager is the successful manager. We become suspicious of persons sitting around for long periods, seemingly not doing anything. Without question, there is much merit in working and in keeping busy. However, we often make one fatal mistake, that is, fatal in the sense that it kills our chances for saving and investing time.

Jean Fabre, the French naturalist, was one day observing processionary caterpillars. These are little fellows, about an inch long, that form up into long strings, and move over trees eating leaves and insects. Fabre was able to get them onto the rim of an old red flower pot and make them close up their circle. As they moved around the rim in an unbroken circle, he figured that they would soon realize they were going in circles and would stop. Yet they starved to death within reach of food because they confused activity with accomplishment. They were active as could be, moving along staying busy; they just weren't getting anywhere.

Many supervisors find themselves in the same situation. They are constantly on the go, moving from one meeting to another, dealing with one crisis after another, fighting "fires," and working out problems. Yet, when everything is summed up, they really haven't accomplished very much. Results are what really count, and only with careful time planning will it be possible for you as a supervisor to focus your time on reaching those results. Often, too much activity is a symptom of time management problems. If you find yourself in the position of never having enough time in the day to do any real planning, then perhaps you're operating like the processionary caterpillar. That is not profitable, either for you or the organization.

Analyzing Your Time

Every so often, it is a good idea to do some self-analysis. Divide the things you do each day into two categories: those actions that tend to be wasters of your time, and those actions that produce real accomplishments. If the second column (the accomplishment producers) is longer, you are in good shape, and producing results. If, however, your first column is longer, you need to do some serious time planning. Look over your last couple of months, and be honest with yourself.

TIME WASTERS
AND ACCOMPLISHMENT PRODUCERS

Many supervisors and managers find it useful in their time planning efforts to think about time as money. In fact, they set up a "T-account" just like the accountants do. However, this Time-Account is headed on the left with "time wasters" and on the right with "accomplishment producers." In Table 15-1, we have outlined some time wasters and accomplishment producers that supervisors have contributed during time management seminars. Some of the wasters and some of the accomplishment producers should look familiar to you. After studying this "account," try to develop one for yourself. The challenge for better time management is to convert time wasters into accomplishment producers, while making sure that the accomplishment producers you identified really are producing accomplishments and moving you closer to your real objectives.

TABLE 15-1 A Sample "Time Account" for Supervisors

TIME WASTERS	ACCOMPLISHMENT PRODUCERS
1. Coming late to meetings and causing all others to wait while they are being briefed.	1. Getting to work early, to give yourself time to wake up and do some forward planning before the employees arrive.
2. Failing to delegate work to subordinates when (the supervisor) feels he or she can do the job.	2. Researching problems and getting the facts before making decisions, and going to the proper sources of information.
3. Unnecessary interruptions.	3. Promptly returning phone calls.
4. Long coffee breaks and gossip.	4. Making and keeping appointments.
5. Unannounced visitors who upset your schedule and that of your subordinates.	5. Keeping extra work in a briefcase or folder to do while traveling to and from work, or on business trips.
6. Meetings too early in the day. People are not yet awake enough to contribute adequately to problem solutions.	6. Using an agenda (and a time limit for items) for every staff meeting.
7. Passing the buck when something goes wrong, instead of working to solve the problem.	7. Holding working lunch meetings.

*This "TIME ACCOUNT" was produced by supervisors participating in a nationwide series of time management seminars conducted by the authors. The "time wasters" and "accomplishment producers" represent actual supervisor responses.

TIME BUDGETING

Assuming that you, like most supervisors, need some improvement in your use of time, you should begin to develop a time budget. It is like a financial budget in that it involves a series of simple but important steps.

1. Make a list of your real objectives. Do some thinking, and establish those things in your life and your job that are meaningful results toward which you want to direct your activities.
2. Arrange your objectives in the order of their importance. Some objectives, while they may be important to you, are clearly less important than others. Set priorities on your objectives.
3. List the actions and requirements that are necessary to reach each of the objectives you listed above.
4. For each of your objectives, assign priorities to the various activities required to reach the objective. You are now assigning a second set of priorities, first to your objectives, and now to the activities necessary to reach those objectives.
5. Begin scheduling your activities according to the priorities you have set. Plan to do the high-priority activities (such as working toward high-priority objectives) first, and work down the list to lower priority activities and objectives. The steps are quite simple, and yet if they are done with the proper amount of thought and serious insight, the exercise can give your life, on the job and off, a real sense of direction. It can be a significant step toward managing your time, and it can lead to some other benefits as well. There is actually one more step to the process of time budgeting, one that is often overlooked.
6. Perform the activities as you have scheduled them. Remember that we have already discussed the problem of "time wasters" in your daily activities. Avoid them, and stay with the activities and objectives to which you assigned high priorities.

Regular Time Planning

Time budgeting is an activity that we should do regularly. It can give you some important insights into just where your time really goes. If you are like most supervisors, you will find that if your time is not invested in significant amounts, you will waste it away on trifles and meaningless activities that don't produce any real or lasting accomplishments. Without time planning (and actions that follow your plan), time seems to vanish. Just as "time flies when we're having fun," it also flies when we fail to plan our time and control it properly.

Photo courtesy of Eastman Kodak Company.

FOOTBALL—LIKE SUPERVISION—REQUIRES CONSTANT TIME MANAGEMENT

ACTION GUIDELINES FOR TIME PLANNING AND BUDGETING

From seminars and discussions with supervisors in hundreds of businesses and other organizations, we have developed a number of time management guides. Not all of these ideas will work for you. Some may fit your situation, others won't fit at all, and still others you may have tried already, and found that (for you) they don't work. The challenge is to develop your own ideas; use ours as starters. Consider each time management guide carefully. Think about the ideas, and don't assume that just because an idea seems unpromising now, it will remain so in the future. It is strange how both reading and thinking about an idea brings it back to your mind later when a new problem or situation comes up. We can't change the clock to give us more time, but we can change the way that we use the time we have available. In many areas of management, time is a resource we have to become more sensitive to. Here are some suggestions:

1. *Get started.* When you arrive at work in the morning, do first the things you may not like to do. Open and reply to your mail. Read the reports. Return the calls.

2. *Remember the early bird.* It's often far easier to perform at your best in the quiet hours of the early morning. Arriving at work a few minutes early can often result in substantial time savings later in the day.

3. *Little things mean a lot.* By starting early, and relying on a staff or a secretary, it means that someone is giving up his or her time for you. Remember the people who make the difference between using your time efficiently and effectively and wasting your time by giving unnecessary instructions. A cup of coffee, or a kind word at the right time, can be the motivator that spurs people to help you save your time.

4. *Answer your own phone and mail.* Do not answer everything in the mail, nor every phone call, but answer enough to get a first-hand feel for the information coming in. Delayed messages, involvement of secretaries, serpentine instructions . . . all take valuable time from more important matters.

5. *Make your telephone calls before 9 A.M. or after 3 P.M.* If you call between the hours of 9 A.M. and 3 P.M., people are often in meetings, and you'll waste a lot of time trying to run them down.

6. *Bug yourself.* For some of your telephone conversations, set up a recorder, and play back the tapes to yourself later. It's amazing how much you can learn about your habits of repeating yourself and wasting time in unnecessary or pointless conversation.

7. *Become "clock conscious."* Check frequently on the time. It's too easy to ignore time for a while, and then suddenly realize that it's later than you think. Don't offend people by constantly looking at your watch while talking to them, but be aware of how much time you're really using.

8. *Move off the dime.* When a problem comes up, don't jump right in with the first thought or solution that pops into your mind. Invest some time planning your response to the problem. But don't plan too long. Often, some serious thought and planning followed by some movement toward a solution can avoid wasting time while all the unknowns fall into place.

9. *Fly to the moon.* Few decisions are made on a one-shot basis. Decision making is a process of taking some initial direction and then making "mid-course" corrections along the way. Too much time is often spent trying to "wrap up the whole problem." The trip to the moon wasn't accomplished by pointing the rocket in the direction of the moon and letting it go. Millions of corrections to the path were made before the objective was reached. The same should occur with your decisions.

10. *Avoid interruptions.* When you're working on projects, plans, or activities that require concentration, put yourself in a place where you can't be easily interrupted. Sitting in the cafeteria working on the next period work schedule is stupid. You are going to be interrupted, and a two-hour job will take six hours to finish. Make it clear by your surround-

ings and your behavior that you don't appreciate it when interruptions occur. People will get your message, and interruptions will decrease.

11. *Don't be a perfectionist when it's not required.* At times high accuracy is required and valued; when it's not, don't waste your time working a problem out to the fourth decimal place when rounding to the nearest whole number is sufficient.

12. *Don't use pencils.* They require sharpening, and the time it takes to walk from your desk uses up more time than the task is really worth.

13. *Play politics when necessary.* In many organizations, moving ahead means playing political games. If you've decided that your career is going to be with a particular company, accept the political game as a fact of life, and play as well as you can. Resisting the "game" wastes time, while accepting the usual political activity in your organization might turn out to be a useful investment of your time.

14. *Use a tickler system.* Have some method to remind yourself of high-priority activities and objectives, and to keep you on schedule. Perhaps a pocket or desk calendar will work, or maybe a notepad clipped to the inside of your jacket, or a corkboard in a place where you stop for writing. Develop a system that works as a reminder for you, but develop it now.

15. *Be a quarterback.* Develop a good team of assistants, and use them. Don't try to handle all the details personally. Call signals for your staff, and let them run with the ball. You will not only save yourself time, you'll motivate your people as well by giving them more responsibility and personal initiative.

16. *An "open door" policy.* An open door can often lead to a steady flow of people with important problems. It can also lead to people with problems that should be solved elsewhere: "Since he's available anyway, why not drop it in his lap." Be ready to listen, but set some ground-rules first.

17. *Open door/open mind.* If your door's open, your mind should follow suit. Nothing is accomplished, and much time is wasted, when those taking advantage of your willingness to listen and discuss find that you really don't want to hear what they have to say.

18. *Work at work.* Somewhere we've learned the notion that successful people are the ones who constantly work after hours. However, a consistent pattern of homework is more likely to be a symptom of a basic failure to organize the hours on the job. It may be a signal that you're wasting too much time at work and not really working productively.

19. *Have a "self time."* Set up (and faithfully keep) a time each day or each week when you can think about your plans and analyze your performance in the past. All the planning and budgeting in the world are wasted if you fail to set aside a time, free from interruptions and other problems, where the plans can be analyzed and changed and where new plans can be made. Find fifteen minutes, a half-hour, or even an hour, and regularly spend it with the most interesting and important person you know—yourself.

20. *Call in.* When you plan to be out of your office for more than an hour, let someone know where you can be reached. This way, you can avoid a pile-up of problems and calls, and you can solve new problems before they mushroom out of control.

21. *Run a tight meeting.* Set strict time limits on all meetings and announce those limits to the people present. During the meeting, stress the time remaining. Have an agenda, and stay on it. Hold meetings late in the day.

22. *Explain "No."* Everyone must veto occasionally. Avoid misunderstandings and later confusion (or worse) by giving an explanation when you turn down an idea, suggestion, or offer. A few words now can prevent many words later. You never get a second chance to make a first impression.

23. *Tighten your schedule.* If you don't make up a daily schedule, start today. If you do schedule your day, pay closer attention to it, and look for places where you might be leaving yourself more time than you really need. Plan alternatives in case an appointment is cancelled.

24. *Daily to-do list.* Begin each morning by listing tasks and activities which will help you achieve high-priority goals. Always start with A's, not C's.

25. *Do it now.* Procrastination is suicide on the installment plan. Get started and follow through on tasks you begin before you begin others.

26. *Odds 'N Evens.* Set appointments at unusual times. We normally think in full-hour and half-hour intervals. Try 10:15 A.M., 2:50 P.M., 3:20 P.M. Keep others on their toes to be prompt, and show that your time is well scheduled.

27. *Lightening strikes anyway, so . . .* You can't do anything about the unexpected, so remain flexible. Have things that can be done when meetings are cancelled. When you're unable to stay on schedule, get back to normal as soon as the unexpected event passes.

28. *Gang up on visitors.* When you have planned a meeting or conference with someone you know will waste your time, plan to have one of your subordinates or coworkers join you. This way, it's possible to close the meeting by prearranging some signals.

29. *Pick up speed, talk first.* When confronted with someone you know wastes your time, stay on the offensive. If you keep moving, you make a poorer target for the "waster." As long as you are in control, you can decide how much time is appropriate for the confrontation.

30. *Avoid temptation.* Stay away from persons and places that chronically take more of your time than you want to spend. Those favorite haunts for the mid-morning coffee or the longer lunch can lead you to forget your carefully made time-saving plans.

31. *Avoid the tyranny of the urgent.* Don't let things control your time. Good planning and faithful following of the plan will help you to avoid always being in a rush. You don't usually perform at your best during a crisis, and this tends to waste even more time later.

32. *Carefully select alternatives.* Being too hasty or not getting all the facts can lead you down the wrong path, and you will waste time retracing your steps. Don't sit on a decision forever, but do look at each alternative carefully before selecting. This is an investment of time that can save time later.

33. *Minimize time on routine things.* We all have to do certain repetitive activities. Plan them so that they are all done at one time, when you're at your best. Putting them off only stretches out the time it will take to eventually get them done. If possible, delegate some routine activities, and save your time for high-priority and goal-oriented activities.

34. *Combine and conquer.* Combine similar tasks and activities. This is the first step in an industrial analysis of a production process, and it should be done occasionally in your own job. Are you doing five routine jobs that could be combined into one report or two operations?

35. *Don't write unless it's absolutely necessary.* Use your phone. You can solve unexpected problems that may take days to solve by written memos.

36. *K.I.S.S. (Keep it short and simple).* When you do write, get to the point. Cut out the flowery phrases and long-winded narratives. Keep your main points logical and easy to understand and follow.

37. *Don't let the computer get you down.* "Our computer's down!" In this age of increased computerization, we all hear this more and more. There are a lot of good reasons for the computer going down. However, few of them really soothe or satisfy us when time is critical. As in the case of so many other uncontrollables, have other things to do while waiting for the system to come back "up." The lost time costs are enormous when tellers, clerks, agents, and others wait for the machine to come back into service. It's good management use of time to arrange for alternate tasks that can be performed while waiting for the computer. Also, it may be wise to instruct employees in the use of manual methods for helping customers or users when the system goes down.

38. *Reduce wayward calls.* This is an office management problem. Time gets wasted when telephone calls are misdirected. Those calling in are inconvenienced, and those in the office waste valuable time trying to help unscramble the mess. A good call director, and good instructions for that person, can help produce a more efficient office.

39. *Travel time.* Going from point A to point B is necessary, but it can be a time waster if not properly used. On planes, trains and other public transportation, it's wise to have some "accomplishment procedures" along. Catch up on required or pleasure reading, complete those expense reports, or do a bit of creative writing. Dictate letters, or read some mail. The time between stops goes faster, and otherwise wasted time turns into real productivity.

Travel time in a car, when you're driving, is another matter. In heavy traffic, trying to pay attention to anything except the other motorists is foolhardy and dangerous. Driving in these conditions is accomplishment producing by itself. However, on the open road, as in light traffic, it may be possible to use the travel time for other purposes. Listen to tapes of meetings, speeches, or classroom lectures. Use the time for thinking about goals, priorities, activities, and time problems. As long as you can keep your attention on the road, it's possible to accomplish more than just travelling.

40. *Return phone calls.* There are several ways to save time by returning calls. When it's possible, and it fits with your schedule, immediately return calls as soon as you can. Further delay may only add to serious situations, and it can create unnecessary anxiety if you do not return them. If returning calls immediately often interferes with other plans and priorities, schedule a certain period for calling each day. If you do all your calling at once, you do not interfere with other plans.

41. *Continually review priorities.* As time moves on, and circumstances change, priorities might need to be revised. When the unexpected occurs, remember that it provides you with a challenge to which you must adjust. Handle the unexpected, and then get back to your plan.

Time planning and time management are supervisory activities that you won't find in any supervisor's job description. They are not usually something that management uses to evaluate your performance. Yet, effective time management is one important key to your being able to perform up to the standards by which others judge you.

HELPING YOUR PEOPLE MANAGE THEIR TIME

In a series of recent time management seminars, we asked the participants to list some of the things that their bosses could do to help them do their jobs better. We also asked them to consider how their bosses could support the goal of better time use and better management. Here are the most frequently mentioned ideas. My boss could help me manage my time better by

1. Developing better job descriptions for me and my coworkers. This would help us to know what he/she expects. Too often, our job descriptions are inadequate or outdated, and that leads to a lot of uncertainty.

2. Delegating more—being more supportive.
3. Once delegating is over, leaving me alone. Stay off my back, and let me do what has been assigned.
4. Discussing staffing and budgeting requirements with me—asking my ideas.
5. Being concise—giving clear instructions.
6. Providing us with the right tools, equipment, and information.
7. Providing the proper training and frequent upgrading of our skills, so that we are working with the best available skills.
8. Following up—showing some interest in the tasks that have been assigned.
9. When we need a decision, giving us the decision as quickly as possible.
10. Being consistent—not constantly wavering, either in instructions or in application of policies.
11. Setting and then communicating the goals to us.
12. Conducting periodic reviews of our performance.
13. Providing rewards and keeping in mind that recognition and praise are powerful incentives.
14. Being available for help–not leaving us to flounder after having made an assignment.
15. When he/she tells me something is needed *urgently*—using it as soon as I give it to him/her. There's nothing more frustrating, and more demotivating, than a "rush" project that just sits there for weeks after I have knocked myself out to get it done quickly.

This list is revealing for supervisors. It covers a variety of topics, including delegation, motivation, communication, managing with objectives, and performance appraisal, as well as time management. From such a list, it is possible to conclude that effective time management hinges on effective supervision.

One supervisor, participating in this exercise, suggested after she saw this list that "I'm going to go back to the office and have my people develop a list like this for *me!*"

The blame for poor time planning and poor time management is not yours alone. Too often, supervisors tend to reward those who are able to come through in a crisis and get the job done. The quarterback who comes into the game late in the fourth period and turns a possible loss into a narrow victory is often praised more than the quarterback who week after week does his job in an unspectacular fashion. Proper time management, coupled with good performance in other areas of supervisory responsibility, should help you avoid crises. Set an example for your employees and for your supervisors as well. Perform your own activities on schedule and with good time planning beforehand, and reward your employees when they do the same for you.

Good time planning and management should mean fewer crises,

smoother interpersonal relations, and a real increase in your productivity and that of your people.

DISCUSSION QUESTIONS FOR TIME PLANNING AND BUDGETING

1. How do you make use of your time? Do you find yourself in control, or do others exercise more control than you do?
2. What are your priorities?
3. Develop a weekly budget for your time. Is it realistic?
4. List three suggestions for time management that can be directly applied to your job.

ACTION EXERCISES FOR TIME PLANNING AND BUDGETING

1. Develop your own list of additional time wasters and accomplishment producers, similar to our list in Table 5–1.
2. The most important time is your own time. What are the three major problems you faced in the past week? Do you really feel you have solved these problems "for keeps" or do you feel you have merely solved the surface symptoms? (Answer yes or no for each problem, and explain your answers.) If these were supervisory problems, could they have been delegated to a subordinate?

CASE 36. The Veteran

Lyle Tatum was coming down the hall, and Alice Gannon knew she'd better think fast. If she didn't, she could look forward to an afternoon of "war stories," and little else being done.

Lyle was a good executive, and was presently doing a fine job as staff assistant to the president of Chamboa College. In this position, he was responsible for coordinating with all supervisors in the college and for maintaining communications between departments. Before coming to the college, he had an eventful career as a military officer, spending eighteen years as an enlisted man and nineteen years as an officer in the army. He retired with the rank of colonel and joined the college at a salary far lower than the college would otherwise have paid for a person with his qualifications and experience.

The problem with Lyle wasn't his ability as an executive. It was his habit of telling war stories whenever anyone would listen. His usual pattern was to come into the office for a meeting (scheduled or unscheduled), discuss the college problem for about ten minutes (being a good executive, problems seldom took long to dispose of), and then quickly jump into his stories. Usually, he would start with "This reminds me of the time with Patton, crossing the . . ." He would then tell as many stories as he could remember, and Alice and others could do nothing except sit and listen.

Lyle's stories were, of course, first-hand experiences. Lyle was in the infantry, and he served everywhere. Unfortunately, after hearing each of Lyle's stories four or five times, all Alice could do was roll her eyes toward heaven, and pray for deliverance. Other supervisors in the college had similar problems with Lyle. No one was able to maintain any sort of daily time plan with him around. Something had to be done, and Lyle was coming down the hall again.

1. What can Alice do to manage her time with this known interruption?
2. Since Alice is not the only one with the problem of Lyle, is there any action that the other supervisors could take to combat the waste of time?

CASE 37. Who's Responsible for What Around Here?

Bill was recently informed by my supervisor that we would have to start calibrating the hydraulic tongue wrenches on the first shift. I arranged to have the second-shift man come in two hours early on two different days to explain the procedure. This was done, and my men calibrated the wrenches.

The next step was to arrange to have a gauge standards man review the calibration and approve it. Bill walked over to the Gauge Standards Department to explain that he was ready to have the wrench approved. Al, the leadman in Gauge Standards, asked Bill to wait, and then he went to get his foreman. The leadman explained to his foreman what Bill wanted, and the foreman immediately got angry. He said he told Al that he would not do this job on the first shift. He said he did not have the manpower, and he wanted the job to remain a second-shift operation.

Bill returned to his section and reported to his supervisor what had happened. He said he didn't know about any conversation between Al and Gauge Standards. He suggested that I talk with Al and find out what was going on. He said that Al was the man who decided to do this operation on the first shift.

I talked with Al and he laughed and said he knew they didn't want to do the job. He added that they would do the job regardless and he would arrange to have a man come over from Gauge Standards.

The man did show up, but in the interim I wasted approximately twenty minutes of my time, and we lost three hours time on the wrench calibration.

1. How was time wasted by these employees?
2. Could this situation have been simplified to save valuable time?
3. Who seems to be the major problem in this case?

The Future Challenge of Supervision

16

After you read this chapter and participate in the "self-audit" for supervisors, you will be able to

1. Understand and discuss with other supervisors the nature and importance of social responsibility for all managers.

2. Evaluate your own behavior and that of other supervisors and managers, and assess how that behavior stacks up with your own personal code of ethical conduct.

3. Relate your organization to the pluralistic system of our society.

4. Evaluate your strengths and weaknesses as a supervisor in all areas of management, and compare your evaluation to that of your colleagues.

Supervision is a great and continuing challenge; it brings together people, materials, and ideas to reach important goals. This responsibility rests on the shoulders of the men and women in supervisory and managerial positions. Decisions that you and your fellow supervisors make about products, methods, services, prices, standards, and actions must take into account a growing variety of pressures from many sources, both public and private.

SOCIAL RESPONSIBILITY

Supervisors are sometimes thought to be unfeeling about their responsibilities to society and the environment. This view is unfortunate. While it is true that many managerial actions have been misunderstood, all organizations and their managers must be responsive to society if they are to survive. The strength of any organization or department has always been its responsiveness to the changing needs of the many publics it serves.

There is a lot of controversy about the social responsibility of management. Some supervisors feel that their only responsibility is to respond to the demands of their superiors. Others contend that the only responsibility that supervisors have is to reach the goals of their departments. While there is no "correct" view of supervisory social responsibility, there are some important factors to consider.

ACTION EXERCISE TO PREPARE YOU TO MEET
THE FUTURE AND CHALLENGE OF SUPERVISION:
SUPERVISOR'S SELF-AUDIT

The purpose of the supervisor's audit is to let you analyze your supervisory skills. This test will help you better focus on the concepts in the text and serve as stimulation for you to become more knowledgeable about the profession of supervision.

In order to score your performance, you should use the following scale:

5—*Outstanding.* Little improvement necessary.

4—*Superior.* Some additional knowledge required.

3—*Average* or *satisfactory.* Additional knowledge would result in improved performance.

2—*Below average.* Some skills and knowledge but not enough to pull present performance up to satisfactory level.

1–*Poor*. Little or no knowledge of the skills involved. Results are not acceptable, and major improvements are necessary.

How do *you* rate in comparison with other supervisors or against your idealized standard of an outstanding supervisor?

PLANNING

SCORE
1 to 5

1. Do you know what the real objectives of your organization are?

2. Can you explain to subordinates how your group's activities relate to the organization's objectives?

3. Do you discuss overall plans with your people?

4. Do you use measurable and approved objectives to guide you and your subordinates in your work?

5. Do you periodically review with your subordinates the procedures used by the group with a view toward improving them?

6. Are your employees involved in the planning process?

7. Do you give your people full recog- nition for their efforts when goals are reached?

8. Do you coordinate the plans of your group with those of your boss, with staff departments, and with other departments with whom you normally interface?

9. Do you convert plans into schedules, budgets, and other action tools?

10. How successful has your group been in reaching its goals?

PLANNING TOTAL:

Continued

STAFFING

1. Do you know the job requirements for the jobs that you supervise?
2. Have you personally reevaluated the job descriptions of your people in the past two years?
3. Do you do your own new employee orientations?
4. Have you developed a strong and positive relationship between performance on the job and rewards?
5. Have you developed a career ladder in your work group?
6. Do each of your employees know and understand performance criteria for the job?
7. Have you developed a systematic technique for interviewing potential employees?
8. Does personnel have enough information about the type of employees you need to do an adequate job of screening candidates for the job?
9. Have you developed a system to identify promotable employees?
10. Does each employee know where he or she stands in the group in terms of performance?

STAFFING TOTAL:

Continued

ORGANIZING

	SCORE 1 to 5

1. Do you maintain an up-to-date organization chart for your group?

2. Do employees in your group understand for whom they are working?

3. Do you develop and maintain an ideal organization plan on a continuing basis to provide both for additional personnel or possible reductions in personnel?

4. Are organizational changes made in terms of your ideal organizational plan?

5. Have you ever computed the span of control that you have?

6. Have you compared that span of control with others?

7. Does each person in your group report only to one person?

8. Do you maintain harmonious and effective working relationships with other supervisors?

9. Do you delegate routine work to subordinates as much as possible?

10. Have you reviewed the structure of your work group in the past two years in search of improvements?

ORGANIZING TOTAL: _____

_____ Continued

CONTROLLING

1. How well do the instruments you use for control relate to your planning documents?

2. Do you have adequate feedback on how well you are reaching your goals?

3. Do you provide your employees with the feedback when you receive it?

4. Are your subordinates fully accountable for the controllable costs that apply to the operations of your group?

5. Do you conduct frequent review sessions designed to seek subordinates' opinions on how to improve performance?

6. Do you encourage or require that your subordinates develop a means of correcting their own variances before you need to tell them?

7. Do you ensure that prompt remedial action is taken to correct any variance as soon as possible?

8. Do you search for the underlying causes of many operational problems that occur?

9. Do you provide for yourself the time necessary to supervise effectively?

10. Is the value of the results achieved by your group substantially greater than the cost of achieving them?

CONTROLLING TOTAL:

Continued

DECISION MAKING, LEADERSHIP, AND MOTIVATION

1 to 5

1. Do you review all the available factors before making a decision?
2. Do you search for and weigh alternatives before making decisions?
3. Do your decisions solve the real problems?
4. Is your present leadership style most appropriate to the group you are supervising and the tasks that you are responsible for?
5. Do the subordinates in your group feel that they have an opportunity to give their views on problems and procedures?
6. Do you give your subordinates the recognition due to them for the accomplishments that they produce?
7. Do your subordinates feel a sense of accomplishment when they complete their assigned tasks?
8. Do your subordinates feel that they have an opportunity for advancement and that you will help them advance if their performance merits it?
9. Do you create a work climate where your people want to accept greater personal responsibility for the work they do?
10. Do you have a satisfied, highly productive team of people working for and with you?

DECISION MAKING, LEADERSHIP,
MOTIVATION TOTAL:

SCORING REVIEW

	YOUR SCORE
1. Planning	
2. Staffing	
3. Organizing	
4. Controlling	
5. Decision making, Leadership, Motivation	
TOTAL:	

	10	20	30	40	50
Planning					
Staffing					
Organizing					
Controlling					
Decision making, leadership, motivation					

The total score and the scores for the individual categories are to be used only for comparison and reflection. Although there is no absolute scale for measuring your audit, you can use these results in two ways: First, review the entire audit for areas where you scored yourself low. These areas are the first to require attention and special treatment. Second, compare your total (or section) scores with those of your colleagues and discuss among yourselves the meaning of the various ratings. How do these self-ratings compare with the performance ratings that your superiors have given you?

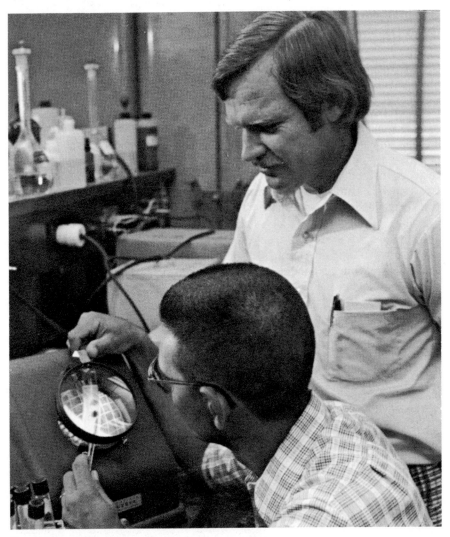

Photo courtesy of Betz Laboratories, Inc.

SUPERVISOR'S SELF-DEVELOPMENT: SOME SOURCES FOR MORE INFORMATION

In order to keep up with the rapidly changing world of supervision, today's supervisor must expose himself or herself to the wide variety of important information that is available. Much of this information can be found in the periodicals and publications written by and for managers and supervisors. As people's needs and work habits become more complex, the supervisor must be able to evaluate and take action. It is only by knowing where to go for information that this process of supervisory "self-development" can continue.

This list is not exhaustive. It does give you a range of publications that are available in college and university libraries, company and agency libraries, union libraries and reference rooms, and in many public libraries.

A good strategy, especially if you are dedicated to continuing your supervisory education, is to spend about a year reviewing as many periodicals as possible, taking from each any ideas that you may be able to convert into better management practice. Once you've identified one or two journals that (for you) contain the best and most relevant information, invest in a subscription. This ensures you of an immediate and personal supply of new ideas and viewpoints. Also, don't forget that supervision is a two-way street. When you read ideas from these periodicals, and profit from them, send a note to the editors of the periodical and outline your experiences. In this way, others can learn from your experience.

Periodicals

Academy of Management Journal.

Administrative Management.

Administrative Science Quarterly.

Advanced Management Journal.
    Society for the Advancement of Management.

American Business.
    Articles on employee relations and industrial relations.

American Federationist.
    Official publication of the AFL-CIO.

Business Horizons.
    School of Business, University of Indiana.

Business Quarterly.
    University of Western Ontario.

Business Review.
    University of Houston's College of Business Administration.

Business Week.

Factory.
    Articles on production, industrial relations, maintenance.

Harvard Business Review.

Hospital Administration.

Human Relations.

Human Resources Management.
University of Michigan (formerly *Management of Personnel Quarterly*).

Industrial Management.
Chicago: Industrial Management Society.

Industrial Relations.
University of California, Institute of Industrial Relations.

Industry Week
Penton/IPC Publications

Journal of Business Administration.

Journal of Business of The University of Chicago.

Journal of Management Studies.

M.B.A.

Manage.
National Management Association.

Management Information.

Management Review.
American Management Association.

Manpower.
U.S. Department of Labor.

Modern Management.
Articles on factory operations, labor relations.

Modern Office Procedures.

Monthly Labor Review.

The Office.
Articles on office procedures and methods.

Office Executive.

Office Management.

Personnnel.
Articles on hiring, training, and managing employees. American Management Association.

Personnel Administration.
(see *Public Personnel Management.*)

Personnel Administrator.
American Society for Personnel Administration.

Personnel and Guidance Journal.
   (formerly *Occupations.*)

Personnel and Training Management.

Personnel Journal.
   Santa Monica, California.

Personnel Management.
   (Includes *Personnel and Training Management.*)

Personnel Management and Methods.
   (see Personnel Training and Management.)

Personnel News.

Personnel Policy.

Personnel Review.

Personnel Training and Management.
   (formerly *Personnel Magazine and Personnel Management and Methods.*)

The Personnel Woman.
   International Association of Personnel Women.

Production Engineering
   Penton/IPC Publications

Public Administration.

Public Administration Review.
   American Society for Public Administration.

Public Personnel Management.
   (formerly *Personnel Administration–Public Personnel Review.*) International Personnel Management Association.

Sloan Management Review

Supervision.
   Burlington, Iowa: National Research Bureau, Inc.

Supervisory Management.
   American Management Association.

Training and Development Journal.
   American Society for Training and Development.

Training in Business and Industry.

Western Business Review.
   Denver University, College of Business Administration.

Working Woman

Yearbook of Labor Statistics.
   Geneva: International Labor Office.

Dictionaries

HOPKE, WILLIAM E., ed. *Dictionary of Personnel and Guidance Terms.* Chicago: J. G. Ferguson, 1968.

BECKER, ESTER R. *Dictionary of Personnel and Industrial Relations.* New York: Philosophical Library, 1958.

Handbooks and Manuals

SCHEER, WILBERT E., ed. *The Dartnell Personnel Director's Handbook.* Chicago: Dartnell Corporation, 1969.

MAYNARD, H. B., ed. *Handbook of Business Administration.* New York: McGraw-Hill, 1967.

HEYEL, CARL, ed. *Handbook of Modern Office Management and Administrative Services.* New York: McGraw-Hill, 1972.

LESLY, PHILIP, ed. *Lesly's Public Relations Handbook.* Englewood Cliffs, N.J.: Prentice-Hall, 1971.

MEE, JOHN F., *Personnel Handbook.* New York: Ronald Press, 1951.

CARSON, GORDON B., ed. *Production Handbook.* New York: Ronald Press, 1972.

Abstracts and Indexes

Employment Relations Abstracts . . . Guide to Current Material on Labor Relations and Personnel Management. Information Service, 1435 Randolph Street, Detroit MI 48226 (semimonthly).

Personnel Management Abstracts. Bureau of Industrial Relations, Graduate School of Business Administration, University of Michigan, Ann Arbor 48104 (quarterly). Summarizes articles on personnel management from a wide range of business periodicals.

Psychological Abstracts. Lancaster, Pa., American Psychological Association. Monthly bibliography of new books and articles on many subjects related to problems of management and supervision.

Professional Publications

There are hundreds of publications written for supervisors in specific professions and industries. Consult your own professional societies, company libraries, or Personnel Department for those that pertain to you. Here is a very short sample list:

Alabama Insurance Executive

American Health Care Journal (Nursing Homes)

Association Management

City Manager

Civil Service Journal

Cornell Journal of Hotel and Restaurant Management

Credit Union Management

Hospital Manager

Hotel and Motel Management

Journal of Nursing Management

Journal of Small Business Management

Monument Builder

Occupational Health Nursing

Paper Industry Management Association Journal

Recreation Management

Steering Wheel (Texas Motor Transportation Association)

Dictionary for Supervisors[1]

Accounting: Often called the language of business. It involves the identification, measurement, collection, interpretation, and communication of events and happenings of business.

Accounting Period: A particular period of time used for computing profits, losses, and various operating statistics of a company. Most companies operate on the basis of a one-year accounting period (corresponding to the calendar year), although with the advent of computers and other accounting aids, quarterly (three month), monthly, and even daily statements can be prepared as an aid to management.

Accrual System: The recording of transactions when they take place, even though the money for the transaction has not yet been received by the company.

Across Communication: Involves the coordination of activities, plans, and communications with other supervisors and other departments in the organization.

American Federation of Labor: An early federation of craft unions, it was founded by Samuel Gompers.

AFL-CIO: A voluntary federation of 135 national and international labor unions which was the result of a merger in 1955 of the American Federation of Labor and the Congress of Industrial Organizations (composed primarily of industrial unions).

---

[1]These terms are commonly used in business (and many other) organizations. While many of these terms were not discussed in the text, they are terms supervisors should understand.

Analytic Production Processes: Processes where basic substances and materials are broken down into new forms of material.

Assembly Production Processes: Those series of operations that take a variety of parts and gather them together in a new product without changing either the physical or chemical nature of the components.

Assets: All properties of value which are owned by the business. Assets may be physical (land, buildings, equipment, inventory, materials) or financial (cash, accounts receivable, securities).

Auditor: An accountant who acts as the accountant's accountant. The auditor reviews the work of other accountants in a business and determines that the procedures and methods used are consistently applied and conform to generally accepted accounting principles. Auditors can be either internal or external.

Autocrat, Benevolent: Sees his or her role in the work group as a "parent figure."

Autocratic Leadership: Work-centered leadership.

Autocrat, Tough: Views leadership as a matter of giving orders.

Balance Sheet: A financial statement that shows the financial position of a company on a particular date. The balance sheet shows what the company owns, what it owes, and what the owner's portion of the business is worth.

Bond: A promissory note which extends over a long period of time, promising that the business will repay the loan along with a specific annual interest payment.

Bondholders: Creditors of a corporation, those who are owed specific sums as a result of a purchase of a company's bonds.

Bonded Public Warehouse: A warehouse owned by an independent company or individual and used for storing inventories of a borrower. Inventory loans generally require the use of bonded warehouses as a means of securing the loan collateral.

Boycott: An attempt to restrict sales by influencing people or firms not to purchase the goods or services of a business.

Break-even Point: A particular level of production that occurs when the monies received by a company on the sale of its products are high enough to cover not only the costs involved in actually producing the units sold but also the various fixed costs and overhead incurred in production.

Budget: The financial plan of a company, it shows the income and expenses that the company anticipates for a future period. The budget is said to be balanced when the amount of income expected during a coming period is equal to the amount of expenses that the company expects to incur.

Bureaucratic Organization: A form of organization in which work is arranged in a precise manner and each individual in the organization knows exactly what his or her job and responsibilties are supposed to entail.

Capital: The investment of various monies that allow for the purchase and maintenance of improvements on the natural resources of a company. Capital is frequently used to include such things as machinery, equipment, and buildings owned and used by the business.

Cash Basis: Recording a transaction in the official journals and ledgers when the monies for the transaction are received.

Cash Dividends: A dividend that is paid as a percentage of the corporation's profits, based on the number of shares of corporation stock one owns on a specific date.

Celler-Kefauver Act: Prohibits companies from purchasing the stock of their competitors, when such purchases would have the effect of reducing the competition that already exists in the market.

Centralized Organization: An organization in which the decisions are made by a limited number of people.

Central Processing Unit: The major part of the computer, which contains the circuits to control the computer and allow the computer to perform the various operations assigned it.

Chain of Command: The linking pattern that connects the top officials in the bureaucratic organization down through the company's structure to the lowest supervisory levels.

Cigarette Labeling and Advertising Act: Requires that a warning statement be printed on each pack of cigarettes and that television and radio advertising of cigarettes be discontinued.

Clayton Act: Extends the regulation of monopolies and trusts beyond the scope of the Sherman Act, and makes it unlawful to discriminate on the basis of price between various purchasers.

Collective Bargaining: The process through which the representatives of organized labor negotiate with the representatives of management to set the conditions of employment for the workers they represent, for a specific period of time.

Common Stock: Securities issued by the corporation. They generally carry no fixed dividend rate and, as such, they offer the owner no guarantee as to a specific return on his or her investment. The owners of a corporation's common stock have voting rights (except in a few cases) and they control the policy setting of the corporation.

Computer: A machine (actually a collection of machines) that can receive, store, manipulate, and report information.

Computer Hardward: Machinery that goes into making up a computer system.

Computer Program: A set of instructions for a computer using an appropriate language of symbols and procedures.

Consultative Leadership: Emphasizes the need for the leader to involve the members of the work group in decisions that affect the group members.

Contingency Management: A view that the managerial style of a supervisor should be based on a variety of factors, including the nature of the work, the employees, the supervisor's talents, and the needs of the organization and its environment.

Continuous Process: Production for long periods of time, with relatively few changes occurring in the set-up or operation of the machines and equipment involved.

Convenience Goods: Goods which consumers can readily purchase at a variety of locations. They are generally low priced and do not usually rely on strong brand-name recognition.

Coordination: The action of several supervisors working together to develop ways of reaching common objectives or to help departments reach complimentary objectives.

Corporation: A group of individuals who join together to create an entity which, by statute, operates as a legal person, authorized to make contracts, own, and dispose of property in the name of the entity, and to otherwise function and transact business within the limits of the powers granted in a state charter.

Craft Union: A labor organization, with membership concentrated on workers who have specific trades or skills which cannot be replaced.

Cumulative Preferred Stock: Stock of a corporation that will require the corporation's board of directors to pay dividends that have been omitted in previous dividend periods, perhaps because of the company's inability to pay them. Cumulative dividends, as well as the current dividends payable, must be paid before any dividends can be paid to the common shareholders.

Current Assets: Assets of a company that can be converted into cash or consumed in a relatively short period of time. Cash is the most liquid of all assets because it can be converted simply into other forms of asset through exchange. Other current assets include accounts receivable, inventories, and prepaid expenses.

Current Liabilities: The debts of the firm which are due and payable within a short period of time. Examples include wages payable and accrued taxes payable.

Current Ratio: The amount of assets (current) listed on the company's balance sheet, divided by the amount of the company's total liabilities. It shows the company's ability to pay short-term claims.

Data Processing: In business, refers to the activities involved in handling the large amounts of data or information generated by the business' operations.

Debt Capital: A term used to distinguish money used for capital expenditures derived from borrowing and the equity capital of the corporation, represented by the investment of the owners or stockholders.

Debt Funding: The acquisition of capital funds through the borrowing of money from outside sources. It involves the execution of short-term and long-term financial instruments, appearing on the company balance sheet as long-term or short-term liabilities.

Decentralized Organization: An organization in which the operating decisions are made at various points throughout the organization structure. It usually involves a company operating with two or more autonomous divisions or departments.

Decentralized Organization: One in which operating decisions are made throughout the organization.

Decision Making: A process of management which takes place at every phase of the operation of a business. It involves the statement of a business problem, identification of alternatives, and selection of an optimal course of action.

Delegation: Process by which supervisors entrust certain employees with the accomplishment of work objectives.

Democratic Leadership: Often described as no leadership at all.

Demographics: The analysis of people by placing them into categories. This would include categories such as sex, age, income, occupation, place of residence, political affiliation, and other personal characteristics. They are used in marketing to determine potential markets and to reach persons who might be more likely to purchase a company's products.

Departmentalization: The efforts of an organization to put employees of similar skill levels, and performing similar or loosely related tasks together in the same administrative unit.

Direct Customer Complaint Lines: A service provided by many companies which enables people with complaints (or new ideas) to be heard directly at the corporate headquarters, rather than having to "go through the red tape and company channels."

Directive Counseling: The supervisor listens to the employee's problem, decides what the emloyee should do, and instructs the employee how to proceed.

Discretionary Income: The income an individual consumer has left after all of his or her necessities have been provided for.

Dividends: The proportional shares of the profits of a business distributed to shareholders of a company's stock.

Division of Labor: Occurs when each job in an organization is broken down into parts that can be performed by a single individual, under the direction and control of a supervisor or manager.

Downward Communication: Involves directing and controlling employees.

Economies of Scale: Occurs when a company is able to spread the fixed costs of doing business over a large number of production units.

Ego Needs: Center around the employee's attempts to get recognition from others in the work group.

Emergency Goods: Goods purchased only in situations where an urgent need becomes evident. Examples might include medication, bandages, or sandbags for flooding.

Enlightened Self-Interest: Business actions that are undertaken partly for providing social good, and partly to improve the profitability of the company.

Entrepreneur: An individual who enters the marketplace and risks his or her money and the money of investors in an attempt to earn a profit by satisfying a portion of the potential consumer demand. The entrepreneur is usually also involved in the management of the business.

Equity Capital: Capital raised through the sale of stock of a corporation.

Ethics: An individual's code of conduct that acts as a guide for personal decision making.

Expenditures: An amount of money that has actually been spent.

Expert Leadership: Based on the individual leader's knowledge and information.

External Variables: The actions of a business' competitors, or those actions that the business decision maker thinks the competition will take, over which the businessperson has no control.

Extractive Production Processes: The gathering of basic materials from the earth or the sea. In extractive processing, materials growing on the ground, living in the sea, or simply lying in the ground are separated from their natural environment and collected for distribution as raw materials.

Fabricating Processes: Materials are assembled to form complete products. In fabrication, the materials brought together are usually changed in form to make them more useable.

Fair Credit Reporting Act: A major step in protecting the rights of consumers in their dealings with creditors and to assure that consumers have access to the files that have been assembled by credit reporting agencies.

Fair Trade Laws: Laws which seek to maintain the price at which products can be sold in a given state.

Federal Regulatory Agencies: Established by Congress to oversee and regulate the activities of certain segments of the American economy.

Federal Tax Policy: Encompasses the whole range of tax laws, as well as the interpretation of the tax laws from the Internal Revenue Service and the various courts involved in tax litigation.

Federal Trade Commission: Established to prevent unfair methods of distribution of goods in interstate commerce.

Federal Trade Commission Act: Designed largely to correct the abuses and the enforcement problems that developed in the application of the Sherman Act.

Feedback: Occurs when information about the progress of a job is measured at different points along the way, and communicated back to management. Information which tells each supervisor if the organization's operations (and those of the department) are working as planned.

Financial Institutions: Organizations whose primary purpose involves the flow of dollars to facilitate trade.

Financial Instruments: Methods used by business to finance its needs for either fixed or working capital.

Financial Ratios: Measures that are calculated from the accounting statements of a business. They are used to help the decision makers interpret financial statements and to determine the progress and performance of the company.

Financial Statements: The summaries of the major financial activities of the business. They present the information that management and outside interests want to know about the operation of the company for a particular period or the present position of the company.

Fiscal Year: Any accounting period, one year long.

Fixed Assets: Assets considered to be permanent, or with a long-term life. A plot of land, buildings, and equipment are usually considered to be fixed assets.

Fixed Capital: Money used by a business to purchase the assets necessary to run the business. These assets usually include what we have defined above as fixed assets.

Fixed Costs: The costs of production and operation of a business that cannot be allocated to a specific unit of production.

Flat Organizations: Have larger spans of control which result in shorter lines of communication between the top and the bottom, especially when large numbers of employees are involved.

Flow Chart: A logical procedure used to solve the particular problem at hand, using a step-by-step detail of the solution. It is often used as a means of developing a program for a computer.

Forecast: A prediction of future activities, usually based on information relevant to that activity's outcome.

Form Utility: The production function of transforming raw materials that cannot be used by consumers into products that have a consumer use provide form utility. It is the usefulness of a product that results from its being in a particular form.

Formal Organization: Consists of the relationship between the various jobs performed in the company.

Formal Work Groups: Consists of those people in a business who work together in reaching specific goals of the organization. They have no particular opportunity to decide on their willingness to participate with the other group members. This is decided by the supervisor or others in the company.

Frequency Distribution: A grouping of raw data, developed to provide more insight into the pattern of the data than would be otherwise available.

Functional Departmentalization: Putting employees in similar jobs together in a single organizational unit.

Functional Group: People who assemble together for the purpose of accomplishing a specific goal or objective.

Functional Organization: An organization that is divided into departments or divisions on the basis of specific activities or functions.

Goodwill: The value placed on the reputation of a business. It is the value of a business in excess of its net assets or equity.

Group: A collection of two or more people who share common beliefs and values and who are working to achieve some common goal.

Grapevine: The path that rumors take in an organization.

Grievance: A formal, written complaint submitted by an employee through his or her union representative, usually the union shop steward. A grievance is raised over an issue where the employees feel that supervision has been unfair, or where the union-management contract has been violated.

Hierarchy of Needs (Maslow): Man's needs have a natural set of priorities for all people.

Human Relations: A school of management thought that recognizes that workers have needs involving social relationships with other workers.

Impulse Goods: Goods bought by consumers on impulse, and sold, usually by a strategic placement of the goods in a store. Examples include such things as candy or shoelaces.

Income Statement: A summary of a business' operations for the preceding accounting period. Its purpose is to show whether the firm made a profit. It is often called the profit and loss statement, and reflects the sources of revenue and the cost and expenses incurred in doing business.

Industrial Unions: Organized across industry lines and include the majority of all workers employed in a given industry, rather than those having some specific skill as is typical of the craft unions.

Informal Organization: The relationships that people as individuals develop within companies and organizations.

Informal Work Group: The relationship of people who work in the same company, based on voluntary membership.

Information System: Interrelated patterns of events and procedures that specify the data to be collected and used by a business and how the collection and use is to be accomplished.

Input-Output Model: This is the flow of material through various stages in the total production process of a business.

Intangible Assets: Assets which have value without any physical form, which have been paid by a firm. The most common examples are patents, trademarks, and goodwill.

Intermediate Consumers: Those who buy goods and services to be used in the production of other goods and services.

Intermittent Processing: Involves the production of material over a limited period of time, while continuous production would be carried out over a longer time period. Intermittent processes are usually short-run processes, operating and then ceasing for a time, and then running again.

Internal Variables: Factors in business decision making that executives must consider that result from forces within the organization.

Inventories: The materials and products held by a company for sale, or the stock of items the company holds to be used in the on-going activities of production.

Inventory Turnover: The financial ratio that indicates the number of times that an inventory level has been sold during the course of an accounting period. It is computed by dividing the cost of the goods sold by the average inventory during the period.

Job-Task Pyramid: The organization of positions, also referred to as the formal organization.

Journal: A book of original entry of a business; it is the first place in an accounting system where a transaction is recorded. In journals, transactions are recorded chronologically.

Laissez-Faire: Primarily a concept that business activity is of no concern to the government, and that businesses will operate properly and be regulated sufficiently if left to the pressures of the marketplace.

Leadership: A personal characteristic, a natural part of authority, it is also determined by whether employees will follow.

Ledgers: The books in which a variety of business accounts are kept.

Liabilities: The legal claims against the assets of a business, held by persons or organizations other than the owner. They are the debts and obligations incurred in normal operation of the business.

Limited Partnership: A form of partnership where one or more of the partners is able to limit his or her liability for the losses of the business, with a corresponding limit on the individual's ability or right to participate in the profits of the business.

Line Functions: Consist of areas in a business that relate directly to the production and sale of products or services.

Line Employees: Employees who are directly involved with the production, distribution, or financing of the products or services of an organization.

Local Union: An organization composed of the members of a national union who work in a particular locality or for a particular organization.

Long-Term Liabilities: Financial obligations of a business which will not be met or come due within the next year.

Management: A process and a group of people. It is the men and women who direct a business organization (group) and the processes and functions by which organizations are guided toward their goals (process).

Management by Objectives: A process whereby the superior and subordinates in an organization jointly identify common goals, define each individual's major areas of responsibility in terms of results expected, and use these measures as guides for operating the unit and assessing the contributions of its members.

Manipulative Leadership: Based on the belief that employees are individuals who can and should be manipulated by the leader in order to reach the leader's goals.

Margin: The percentage of the total price of a share of stock that must be paid immediately on purchase.

Marketing System: The process or series of activities that brings products and services from the manufacturers to the ultimate consumers.

Matrix Organization: An organization that is usually structured around the completion of certain projects or jobs.

Mean: The arithmetic average of a series of numbers.

Median: A measure of central location, often used in place of the mean. It is not as susceptible to distortion from extreme values as is the mean.

Memory: In computer terms, the storage component of a computing system.

Message: The content of communication.

Minimum Inventory: The quantity of a particular raw material or component that a company should have on hand to meet current production commitments.

Mode: A measure of central location, it is the item that appears most frequently in a series of values or characteristics.

Monopolistic Competition: A condition that exists where a market contains many producers who engage in nonprice competition.

Monopoly: A condition of the economy that exists when there is only one provider of a product or service. In a monopoly, the consumer has no choice but to purchase from the one supplier who can control the price of the product or service and determine the conditions of sale as well.

Mortgage: A financial instrument, a loan, that is provided by a bank or other financial organization for the purchase of a specific asset. The asset purchased is usually used as the collateral for the loan, with the buyer putting up a portion of the total price of the asset as a "down payment."

Motivation: Creation of a work climate in which employees work willingly to reach the goals of the organization because they find doing so to be in their own best interests.

Motivation-Hygiene Theory (Herzberg): Stresses the factors which exist in the work environment (such as achievement opportunity, recognition, responsibility, and personal growth) and are the true motivators.

National (or International) Labor Union: Normally a federation of regional and local labor organizations whose chief function is to act as the primary negotiator in dealing with large employers.

National Labor Relations Act (The Wagner Act): The beginning of the national legislation affecting the rights of labor to organize and bargain collectively.

National Traffic and Motor Vehicle Safety Act: Specified standards for automobile safety and required that automobile companies notify owners of their products about safety defects.

Noise: Can be physical (interruption of or distortion of a message) or nonverbal.

Nondirective Counseling: Does not involve the supervisor directly, in an advice-giving situation. Rather, employees are encouraged to express their true feelings about a situation or problem.

Nonvoting Preferred Stock: Stock of a company that does not give owners the right to vote, or that restricts the voting rights to certain issues.

No-Par Stock: Stock of a company that is issued with no specific monetary value designated.

Oligopoly: An economic condition that exists where there are few producers and where there is little or no difference between the products they sell. Under oligopoly, there is usually one large business that dominates the market, setting prices and conditions for sale that the other companies in the industry tend to follow.

On-Line Operations: A condition that exists in a business when all data produced by the business is immediately available to the computer, with no delay between transaction and recording.

On-the-Job Training: Training which is conducted in the department using machinery, equipment, and personnel actually involved in the department's activities.

Open-System Management: View of the organization recognizing that people and organizational objectives are a part of a larger and more complex environment.

Organization: A collection of people, arranged into groups, working together to achieve some common objective.

Organizational Complexity: The division of labor within an organization.

Organizing: Establishing the functions or activities to be performed and the sequence of those activities in the overall meeting of objectives.

Orientation: A period of time set aside for employees joining an organization. Its purpose is to acquaint these new employees with the organization and its policies.

Ownership Funding: The money obtained by the organization from the owners through their purchase of stock or shares in the company.

Partnership: An association of two or more persons who engage in a business as coowners. They share the assets and the liabilities of the business and are entitled to a share of the profits of the business.

Partnership Agreement: A document, signed by each of the partners in a business venture, that specifies the legal details of such matters as the extent of individual liability of each of the partners, the manner in which the profits or losses of the business will be divided, and the general conditions that will govern the partnership.

Par-Value Stock: A security carrying a specific monetary value printed on the stock certificate.

Patent: A legally enforceable right to a product or process.

Performance Appraisal: The process by which employees at each level in the organization are evaluated by their superiors at the next highest level. Most such systems include provisions for the employees to share in a discussion of their evaluation with their superior. The results of these evaluations are often used for determining promotion, pay conditions, and changes in job assignments.

Peripheral Equipment: Refers to the input equipment, output equipment, and the attached memory or storage units of a computer.

Perpetual Inventory: An accounting device or system used to keep a complete, up-to-date record of all items on hand in the inventory of a company. Each time an item is put into the inventory, or sold from the inventory, the perpetual inventory records are adjusted to reflect this inventory "transaction."

Personality: The way an individual thinks, feels, behaves, and views the world.

Personnel: Involves those activities of a business that are concerned with the welfare of the employees.

Physiological Needs: Food, water, air, shelter, clothing.

Picketing: The actions of union members in carrying placards and banners in front of a business to win support for their position in a labor dispute.

Place Utility: The value that is added to a product when the product is moved to a location that is close to the consumer at the time of purchase.

Planning Function: Includes all the managerial activities which lead to the defined goals and the determination of appropriate means to achieve these goals.

Pluralism: A condition of society that develops when diverse groups, with diverse needs and objectives, participate in and influence the social system.

Population: A group of items or persons that includes all items or persons who have a common characteristic.

Preferred Stock: Securities issued by a company that usually carry a specific dividend rate to be paid by the company in all years when the company earns a profit. This dividend is paid before any earnings are retained or paid to common stockholders.

Price-Earnings Ratio: The market price of a share of stock of a company, divided by the last year's earnings per share of stock.

Primary Boycott: Occurs when employees and their supporters refuse to purchase the products or services of the employer.

Primary Data: Information that comes from original sources.

Primary Relationships: Exist when people have an opportunity for continual face-to-face contact with other members of a group.

Primary Securities Markets: Occur when funds are channeled directly into the issuing company in exchange for securities. When a corporation receives money for the sale of its securities, it is dealing in a primary securities market.

Procedures: Guidelines for action in organizations that seldom involve disciplinary measures for noncompliance. Used to indicate the proper steps to be followed to reach a particular result.

Product: Any good or service which satisfies the needs of a consumer. Products may be material or physical in nature, or services which have no physical form.

Product Management: Refers to the operation of a matrix organization.

Product or Service Organization: An organization that is a form of bureaucracy, with the same general characteristics as the functional bureaucracy, but with divisions assigned to the production of specific products.

Production: The activity of a business that takes the raw materials and other inputs (including labor) and manufactures the goods sold by the company.

Production Planning: The activity of a business that involves the determination of inputs and materials used in production, the choice of machinery and equipment, and the integration and operation of the production facilities.

Production Records: All of the information that relates to the production of goods of a business.

Product Shipping Schedules: Records that show in detail the goods to be shipped to each of a company's customers—when, how, and the terms of the sale.

Production-to-Order: Involves products that are made only after an order for them is received by a company. This custom production is usually found in the manufacture of large and expensive items, or for those goods (or services) that have a very specialized use.

Production-to-Stock: Occurs when the production of products is carried out with the outputs going into inventory. This usually is the case when the products have a wide and general use.

Professional Association: A group of individuals with common skill or educational backgrounds, who join together to further the development of a particular occupation or to establish standards of performance and conduct for those in that profession or occupation.

Profit: The resources that remain when all of the factors of production have been given a fair share of the proceeds from the operation of an enterprise. In accounting terms, it is the difference between the revenues generated from sale of products and the expenses incurred in producing and marketing the products.

Project Management: Employees are assembled from various departments and functions to work on completing a specific project.

Prospectus: A detailed analysis prepared to accompany the sale of a new issue of stock to the public. It shows the financial condition, capitalization, record of earnings, and profits of a company.

Pure Competition: A condition that exists in an economy where there are many producers or sellers of goods and services bringing similar or identical products to the market, and where price is the main form of competition.

Questionnaire: A list of questions that is designed to elicit facts or opinions.

Random Sample: A group chosen from a population in which each of the items in the population had an equal chance of being selected.

Real Time: In computer language, it refers to data processing that occurs at the same time as the occurrence of the actual business transaction.

Regional Union: A labor organization composed of a number of local unions within a larger geographic area. It generally provides coordination between the locals and the national or international union.

Remote Computer Terminals: Allow access to a computer from a variety of locations at some distance from the main computer.

Reporting Chain: More commonly called the organization chart of the job-task pyramid. Each person in the organization is responsible to one other person.

Role Conflict: Occurs when an individual is asked to think or behave in contradictory ways.

Scab: A person who accepts work at a business firm during a strike. Generally refers to one hired for the purpose of replacing individuals who have honored the strike.

Scientific Management: The first recognizable step in attempting to develop a unified set of ideas to improve management by quantifying workers' actions and logically arrange the flow of work.

Secondary Boycott: Occurs when employees of one company try to force others who do business with their employer to refuse to do so for the duration of a strike action.

Secondary Data: Information that comes from books, journals, periodicals, and other sources that, in turn, rely on primary data.

Secondary Markets: Refers to the buying and selling of securities by investors. In secondary market exchanges of securities, the company issuing the securities receives no direct benefit from the transaction.

Secondary Relationships: Exist when there is no opportunity for face-to-face contact among members of an organization.

Secured Loans: Money that is lent after the assets of a business have been pledged as collateral.

Securities: The documents that provide businesses with a source of funds. They usually include two major types: stocks and bonds.

Security Needs: Those human needs which relate to one's desire for a continued source of income, or for shelter, food, and clothing. Often satisfied by organizations when they provide an individual with the means to achieve physical security as well as some measure of continued employment (job security).

Self-Actualization Needs: Involve the desire for challenge, self-expression, and commitment.

Self-Image: The views that we have of ourselves, which we reinforce with events or situations that are favorable.

Shop Steward: An elected representative of the employees of an organization working under a labor contract.

Silent Partner: An individual who provides a partnership with financial support in return for a share of the profits of the business, but who has no rights to participate in the management of the firm.

Small Business Administration: A federal agency that provides the owners and managers of small businesses with help in finding money at terms and rates that will allow for profitable investment in additional assets. The SBA supplies managerial consulting as well.

Social Distance: The ability of a supervisor to evaluate the behavior of those working for him or her, without letting personality issues interfere.

Social Needs: Stem from people's desire to be with others.

Software: The programming material and the various instructions developed by computer programmers to tell the computer what to do.

Sole Proprietorship: A business enterprise that is owned and usually managed by one person.

Staffing: Involves the assembling in a department or organization the proper mix of people to perform the tasks for which the department or organization is responsible.

Staff Employees: Those employees whose activities serve and support the line functions.

Staff Functions: Activities such as personnel, plant maintenance, and public relations that do not directly contribute to the production of goods or services sold by a company.

Standard Deviation: A measure of the variability of a distribution of values.

State of Nature: A condition which affects the payoff (outcome) of a decision, over which the decision-maker has no control.

Statistical Group: A collection of persons who share a common characteristic, such as age, race, sex, height.

Stock Certificate: A contract between the investor and a company that the investor is entitled to share in the profits or losses of the business on the basis of the number of shares that the investor owns.

Stock Dividend: Issued by a corporation either with or in lieu of cash dividends, a stock dividend is a share (or portion of a share) of stock issued to shareholders for each share previously owned.

Strike: The action of workers who refuse to work due to a failure of their union to agree with the management of their company on the wages or conditions of employment.

Supervision: Overseeing a process, a worker, or workers during execution or performance, to provide direction and link employees with the top policy-making levels of management.

Synthetic Processes: The production of products in which a number of different materials go into a process, and chemical or physical changes take place.

System: Any collection of activities or events that are interrelated.

Taft-Hartley Act: Defines secondary boycotts as illegal.

Tall Organizations: Have relatively few people reporting to any one person.

Taxes, Progressive: Levied with a tax rate that rises as the tax base rises. Example would be the Federal Income Tax.

Taxes, Proportional: Levied on the basis of a specific tax rate. Example would be the property tax.

Taxes, Regressive: A feature of some taxes that causes the tax to have a greater impact on low-income people who have to spend more of their income for certain taxed items. Regression is one feature of sales taxes.

Theory *X* Assumptions (McGregor): Employees are not self-motivated, they are lazy, and they take no real interest in the goals of the organization.

Theory *Y* Assumptions (McGregor): People are generally well educated and trained, and have the ability to accomplish the tasks required and assigned. Employees can become committed to the attainment of the organization's goals, both in the short run and the long run.

Trade Association: A group of competitors, usually in a single industry, who join together to improve members' production or marketing, or to influence legislation affecting the membership.

Time Sharing: A concept that essentially permits several users to have a share of the total time available on the central processing unit of a computer.

Transformation Process: A production process whereby materials that enter the business in one form leave the production facilities in another form.

Treasury Stock: Capital stock originally issued by the corporation as fully paid and subsequently reacquired, but not fully retired.

Truth-in-Lending Law: Requires lenders to specify the rate of interest charged on loans, and to discontinue the practice of concealing charges under a variety of names.

Tunnel Vision: Looking at the organization through a long tube, or with a set of blinders. We see only a part of the entire picture, usually the part in which we are personally involved.

Ultimate Consumer: An individual, household, or company who buys goods and services for the satisfaction of immediate needs.

Unfair Trade Laws: Laws which are aimed at particular marketing practices that result in unfair competitive advantages for certain merchants.

Unity-of-Command Principle: Employees receive their orders and instructions from only one boss.

Unsecured Loans: Loans granted to a borrower on the basis of the borrower's character and past debt performance.

Update: The ability of a computer system to show continuously what is currently the status of a problem in process with no time lag between transactions and the availability of correct information.

Upward Communication: Involves the upward flow of information from the employees to the supervisor.

Value: What people accept as the price they will pay for a product or service.

Variable Costs: Costs that refer directly to the product or service produced.

Vertical Integration: The bringing together of the various production steps leading from raw materials to finished products. It is common in high technology industries such as petrochemicals, automobiles, lumber, etc., where the costs of technology make such integration an economic necessity.

Vestibule Training: Training which takes place away from the actual work being done in the department.

Voting Preferred Stock: Stock of a company that permits a voice or vote in the corporation policies.

Wagner Act: See the National Labor Relations Act.

Wheeler-Lea Act: Designed to broaden the original prohibition of the Federal Trade Commission Act against ". . . unfair methods of competition," to include also what the law designated as ". . . unfair or deceptive acts or practices."

Working Capital: Money of a business that is used to cover its current bills. It is the excess of current assets over current liabilities.

Footnotes

Chapter One

[1]F. J. Roethlisberger and W. J. Dickson. *Management and the Worker* (Cambridge, Mass.: Harvard University Press, 1939).

[2]*The Holy Bible,* Exodus 18: 13–16.

[3]Henry Minzberg. *The Nature of Managerial Work* (New York: Harper & Row, 1973).

[4]Paul Preston. "Self-Analysis: The First Step in Effective Management," *Credit Union Management,* November–December 1978. © Copyright 1978 by the Credit Union Executives Society. Used with permission.

[5]Joel Ross and Michael Kami. *Corporate Management in Crisis* (Englewood Cliffs, N.J.: Prentice-Hall, 1973), p. 21. Reprinted by permission.

Chapter Four

[1]This section based on an article by Paul Preston and Billy M. Thornton, ". . . Better Than Guessing: An Introduction to Bayesian Decision-Making," *Industrial Management,* September 1975, pp. 5–9. Used with permission of the Industrial Management Society.

Chapter 5

[1]D. G. Bowers and S. E. Seashore. "Predicting Organizational Effectiveness with a Four-factor Theory of Leadership," *Administrative Science Quarterly,* 1966, 11(2), 238–263.

[2]FRED E. FIEDLER. *A Theory of Leadership Effectiveness* (New York: McGraw-Hill, 1967).

Chapter Six

[1]ABRAHAM MASLOW. *Motivation and Personality* (New York: Harper & Row, 1954).

[2]FREDERICK HERZBERG. *Work and the Nature of Man* (New York: World Publishing Co., 1966).

[3]RENSIS LIKERT. *New Patterns of Management* (New York: McGraw-Hill, 1961).

[4]This section is from an article by Paul Preston, "How to Turn your Staff into a Working Team." It is reprinted with permission from the August 1982 issue of *Association Management*. Copyright © 1982 by the American Society of Association Executives, Washington, D.C.

Chapter Seven

[1]This section is based on Paul Preston, "The Critical Mix in Managerial Communication." Reprinted with permission from *Industrial Management* Magazine. Copyright Institute of Industrial Engineers, Inc., 25 Technology Park/Atlanta, Norcross, GA 30092.

[2]This section is from Paul Preston's article, "Feedback," *Credit Union Management,* March 1982, pp. 24–27. © Copyright 1982 by the Credit Union Executives Society. Used with permission.

[3]RALPH NICHOLS AND LEONARD STEVENS. *Are You Listening?* (New York: McGraw-Hill, 1957).

Chapter Ten

[1]This section is based on an article by Paul Preston and Brian L. Hawkins, "Performance Appraisal: Evaluation and Communication," *Industrial Management,* January–February 1978, pp. 13–17. © Copyright 1978 by the Industrial Management Society. Used with permission.

Chapter Twelve

[1]This section is from Paul Preston's article, "How to Deliver the Bad News," *PIMA Magazine,* April 1981, p. 26. © Copyright 1981 by the Paper Industry Management Association. Used with permission.

Chapter Thirteen

[1]This chapter is based on an article by Paul Preston, "Successful Conflict Management," *The Steering Wheel,* May 1979, pp. 10–13. © Copyright 1979 by the Texas Motor Transportation Association. Used with permission.

Chapter Fourteen

[1]"Federal Labor Laws and Programs," U.S. Dept. of Labor, Bulletin 262/Revised Sept. 1971. (Washington: Government Printing Office, 1971), pp. 12–15.

Chapter Fifteen

[1]Portions of this chapter are from an article by Paul Preston and Thomas W. Zimmerer, "How to Make the Best Use of Your Time." It is reprinted with permission from the January 1976 issue of *Association Management.* Copyright © 1976 by the American Society of Association Executives, Washington, D.C.

INDEX